In Wisdom and in Passion

In Wisdom and in Passion

Comparing and Contrasting Buddha and Christ

JOHN QUERIPEL

WIPF & STOCK · Eugene, Oregon

IN WISDOM AND IN PASSION
Comparing and Contrasting Buddha and Christ

Resource Publications
An Imprint of Wipf and Stock Publishers
199 W. 8th Ave., Suite 3
Eugene, OR 97401

www.wipfandstock.com

PAPERBACK ISBN: 979-8-3852-0697-1
HARDCOVER ISBN: 979-8-3852-0698-8
EBOOK ISBN: 979-8-3852-0699-5

06/27/24

Contents

Introduction

IN THIS WORK I wish to both compare and contrast two great religious figures, those after whom religions were founded. It is not my belief that such was the intention of either, yet so radical was each within their own religious tradition that their followers soon developed new faiths which became named after them. Both clearly have had a profound effect on the world.

From each we can learn much, with their different approaches representing the creative tension of opposites. I believe that in both their oppositions and commonalities, there is much needed wisdom to be mined for a modern age.

At this point some self-disclosure is in order. I come to the task as a Christian, indeed a minister, now retired, within the Uniting Church in Australia, though there are many Christians for whom my views would be viewed as unorthodox, indeed even anathema.

Having so declared, I have sought to give even-handed treatment to the comparison of the figures before me. I cannot, of course, speak as a Buddhist, so I am unable to know that faith in the deep internal or existential manner that an adherent of any religion knows their faith. On the other hand, I am aware of how a confessional believer can so easily misunderstand their own faith, given both their acculturation within their tradition and their self-interest in preserving or perpetuating it. This can often result in a blinkered approach, which may limit the ability to see the radical insights one's own faith founder is presenting, never mind appreciate the insights of another. For me, this danger of course arises from a commitment to Christian faith. I would hazard a guess that like dangers lurk for those committed to Buddhism.

Further to this preface, I must say that I have no intention to cause offense to those of the "other" faith. If there be mistakes of understanding or interpretation concerning Buddhism, these I regret, and I would ask for response given that this may be but one statement in a needed ongoing dialogue. As for my understanding of Christianity, though it differs from many others, I am more than prepared to stand my ground.

Before we begin our task we need recognize we can only deal with the accounts of Buddha and Christ as they come to us, framed through the eyes of their followers' faith. We can never get at the actual historical reality of either. We have, however, virtually no other writings contemporary with either figure and so are greatly reliant on seeing them through these lenses.

Scholars attempt to see back to the actual figures, behind the faith commitment, by trying to get rid of the lens, but this is no easy task and is always filled with conjecture. Whenever we try to do such, we are faced with two essential questions: Is such insight possible, and when we seek such insight, how influenced are we by our own commitments and biases in our search and what we find? We can conclude, despite the best scholarly efforts, that we can never get at the actual historical reality of either. We do not have histories but rather faith accounts of each figure.

A faith lens is evident even in the honorific titles they acquire—Buddha and Christ—these faith titles, given by their followers, intensely coloring the accounts they give to us.

Buddha means "enlightened being," clearly a title of belief, while Christ is the Greek form of the Hebrew Messiah, best understood as "the anointed one, come to bring God's reign," being likewise a title of faith.

To speak of the supposed actual historical figures, we ought use their names, Siddhattha Gotama (I have chosen to use the earlier form of name in the Pali rather than the Sanskrit form when speaking of the actual life of the one to become Buddha), and Jesus, the one to become Christ.

When I use their original given names I am doing so when speaking of both Gotama and Jesus in their "historical" manifestations, though in reality, as said, they always come to us through accounts colored by their author's faith. In the supposed "historical" narratives given of each, they are both already understood to be far more than mere historical actors, the "history" given being profoundly colored by faith.

The earliest account we have of Jesus' life is contained in the Gospel of Mark, written some forty years after his life. Given that in Paul's letters, composed just twenty-five years after Jesus' life, we already have a Christ of faith as distinct from the Jesus of history, in whom Paul seems to have little interest save his death and resurrection; clearly Mark's composition is not an attempt at historical biography as we know it, but rather a hagiology intended to bring the reader to faith. The impossibility of accessing the historical life of Gotama, as distinct from the Buddha of faith, is even more difficult, as the earliest Buddhist texts come from much later, at least three hundred to four hundred years after his life.

Before these earliest accounts there were oral traditions, but for obvious reasons these are not before us, and any statements as to what these were is speculation, even if it be scholarly speculation.

Of both figures I have taken the practice of referring to them by their given names when speaking of each before that event understood to be central to their lives, enlightenment for the one who would come to be known as Buddha and death and resurrection for he who would become recognized as Christ. This presents some difficulties, for the event which leads to Gotama being understood as Buddha occurs at a point in his life prior to most of it, before he commences his mission. For Jesus, however, that understood by his followers as causing him to be identified as Christ comes at the very end of his life, or more accurately after it, in his resurrection, that clearly being after his teaching. Gotama teaches as Buddha, his elevation already having been achieved, while Jesus teaches as Jesus, elevation to being Christ coming later. This is in no way to suggest that Jesus' teachings are in any manner to be seen to be inferior to those of Buddha. It is merely an indication of when each transformative experience, in the eyes of their followers, took place.

Most of the information, as distinct from analysis, I will give concerning these figures and the faiths which spring from them will be around Buddha and Buddhism. The reason for this is because I assume most readers will be more familiar with the Jesus story and the development of Christianity, though as said, this familiarity creates its own problems. In the West we are so acculturated in the Christian story that we are often unable to see it for what it really is. We have been taught to understand it, even subconsciously in a certain manner, and so taught, can easily miss both its actuality and profundity, often through domesticating it.

Last, as with my use of the earlier name for the one to become Buddha—Gotama, rather than Gautama—I will generally use the earlier Pali word in speaking of aspects of Buddhism, except when specifically referring to Mahayana.

With this in mind we commence our journey.

1

MISSIONARY FAITHS

Historian Arnold Toynbee stated that the encounter between Buddhism and Christianity is "one of the greatest collisions of the twenty-first century."[1] It is the dialogue both between East and West and between fundamentally different systems, framed by very distinct cultures.

Buddhism is the world's fourth largest religion, with some 520 million adherents, while the 2.5 billion professing Christianity, the world's largest faith, represent 31 percent of the global population. Given such massive numbers, dialogue is essential but also unavoidable.

The recent interest in dialogue is further stimulated by the widespread contemporary interest in Buddhism in lands traditionally associated with Christianity. This interest, expressed by numerous Westerners, has been joined by large scale migration of Buddhists to the West, much of that being a result of recent conflicts in Southeast Asia. Meanwhile, in some lands (China and South Korea), long associated with Buddhism, indigenous Christian churches are making rapid advances.

Both Buddhism and Christianity are missionary faiths. Of the other major world faiths only Islam shares this attribute; the others, Judaism and Hinduism, being faiths of a people, making very little attempt to convert outsiders. Essentially one is born Jewish or Hindu.

That both faiths are missional faiths has meant they have come into contact, and therefore dialogue, though that missional emphasis obviously also creates problems in that dialogue.

---

1. Keown, *Short Introduction*, 145.

While conversations between Buddhists and Christians, given the globalized world with its swift means of travel and advanced technologies, are primarily a modern event, its roots go back a long way.

In the West knowledge of India is found as early as the fifth century BCE, in such writers as Hecataeus and Herodotus. This knowledge, over a century later, no doubt stimulated Alexander the Great's desire to conquer those distant lands. With his army he reached as far as North India, vanquishing many places where Buddhism was the majority faith, before his troops rebelled, forcing him to turn back west toward home.

Buddhist sources also tell us that at this time there were Buddhist missionary endeavors to the West. From India we have accounts revealing how Buddhism had reached such places as Egypt, Syria, and Greece as early as the third century BCE. A non-canonical Pali Buddhist text, Milinda Panha (Questions of Milinda), tells of a successful attempt by a Buddhist monk, Nagasena, to convert a second century BCE Bactrian-Greek king, Menander (Pali "Milinda").

While the story is almost certainly not factual, it does show Western exposure to Buddhism from a time not too distant from the Buddha himself. That Nagasena travels west implicitly suggests that Hellenic culture was likewise known in India. That is evidenced by a rock "Edict XIII" of the third century BCE king Asoka, mentioning a Buddhist mission to Antiyoko (Antiochus II of Syria), Purumeya (Ptolemy of Egypt), Antakini (Antiochus of Macedonia), Alikasundara (Alexander of Northern Greece), and Magus of Cyrene.

Buddhism became widespread in some areas under Greek influence: Bactria (centered on modern-day Afghanistan) and the Hindu Kush. From these contacts stories of the spectacular feats of Indian holy men found their way back to Greece, though little detail of their actual religion. Later, Buddhist teachers were present in Alexandria in the first century, a city containing a massive Jewish population as part of the diaspora, some of whom no doubt were followers of Jesus.

Greek culture, however, was strong and resisted this missionary faith, so successful in the other places to which it traveled. Presumably this was due to their perception of the fullness of their own religion and philosophy. For like reason, India has not been a fertile ground for the Christian gospel.

Again we have further evidence from the time of the Roman Empire of Buddhist missionary efforts to the west. We are told of emissary, Porus, sent by an Indian king, Pandion, perhaps referring to the South Indian Pandya dynasty, to Augustus around 13 CE. Later, Christian writers such as Hippolytus (deceased c. 236) and Epiphanius (310–403) speak of a figure, Scythianus, who visited India around 50 CE bringing back with him a doctrine of

"Two Principles." Cyril of Jerusalem (313–386) informs us that Scythianus' pupil Terebinthus presented himself as a Buddha, while teaching in Palestine, Judea, and Babylon.

An early Christian father, Clement of Alexander (c. 150–c. 215), one of the founders of Christian Gnosticism, informs us that Buddha was thought to be divine (*hos theon tetimekasi*) by those in Buddhist monasteries due to his "superlative sanctity" (hypberbolen semnotetos).[2] One may speculate that Clement's gnostic interests may have been stimulated by some familiarity with Buddhist teachings.

Even the story of Buddha's virgin birth was known, with Archelaos of Carrha (278 CE) mentioning it, while later the fourth century Christian saint Jerome says Buddha "was born from the side of a virgin."

Traces of Buddhist thought are found in the works of Evangrius Ponticus, whose fourth century CE works on human covetousness clearly exhibit Buddhist ideas.

From these East-West contacts, some have asserted that Jesus was influenced by Buddhist teaching, this based on the supposed similarity between the teachings of both Buddha and Christ. Given Jesus' hometown of Nazareth was only a few kilometers from the substantial Graeco-Roman city of Sepphoris, it is claimed therefore that some Buddhist teachings may have been present, making it possible Jesus may have been partially influenced by Buddhist teachings. This influence however, if any, would be extremely minimal. Jesus was deeply nurtured within the Jewish tradition, and it was this, not any exotic tradition, which shaped his teaching and life. Without actual evidence the only grounds for this influence are the supposed similarities between the teachings of Buddha and Jesus. These similarities, however, do not suggest cultural borrowing, for they are not at the level of specific images or language. Rather Buddha and Christ each offer diagnosis for both the human condition and a prescriptive cure. Both give what William James noted in his classic work *The Varieties of Religious Experience* a model of the human condition and a spiritual solution. What we find is not a cultural borrowing but more so a commonality of religious experience, arising from common human experience.[3]

There are stories of Jesus having travelled to India, supposedly where he absorbed local teachings, including those of Buddha, in the lost years, between his adolescence and the commencement of his ministry, and even being a type of proto-frequent traveller, returning to India to die, where supposedly his body is buried. There is however, no actual evidence for any

2. Pieris, *Love*, 125.

3. James, *Varieties of Religious Experience*.

of this, and it is hardly likely that Jesus, as a peasant, would have travelled such great distance. As we shall see, influences exercised upon Jesus were entirely Jewish.

We do know, however, that early Christians found their way to India, tradition telling us that even one of Jesus' apostles, Thomas, made the journey to that land. If not he, we do know that the Thomas tradition, which survives to this day in the Mar Thoma Church, was established in India not long after the time of Christ. Already present in India was a Jewish community, albeit very small.

Later, in the thirteenth century, Marco Polo made his famous journey to the East where he encountered Mahayana Buddhism. Of Buddha he wrote, "But it is certain, had he been baptized a Christian he would have been a great saint alongside Our Lord Jesus Christ."[4] Other western travelers of that time, Giovanni de Piano Carpini, and William of Ruysbroeck, sent reports of Buddhism, noting its similarities with the Nestorian-Christian communities long present in that part of the world, reaching even to China.

Within Europe, around the same time, the story of Barlaam and Joasaphat became hugely popular, though its medieval readers would hardly have suspected it was based on a narrative of the life of Buddha, Josaphat being a corruption of Bodhisattva. Joasaphat became very popular, and numerous documents were made purporting to be his teachings, there even being a thirteenth century document, "Life of St. Joasaphat." This transition happened, it seems, through the term Bodhisattva becoming Budasaf in Arabic, before the saint's name reached the West through the Georgian church, where St. Euthymius (955–1024) introduced him in the tenth century as Iodasaph. The outstanding feature associated with Iodasaph in Euthymius's writings was his life of asceticism and worldly renunciation.

He remained a saint until recent times before being quietly dismissed from such company. In more interfaith times perhaps he may be due for a return!

Buddhism finds its missionary impulse in the words of Buddha: "Go monks, and wander for the good and welfare of the multitudes, out of compassion for the worlds; go forth for the welfare, the blessing, the happiness of all beings . . . Go forth and spread the teaching that is beautiful in the beginning, beautiful in the middle, and beautiful in the end" (Samyutta Nikaya 4:453, Vinaya 4:20). Buddha, himself following his enlightenment, travelled widely for forty-five years propagating the way he had discovered. Accounts we possess tell us his followers clearly fulfilled his command.

---

4. Keown, *Short Introduction*, 129.

The spread of Buddhism, contrary to that of Christianity, has never been facilitated by use of the sword.

Buddhism's spread was greatly accelerated by the actions of the afore-mentioned third-century BCE Buddhist king, Ashoka Maurya. Through conquest he extended the Mauryan empire, making it the largest empire in India until the coming of the British Raj some two thousand years later. Ashoka's conversion to Buddhism came after a bloody campaign in the east, around present-day Odisha/Orissa, where he, overcome by great remorse for the destruction his actions had caused, turned to Buddhism, under which principles he ruled for the rest of his reign. While he extended the influence of Buddhism in India, he also sent emissaries to the Near East, as far as Macedonia, Syria and Egypt, and also in the opposite direction, to Southeast Asia.

On one stele erected by Ashoka come the following words. We do well to be guided by them in our exploration.

> One should not honor only one's own religion and condemn the religions of others, but one should honor others' religions for this or that reason. . . . In acting otherwise one digs the grave of one's own religion and also does harm to other religions. Who-soever honors their own religion and condemns other religions does so, indeed, through devotion to their own religion, think-ing: "I will glorify my own religion." But on the contrary, in so doing they injure their own religion more gravely. So concord is good: let all listen, and be willing to listen to the doctrines professed by others (Ashokan Rock Edict 12).[5]

It was also at this time that the faith came to the Kathmandu Valley in Nepal, where it remains popular to this day, coming first in the form of Theravada, before later being superseded by Mahayana, especially in its Tantric forms.

Again, another ruler, a second-century CE king, Kanishka from north-ern India, was responsible for facilitating the later spread of Mahayana to the north and east.

The dissemination of Buddhism was often at this elite level with kings like Ashoka dispatching monks to accompany diplomatic missions. With the acceptance of Buddhism at an elite level in a kingdom, the faith would soon then pass to the wider populace.

Buddhism was also spread by prominent scholars and philosophers, for possessing a dynamic philosophy, the faith contained many ideas which intrigued and attracted thinkers. Such philosophical questioning made

5. Shearer, *Buddha*, 25.

Buddhism popular in places possessing an already rich philosophical tradition, such as China.

The Silk Road also greatly facilitated the spread of ideas, carried along the series of roads between East and West, by merchants and traders, with whom Buddhism had found initial acceptance. Due to this trade many of this class had become sufficiently wealthy so to be able to indulge their curiosity around ideas and thought, such as Buddhism.

Both faiths were responsible for establishing great centers of learning during the medieval period. In India, under Buddhist influence, were established great universities, such as that those at Nalanda and Vikramashila, which flourishing between the seventh and twelfth centuries CE had as many as ten thousand students enrolled at any one time. Areas of inquiry included logic, grammar, epistemology, medicine, and philosophy, particularly that pertaining to Madhyamaka thinking. In like manner Christian thought was the stimulus for the great Western universities of Europe, the earliest being at Bologna, Oxford, Salamanca, Cambridge, and Padua. Through their preparedness to struggle with rigorous thinking, while developing new teachings, these great institutions facilitated the spread of both faiths, particularly through the intellectual elites.' Each were able to incorporate learning into their faiths, to the point that learning became almost synonymous with each religion.

The two Buddhist schools, Theravada and Mahayana, whose differences I shall later examine, moved in two different directions geographically, as well as doctrinally. Theravada became popular in the south of India, from where it reached into Sri Lanka, Indonesia, and Indochina, while Mahayana spread northeast to China, and thence to Japan, Korea, Tibet, and Vietnam. There are exceptions to this general pattern, however: the Borobudur shrine in Indonesia is adorned with many scenes from the Mahayana sutras, while Sri Lanka developed Mahayana schools, with Theravada not becoming the official faith until the twelfth century CE.

Buddhism had arrived in Sri Lanka very early, around 250 BCE, brought by two monks, Mahinda and Saṅghamittā, envoys of Ashoka, said to be his son and daughter respectively. They may have also been responsible for also introducing Buddhism to Burma and Thailand. Sri Lanka was the locale where Buddha's teachings were first put into writing, some four hundred years after his death.

Buddhism, in a nascent Mahayana form, reached China by the first century CE, during a time of great stability and strength for China under the Han dynasty. This stability greatly assisted the transmission of the faith through that extensive empire. The major existing Chinese religio-philosophical system of Confucianism lay great store on the family and service within the social order, while the more mystical Chinese religion of Taoism spoke of reverence for the elders and of not moving against the flow. Buddhism, with its call to leave families and society, to establish an alternative society in the sangha, came as a countermovement and threat to both. Over time similarities were found between the Tao and the dhamma (Buddhist teachings and also cosmic order), each being viewed as the aligned way to live. The sangha represented another locus of power away from the social order headed by the emperor, with Buddhist monks refusing to bow to him. This resulted in Buddhism being viewed sometimes with suspicion, including four major suppressions between the fifth and tenth centuries by four different emperors during the Northern Wei, Northern Zhou, later Zhou and Tang dynasties. This suppression included the destruction of monasteries, confiscation of lands, and defrocking of monks.

Buddhism held appeal to those who could never climb the stratified social hierarchy as represented by Confucianism, with its orientation to the ruling class, while also answering many metaphysical questions, left unanswered by this Chinese belief, with its more practical earthly orientation. Particularly in providing answers concerning the afterlife Buddhism resonated with the Chinese strong ancestral interest. Further, with its concern for inner stillness, Buddhist meditation also fitted well with the Taoist concern for harmony. The interaction of Buddhism and Taoism would be instrumental in developing the Ch'an Buddhist school, better known in the West by its Japanese appellation, Zen. The terms Ch'an and Zen both derive from the Sanskrit dhyana, meaning meditation, something at heart of this school of Buddhism. Along with Ch'an, the Ti'en Tai school, centered on the Lotus Sutra, also became very popular in China. Finally, Buddhist concern for scholarship also appealed to the strong Chinese scholarly tradition. In time, with Confucianism and Taoism, Buddhism became one of the triad of Chinese religions.

From China, Buddhism spread to Korea during the fourth century and hence to Japan in the sixth century, greatly influenced by the land from whence it had come. Thus the Japanese schools such as Tendai and Shingon, the Japanese form of Pure Land Buddhism, all find their roots in China, as does, as just seen, that school most identified with Japan, Zen.

Buddhism first came to Thailand in the 3rd century CE and gained such traction that today in its Theravada form it is the constitutional religion of that land. Great Buddhist centers were established at Sukhothai and Ayuthaya, while all Thai males until now are expected to spend time in the sangha.

Buddhism in both Theravada and Mahayana form reached Burma in the fifth and sixth centuries CE, though eventually the former prevailed.

The great medieval city of Pagan became one of the great Buddhist centers adorned with many thousands of Buddhist temples.

The faith arrived in Vietnam during the seventh century in Mahayana form, with the source again being China. Later it would come to Cambodia, the time of its arrival marked in the changing of temples in Angkor from Hindu to Buddhist during the twelfth century.

Another place strongly associated with Buddhism is Tibet, where again the source was China. Due to Tibet's remoteness the faith didn't find its way to that domain until the seventh and eighth century CE. The form of Buddhism most associated with Tibet is Vajrayana "the thunderbolt vehicle," sometimes known as Tantra or Mantrayana. Vajrayana is essentially a part of Mahayana Buddhism, but adds to that school its own rich symbolism and religious practices. Central to practice is a series of Scriptures, known as Tantras, composed in India in the latter part of the first millennium.

Christian missionary impulse likewise finds roots in the words of the one at its heart. In Matthew's Gospel, Christ in his parting words commands the apostles "make disciples of all nations, baptizing them in the name of the Father, Son and Holy Spirit" (Matt 28:19).

The land where the faith was born, Israel, lay at the crossroads of numerous trading routes, facilitating the initial spread of that faith. This is clearly evidenced in the journeys undertaken by Paul, who was able to found many churches across a wide domain using the networks of the Roman Empire. The Acts of the Apostles details, though only partially and selectively, the rapid expansion of Christianity. Centering on Paul's efforts, it omits those of others, the most famous being the spread of the tradition, centered on Thomas, to India.

Expansion was, as with Buddhism, facilitated by an empire, in this case, Rome. The Pax Romana, along with the empire's road infrastructure, and naval links between large ports, assisted travel, and with that the dissemination of ideas. Thus, the major urban centers, mostly linked with trade, became the hubs of missionary expansion, with Paul's epistles all being to churches he had established in such places. A lingua franca, Koine (common) Greek, used across the empire, also helped in the spread of Christianity.

It is a moot point as to whether Christians converted Rome or the empire converted Christianity. Whichever the case, by the early fourth century, Rome, which had earlier declared Christianity an illicit faith, had become, following Emperor Constantine's conversion, its great promoter. Judged by him to be the best faith to cement the empire, now with imperial support, Christianity quickly spread to all parts of the empire.

It need be remembered however, that Christianity, with royal patronage, become the faith of the empire, only due to its prior widespread propagation.

Before the Roman Empire took the mantle of Christianity as its official religion, persecution against Christians was constant, on occasions being extreme. That persecution also helped in the growth of the faith, for many in the populace were drawn to the bravery of Christians facing martyrdom, such growing the faith's reputation. It has been said, "the blood of the martyrs was the seed of the church."[6]

Though it was now the religion of empire, Christianity still consisted of different strands. As such it would not do to unite the empire, so Constantine quickly set to work, enforcing a unity. His and his successor's efforts were successful in that an orthodoxy was established, built on common Scriptures, creeds, and leadership (bishops), that unity and assurance of message further facilitating mission.

While it became the official faith of the empire, Christianity had also spread beyond the empire's domain, found in Odessa, Armenia and Ethiopia, with Armenia in 301 CE becoming the first nation to become officially Christian.

Within the empire Christian dominance grew sufficiently strong that a successor fourth century emperor to Constantine, Julian the Apostate, was unable to restore the pagan cults as the official Roman religion.

Under Constantine the empire had split into east and west, Constantine moving his capital to the city that was to bear his name, Constantinople. Increasingly a division grew politically, but also ecclesiastically, between the eastern and western parts of the empire. The Roman church began to view itself, given that it bore the name of the empire, as the preeminent church, that being resisted by the eastern churches, the patriarchs of Constantinople, Alexandra, Antioch, and Jerusalem. This split continued to deepen due to political, cultural and theological factors until finally both mutually excommunicated the other in 1054. That division continues until this day between the Eastern Orthodox Churches and the Roman Catholic Church, with relations only warming in recent decades.

By the seventh century, Christianity had spread halfway around the globe. Nestorian Christians as seen, having propagated the gospel as far east as China while a Celtic Christianity from the most western parts of Europe, was also progressing the gospel through Britain and from there to the Germanic tribes and Scandinavia. That same century however, saw many

---

6. Attributed to Tertullian, late second century.

Christian lands in the Middle East and North Africa lost to a new resurgent faith, Islam.

Orthodox Christians carried the gospel into Moravia and to the Slav peoples and further east. The conversion of Vladimir of Kiev in 988 was significant, resulting in the Russian Orthodox Church, which in turn propagated the faith across the Russian territories as far as the Pacific Ocean, and even into modern day Alaska.

It was, however, mainly the Western church which was responsible for the greatest expansion of the Christian faith. Though that church split in the sixteenth century due to the Protestant Reformation, both Roman Catholics and Protestants, often in competition, backed by their respective states' colonizing efforts, took the faith to North and South America, Asia, Australasia and the Pacific, and to Africa. It is in these colonized lands that Christianity today is overwhelmingly found, while in the western European centers from which it was propagated, its influence has greatly diminished in the face of a growing secularism.

A major part of each faith's rapid expansion was the ability to incorporate preexisting faiths with which they came into contact.

Buddhism readily embraced preexisting religions, Confucianism and Taoism in China, Shinto in Japan, and Bon in Tibet. In China today, a major part of the population (in an officially atheist state) follows a faith combining Mahayana Buddhism, Taoism, and Confucianism, with many pagodas dedicated to both Buddhist and Taoist deities. Across the Buddhist world many local gods and spirits have been incorporated into Buddhism, while people's religious practices, making use of older myths, still include devotion to the older localized deities and spirits, with practices such as astrology, magic, and devotion around relics often continuing. Even within the sangha there may be buildings devoted to the gods.

Often these deities and spirits guide immediate decisions, while larger existential questions of being, and purpose are referred to Buddhism. A preexisting pantheon was frequently retained, but with Buddha placed atop it. While Buddhism is quite accommodating of the worship of other gods it insists on the primacy of the dhamma.

Christianity, despite proclaiming its uniqueness and opposition to preexisting faiths, in actuality also tended to incorporate them. Christianity's two largest festivals, Christmas and Easter, have clear pagan roots, while several preexisting divinities were incorporated into Christianity as saints. Among the earliest was Demetrius of Thessaloniki, who in the fourth century inherited the role of being the patron saint of agriculture. There is an obvious connection to Demeter and the Eleusinian Mysteries, in the common concern for agriculture. Christian practices associated with All

Saints Day, as witnessed in visits to cemeteries and the leaving of food for the deceased in many countries, clearly hearken back to pagan roots.

The church has assimilated many of the ideas of the pre-Christian philosophical ideas, particularly those of Plato and Aristotle, making extensive use of them to frame Christian theological understanding. Thus, Neoplatonism was a powerful philosophical movement in the church, culminating with the great systems, built around Platonism, constructed by Augustine in the fifth century. A half millennium later this was largely replaced by that of Thomas Aquinas, drawing upon the ideas of Aristotle.

The colonial expansion of Christianity led to further co-option of pre-existing religious forms. Catholic practices in the Andean region of South America still contain strong influences of Quechua culture originated from the Incas, with holy days and festivities featuring Quechua dances or figures, notably fertility celebrations linked with Pachamama. Further north in Mexico, both the image and devotion to Our Lady of Guadalupe assimilate elements of native Mexican culture. In Africa the Kimbanguist church is the strongest example of Christianity taking African form. The founder, Simon Kimbangu, rejecting the idea that God would send a white man, asserted instead that Jesus was black. Adherents also retain traditional African practices as polygamy. Despite these features, the church is accepted as a member of the World Council of Churches. In Asia the contextualization of Christianity most famously inspired the nineteeth-century Chinese revolutionary Tai-ping movement. Elsewhere, South Korean Catholics continue to practice a modified form of ancestral rites along with many Buddhist and Confucian customs and philosophies. In the Pacific, Australian Aboriginal forms of Christianity are informed by traditional concepts of the sacrality of the land, while in Aotearoa-New Zealand, a strong form of Maori Christianity is found in the Ratana church.

A final interesting parallel is found in that while both Buddhism and Christianity are strongly missionary faiths, having spread around the world, they find hardly any acceptance in the lands of their births, India and Israel respectively. That is due primarily to reform movements occurring in the faiths from which they came, Hinduism and Judaism, around the same time as the genesis of the two faiths of which we are speaking. Those reform movements successfully caught the changes which had given rise to the new faiths, and directed back into the older, now greatly reformed, faiths.

Predominantly Christianity come to lands, traditionally Buddhist, as part of Western colonization from the 16th to the 20th century. That style of arrival has acted as a great hindrance to Christian-Buddhist dialogue. This colonial enterprise was so successful it reduced economically the former dominant economic powers of China and India to beggar status, something now only being reversed. For many Buddhists the nexus between Christianity and Western colonialism of their lands remains overwhelmingly powerful, making open-minded engagement with Christians extremely difficult. Given such, Aloysius Piernis charges, "For the most part Buddhist-Christian encounter has been a matter of a deformed Christianity colliding with a mis-apprehended Buddhism."[7] It was primarily through this colonial conquest that Christians and Buddhists initially came into contact—and often conflict. It still colors much dialogue today.

    The initial colonial contact came with the opening, by the Portuguese, of the first sea routes to the East, with others—Dutch, English and French—soon following. Christianity, viewed as the religion of the colonizers, has been therefore established with varying levels of success in Buddhist lands.

    For most colonialists their main interest was the accumulation of wealth, with faith peripheral. Where religious motivations were prime, the majority, rather than being scholars, were missionaries, meaning that interest in Buddhism and the surrounding culture was motivated by the goal of conversion, rather than dialogue. This is not to say, however, that there was not an appreciation of Buddhism, along with the surrounding culture, particularly among the Jesuits, who began to make a serious study of Buddhism from the sixteenth century.

    Though there are claims that the apostle Thomas preached there during the first century, followed by a long Nestorian presence, Ceylon (current day Sri Lanka) was the first Buddhist land in 1505 to suffer the effects of colonialism by the West and to have Christianity come as part of that colonial dominance. The church in Sri Lanka is the result of the Portuguese, Dutch, and British, who brought Christianity in Catholic and Protestant forms in successive waves.

    In reaction, asserting its dominance, Buddhism in Sri Lanka has frequently been conservative and reactionary, linked closely with a chauvinist nationalism, particularly following the decades long Tamil rebellion, only recently brutally suppressed. Such is recognized in Buddhism's privileged position in the Sri Lankan constitution. Christianity, along with Hinduism and Islam, are viewed by most as "foreign" religions. Despite this Buddhist/Christian dialogue does take place in Sri Lanka, though it is largely marginal.

    Later the French and British propagated Christianity in their colonial conquests of Indochina and Burma respectively. In all those lands, though significant Christian minorities remain, they still struggle to rid themselves of the taint of colonialism. Many are tribal groupings, using Christianity as part of defining themselves against the ethnic majority.

7. Pieris, *Love*, 83.

Christianity, though it was a French colonial plant, has found success in Vietnam. Its genesis in colonialism, however, makes Christianity suspect for many, including the current government, which came to power following long struggles against Western colonial powers identified with Christianity, France, and then the US. Christians were strongly identified with French colonialism and then later supported US involvement in Vietnam, those loyalties being displayed when many fled to the south following the proclamation of Vietnamese independence by Vietnamese nationalist Ho Chi Minh and the subsequent division of the land between south and north. Later, Christians again would make up a disproportionate number of those fleeing following the defeat of the South Vietnamese regime in 1975.

The colonial manifestation of Christianity in Vietnam was most graphically seen in the Western, particularly US backing, for the Ngo Dinh Diem government (1955-61) in then South Vietnam. The backing for this strongly Catholic leader led to many widespread protests from Buddhists, including monks, most famously seen in self-immolations. Following the Communist victory and reunification of the country, the church has now increasingly had to become indigenous, the strong identification of Christianity with colonialism gradually fading as the long wars for independence recede into history.

In Burma, Christianity came as part of the British colonial baggage. As in Sri Lanka a strongly nationalist Buddhism has taken hold, shaped by many of the same forces. Following the ending of British colonialism, Burma has been ruled by a military, identifying themselves closely with Buddhism. As in Sri Lanka, in Burma, Buddhism has been used to repress minorities of other faiths, most recently the Rohingya Muslims, while Christians are mainly present in the "hill tribes," long in conflict with the central Buddhist government.

Christianity arrived in another largely Buddhist land, Japan, in 1549, though there are again suspicions that Nestorian Christians may have arrived earlier. The Jesuits were responsible under their cofounder Francis Xavier, assisted by other members: Cosme de Torres and Juan Fernandez. At first, as they would be in China, the Jesuit order was held in good esteem, largely due to the Western scientific and technological knowledge they brought. Received positively at court, soon a thriving community of converts was formed.

Though not initially strongly entangled with European colonialism, when later it came to be so identified, Japanese opposition to the faith grew. Under the regency of Toyotomi Hideyoshi (1537-98) Christians were increasingly suspected of being foreign agents. This resulted in the shōgun Tokugawa Ieyasu (1543-1616) banning Christianity and closing Japan off from the West, a policy which endured for 250 years. This suspicion was confirmed by the larely Christian revolt which took place in 1637, led by Matsukura Katsuie, in Amakusa and Shimabara. Japanese opposition toward Christianity became fierce, with adherents to the faith, both foreign and Japanese, violently persecuted. Until today Christianity has remained very peripheral in Japan.

The modern Chinese church traces its roots to the arrival of sixteenth-century Jesuits. Francis Xavier had died trying to enter China, but the mission was carried on by others, most famously Matteo Ricci and Michele Ruggieri. Along with their missionary endeavor, the Jesuits undertook a century-long effort in translating the Chinese classics into Latin, while later spreading knowledge of Chinese culture and history to Europe. The scientific and technological knowledge they shared helped greatly in their reception in the Chinese court. An indigenous church was established and initially Christianity found some fertile ground, but again as it became more associated with colonial exploitation, the missionary project became increasingly opposed.

Yet alongside rejection of Christianity in its foreign form, later the faith, taking a hybrid indigenous form, played an important role in the Taiping rebellion against the Manchus (1850–64). Led by Hong Xiuquan, the self-proclaimed brother of Jesus Christ, the rebellion was religious, nationalist, and political in nature including the conversion of many Chinese to the Taiping's syncretic version of Christianity. Christianity however, only remained peripheral to a China, deeply imbued with a triad of religions, Confucianism, Taoism, and Buddhism, until the contemporary era.

After the revolution of 1949, with the founding of the People's Republic of China, Christianity became viewed as an unwanted Western influence, with foreign missionaries compelled to leave. Following its violent suppression during the Cultural Revolution in the 1960s and 1970s, recent decades have seen a massive growth in the church. This growth has been exclusively driven by the indigenous Christian community that been necessary as the Communist Party government is still very wary of foreign influence in religious affairs.

This current newness of the faith for many in China gives it an energy and vitality founded in conviction, this in turn driving further expansion. Thus, while in pre-revolutionary China, Christianity, with the exception of the Tai-ping hybrid, was largely identified as a colonial religion, it has re-emerged now as a strongly indigenous vibrant faith. Estimates of numbers vary but it is likely that in the past thirty years the Christian populace has quadrupled. Numbers are highly elastic, but some place numbers of

Christians as high as 50–80 million, though in a country of some 1.4 billion people.

The first European to reach Tibet was Ippolito Desideri (1684–1733), an Italian Jesuit who travelled to Lhasa in 1716, where, having learned the language, made a study of Tibetan texts and doctrine at the Sera monastic university debating Christian and Buddhist doctrine with Tibetan scholars. Tibet was a "hermit kingdom," however, until recent times, with little contact with the outside world, meaning Christianity essentially has no foothold.

The only Asian lands where Buddhism is historically dominant, in which Christianity has found success are those in which the faith has grown through indigenous efforts: Korea and China.

Missionary efforts made by Koreans themselves have rapidly spread Christianity through a previously almost exclusively Buddhist land. It was a Korean, Lee Sung-Hun, returning from China in 1784 as a baptized Catholic, who was responsible for bringing the faith to Korea. Despite the following century including four persecutions unleashed against Catholicism, the faith grew with very limited foreign input. Protestantism arrived later in 1884, likewise introduced by a Korean, Suh-Sang-yan, again converted in China. Foreign missionaries followed, with Protestant missionary endeavor being so successful that Korean Protestants outnumbered Catholics by over two to one just twenty-five years later.

The Japanese annexation of Korea in 1910 brought renewed persecution, though Christian identification with Korean nationalism brought respect and growth for the church. Following the end of WWII and Korea's release from the Japanese yolk, Christianity has experienced massive growth, despite the loss of the north to the communists. Protestantism, mostly Presbyterianism, from that time has been doubling each decade. Christianity by some counts is now the largest faith in Korea, surpassing the older faiths, Buddhism and Confucianism. With Buddhism and Christianity both viewing themselves in competition for converts, dialogue in Korea is limited.

In both China and Korea the current rapid growth of Christianity is completely indigenously driven. In both these lands, however, Christianity is primarily a proselytizing faith and so has little time or interest in dialogue. Buddhism, on the defense, likewise has little interest in dialogue.

In China, as with Vietnam, the nation is ruled by a Communist party, with atheism as part of their ideology, so both Buddhist and Christian energies are more directed toward their relationship with secular authorities than to dialogue with each other.

The European colonial conquest of the East obviously represents the greatest contemporary hindrance to Christian-Buddhist dialogue. For many Buddhists the nexus between Christianity and Western colonialism is too tightly intertwined to be easily pulled apart. Christianity is still widely understood as the religion of the colonizer, perceived not only as foreign but also as oppressive.

The appetite of the Europeans in conquest during the colonial period seemed insatiable, that rapaciousness understood in stark contrast with Buddhist culture and philosophy. From the other side, Christians frequently disparaged Buddhist belief for what they judged to be its otherworldly lack of material concern and disinterested passivity, that often confirmed by the levels of poverty they found, and also to how easily they had come into possession of those lands, Buddhist passivity apparently having enabled that. This understanding of perceived passivity was reinforced by the great number of monasteries encountered, wherein monks were seemingly idle.

That judgment of "passivity" and "non-worldly concern" still informs many Christian views of Buddhism. It is to ignore however the great historical Buddhist civilizations, such as Angkor in Cambodia, Ayuthaya in Thailand, and Goryeo, whose capital was Songdo (modern Gaesong) in Korea. These societies were highly sophisticated, abounded in wealth, and were expansionist. Further, as we have seen, China, which has mostly been the world's preeminent economic power, has been strongly influenced by Buddhism.

Modern events also show how Buddhism has been misrepresented as a type of political passivity. Buddhists were strongly involved in the independence movements in Ceylon, throughout Southeast Asia and in Korea, the latter in opposing Japanese rule. One of the most graphically horrifying pictures of Buddhist political protest was Thích Quảng Đức, a Mahayana monk who self-immolated protesting the South Vietnamese political leadership in 1963. Recent resistance to military rule in Burma has frequently found its genesis in Buddhism, with many Buddhists, including monks, at its heart. On the other hand Buddhist social and political involvement has also been present in negative ways, giving ideological justification and succor for past Japanese militarism, and current repression of minorities in Burma and Sri Lanka.

We may conclude that in Asian lands where Buddhism dominates, Christianity is often viewed as a late interloper associated with colonialism, causing dialogue between Buddhists and Christians to be often problematical. In those lands strongly traditionally Buddhist (Korea and China), where indigenous forms of Christianity been established, there is, for reasons given, little interest in dialogue.

Though limited due to the combative Buddhism found in the land, from within a Buddhist context perhaps the most fruitful place for

Buddhist-Christian dialogue has been Sri Lanka. Here, the roots of the church reach back further, while also becoming more indigenous, that serving as a stimulus for dialogue. Dialogue between the two faiths has taken place mainly in the West, due to a growing interest in Buddhism in Western lands.

That wider Western interest in Buddhism did not occur until the nineteenth century, a time when numerous scholars began to be seriously involved in the subject. Impressed by Buddhism having such similarities, as monastic orders, a virgin birth for its founder, and a belief in heaven and hell, many of these first encountering Buddhism viewed it as a legitimate alternative religious form to Christianity. For like reason others understood it negatively as representing a form of Christianity corrupted by the devil. This later group also vehemently rejected all Buddhist concepts absent from Christianity—rebirth and impermanence, especially the soul's impermanence—while also charging Buddhists with idolatry, mainly due to the dominant place of statues of the Buddha and Bodhisattvas.

Of particular import for the initial Western interest in Buddhism was the work of colonial officials serving in the East. Prominent among these were the French scholar Eugène Burnouf, who wrote *Introduction to the History of Indian Buddhism* in 1844, followed seven years later by a translation of the Lotus Sutra, while the British Resident in Nepal, B. H. Hodgson, was responsible for collecting many Mahayana texts. Sir Edwin Arnold's book-length poem, "The Light of Asia, A Life of the Buddha," published in 1879, became an influential best seller, eventually going through eighty editions, selling between half a million and a million copies. In 1881 the British civil servant T. W. Rhys Davids (1843–1922), who had made an extensive study of Theravada Buddhism during his time in then Ceylon (current-day Sri Lanka), established the Pali Text Society.

Scholars also became involved. Max Müller's edited Buddhist texts were published in 1881 in the Oxford series known as Sacred Books of the East, while in that same year the German Herman Oldenberg published *The Buddha, His Life, His Doctrine, His Community*. Later, in the US, Henry Clarke Warren's *Buddhism in Translation* (1896) was published as an anthology from the Pali canon. All of these texts were received eagerly by many Westerners, fascinated by what they viewed as the "oriental wisdom" contained within them.

In Britain the intense interest of the Victorians in the supernatural, through movements such as the Theosophical Society, was instrumental in igniting interest in Buddhism. The founders of that society, Colonel Henry Olcott (1832–1907) and Madame Blavatsky (1831–1891), committed themselves to uncovering what they understood to be the common esoteric truth lying at the heart of all religions and in that search focused primarily on faiths exotic to them, those of the East. Both converted to Buddhism, with Olcott doing much work, still held highly by many Buddhists, to make the faith less superstitious and more rational, so as to appeal to the rationality of the nineteenth-century West. This style of Buddhism became strongly linked not only with Theosophy but with numerous syncretist movements.

In an age of rationality, a non-religious Buddhism appealed to many who had rejected Christian metaphysics. This type of contrast between a religious Christianity and a rational philosophical Buddhism could only survive until the modern era, when vastly increased contact made clear just how forced this contrast was, with the deep springs of Buddhist spirituality becoming clearly evident.

For many such, fascination with the East often was compensatory, coming at a time of secular disenchantment in the West, with religious and spiritual impulses marginalized. Also, much of Western religion, being informed by the wider spirit of the times, had been reduced to moralism or was understood as part of the liberal Western project of making the world "better" through gradual progress. This left a spiritual vacuum, which for some, Buddhism, among other Eastern religious forms, filled.

A powerful stimulus for Buddhist-Christian dialogue came with the inaugural Parliament of World's Religions, held in Chicago in 1893, during which the Ceylonese Buddhist scholar Anargarika Dharmapala (1864–1933) made a strong impression. On following visits to the US, he founded the Maha Bodhi Society, the first international Buddhist association. Along with Dharmapala at that conference, there was present a strong Japanese delegation representing varying Japanese Buddhist schools: Rinzai Zen, Jodo Shinshu, Nichiren, Tendai, and Shingon.

Following the turn of the century the Belgian scholars Louis de La Vallee Poussin and Etienne Lamotte did much for Mahayana scholarship, while later again Zen Buddhism was popularized in the West, by the well-known Japanese scholar D. T. Suzuki (1870–1966), during his time in the US in 1897. Suzuki's writings had a powerful impact on Western intellectuals such as psychologists Erich Fromm and Karen Horney, Beat writers Allen Ginsburg, Gary Snyder, and Jack Kerouac, as well as on other figures like Alan Watts and Edward Conze.

Buddhism found fertile ground in some circles, particularly among the intelligentsia, among whom it is often (mistakenly) embraced as a type of rationalist secular philosophy, in contrast to a Christianity, so linked with speculative metaphysics. This type of Buddhism, stripped of its essential sap, while it was appealing to some, could never speak to the broad masses.

Often, Buddhism has often become part of a movement, marked by a fascination with the mysterious East, as a place of the "other" supposedly possessing a deep wisdom. Such was later negatively connoted by the Palestinian scholar Edward Said as "Orientalism."

The first major school of Buddhism to have wide appeal in the West was Zen. Following World War II, numbers of the occupying forces in Japan observing it were drawn, taking it back then to the US following their term of duty. Zen appealed as a type of rational stark meditative practice, lacking many of the accessories of religion. The iconoclastic and spontaneous nature of Zen attracted first the 1950s Beats and then later many hippies, with the idea that it was mind-expanding, meshing with widespread drug experimentation. In an age of disenchantment with much of mainstream culture Zen was seen as another type of countercultural protest.

Another group which rapidly expanded in the West was Soka Gakkai International (lit. "value creation society"). In both its rapid growth and upbeat good news emphasis, it has many parallels with evangelical Christianity. At the core of its teaching is that all its members can reach their goals by constant repetition of the words *Namu myoho renge kyo* (Honor to the Lotus Sutra of the True Dharma), coupled with a positive mental attitude.

In stark contrast to the simplicity of Zen Buddhism, another form of Buddhism which has become attractive to the West is Tibetan Vajrayana, its ornate rituals, symbols, and ceremonies, including those believed to be magical, proving popular. The attraction to this style of Buddhism was at total odds with what previously had attracted most Westerners to the faith, for here it was the deeply mystical, and metaphysical, which was the attraction. The deep secrets and powers, understood to be held by the Lamas or Rinpoches, often associated with mandalas, mantras, and mudras, deeply fascinate many, as do ornate rituals featuring drums, cymbals, trumpets, and incense. Further interest in Vajrayana is sparked by the land with which it is identified, Tibet, the mysterious hermit kingdom. Issues surrounding the current Dalai Lama, his exile from his homeland and constant traveling, have also been instrumental in further cultivating this interest. The high profile of the current Dalai Lama has led many in the West to think of him, erroneously, as a Buddhist pope.

Contact with this form of Buddhism was initially stimulated by the famous Christian Cistercian monk Thomas Merton who met with the Dalai Lama in 1968, on his way to a conference on Eastern spirituality in Thailand at which he died by tragic accident.

Another important dialogue has been built around the Vietnamese monk Thich Nhat Hanh, who after leaving his homeland during the Indo-China war, settled in France, establishing a Buddhist community in

Bordeaux, with later a number of communities springing from that. He has been instrumental in developing a socially engaged Buddhism. Likewise the Indian scholar, Ambedkar, a Dalit (at that time known as "untouchable") developed a similar social activist style of Buddhism. He was largely responsible in reintroducing the faith back to its homeland.

Today Buddhism is well-established the West. Culturally it has been popularized through such writers as Herman Hesse, while numerous recent Western celebrities identifying as Buddhists have facilitated the faith's spread. These have included George Lucas, David Bowie, Orlando Bloom, Goldie Hawn, Tina Turner, Tiger Woods, Oliver Stone, Leonard Cohen, and Richard Gere.

In recent times dialogue has expanded and encompasses many schools and traditions of both faiths.

Along with this, easier and therefore increased travel has also facilitated contact between Buddhists and Christians, with Buddhist countries being some of the most popular travel destinations for Westerners. This increased contact has also been assisted by advances in modern communications.

Though Buddhism has not gathered massive numbers of Western converts it has been successful in appealing to many who do not formally embrace it, as a type of lifestyle philosophy more than a religion. They are drawn to it by its lacking a deity, not therefore being encumbered with a theology built around such. For many it is still viewed in the rationalist manner in which it was brought to the West in the last century, often appearing as essentially a self-help means. A plethora of book titles around Buddhism will attest to that. In that form it appeals as an alternative to an often-discredited Christianity. Only rarely do these people however, formally become Buddhists.

Thus, paradoxically, despite the centrality of the sangha to it, Buddhism is understood by many in the West as something which is best pursued individually, without need to join an organization. This style of both Buddha and Buddhism seems also appropriate to a Western environment of post-structuralism with its ever-rising mistrust of authority and authoritative statements. The Buddhist admonition to always test one's own experience against any teaching seems most appropriate to the age.

As we have examined, much of the appeal for many regards Buddhism is in that it appears to be much less superstitious than Western faiths like Christianity. That, however, is to ignore miracles, especially those of Buddha, being widely accepted within Buddhism, along with such things germane to Vajrayana as magical amulets, mantras, mudras, and spells. Particularly in Tibet, what Westerners would call magic and superstition is widely associated in such things as the selection of lamas, understood as reincarnations of deceased lamas, including major figures such as both the Dalai and Panchen Lama, while political decisions by the Tibetan government in exile are often referred to the state oracle. Within Buddhism there is also a belief in an ornate cosmology of other realms, both below and above this one, populated by gods and other beings. Further, the unseen, immeasurable power of kamma (karma) as something determinative of all things is central to Buddhist belief. Though Buddhism is often popularly understood in a non-metaphysical automative manner, that is to misunderstand its depth and intricacy, especially the speculative metaphysics strongly present in Buddhism, particularly in the Abhidhamma Piṭaka, the third section of Buddhist Scriptures.

Buddhism is attractive to many in the West as it seems more in alignment with modern cosmology and discoveries in physics. Whereas Christianity seems to be fighting a losing, rear-guard action against the advances of science, Buddhism with its understanding of impermanence seems almost prophetic with regards to quantum physics, much discourse having been expended on this connection. Further, Christian cosmology, long geocentric, with creation having recent naissance, seems quite quaint and limited in terms of what modern science is informing us concerning both the size and age of the universe. Buddhist, or more widely Indian cosmology, with its massive timeframes of kalpas and eons, seems far more appropriate.

The practice of meditation, central to Buddhism, is also appealing to many. Meditation, in contrast to prayer—particularly petitionary prayer, of which increasing numbers are skeptical—often appears attractive. While prayer may be viewed as being speculative, meditation is understood to have many quantifiable benefits such as overcoming stress and other psychosomatic problems, along with providing clarity of mind and insight.

Most of the modern missionary impetus for Buddhism in the West is different however, in that it has come not from elites and scholars but from peoples displaced, or who have chosen to move from their homelands. Migration of Buddhists to the West began on a significant scale in the 1850s, when large numbers of Chinese in particular found their way to the goldfields of the US, Canada, and Australia, while other Chinese and Japanese came later as laborers to North America to work on the rapidly expanding rail network. Later, during the second half of the twentieth century, many Buddhists fled from Vietnam, Cambodia, and Laos due to the massive conflicts, and the subsequent aftermath which embroiled those lands. Some 500,000 found their way to the US, while another 70,000 arrived in Australia. They brought with them their primarily Buddhist religion and soon established places for worship. These temples, however, primarily serve as places for cultural and religious preservation rather than for proselytizing.

There has also been a gradual Tibetan diaspora since the Chinese occupa-tion and incorporation of Tibet into China from 1959.

It is this migration which has been the main cause of the growth of Buddhism in the West, rather than the conversion of Westerners.

While Buddhism has found success in the West, so likewise has Chris-tianity found success in the East. There are a number of reasons for this.

We have already examined the effect of Western colonialism. One re-sult of this has been that in some cases the attraction to Christianity is due to a cargo cult mentality, in that the West was seen as materially rich and technologically advanced compared to Eastern Buddhist civilizations. That wealth and technology had enabled them to conquer Buddhist lands, bring-ing "the modern world" to the East. Those things driving current economic progress in the East, science and technology, have also largely come from the West. This seemingly serves as justification that the Western way, and therefore its faith, must be superior.

Western culture, ranging from Hollywood to sports, is also attractive for many Easterners, and with that often comes Christianity. For others Christianity is understood as modern, serving as a means of breaking free from the constraints of tradition, especially around Confucian roles and responsibilities, that faith being traditional in both lands where Christianity is fast growing, China and South Korea.

Some in traditionally Buddhist lands are drawn to Christianity because of its vitality. That particularly seems to be the case with the above-men-tioned lands, China and South Korea, where an indigenous church has great vigor. The indigenous nature of the church in these two lands is important as it has allowed the faith to escape being categorized as a Western import.

Being vital faiths, both Buddhism and Christianity seek to convert and convict. That missional aim has led to their expansion across wide domains. This, missional goal however has often served to make dialogue difficult. That particularly is the case in traditional Buddhist nations where Christi-anity is still often seen as an interloper associated with colonialism, or when taken indigenous form, is understood as a competitor. In the West dialogue between Christians and Buddhists is still nascent. It has more possibilities given that Buddhism does not present the core challenge to Christianity, that challenge coming more from a generalized secularism. Often churches, however, beset by secularism's challenge, and their diminishing presence, seem not to be strongly disposed to such dialogue. In decline, many church-es are increasingly retreating into more conservative domains, choosing to identify themselves over and against outside influences, including other faiths. With walls raised and doors shut, there is little space for dialogue.

Further, in Western lands, Christian and Buddhist communities are often culturally separated from each other, Buddhists being almost exclusively composed of an ethnic minority. Perhaps with intergenerational change this may become different.

For now we may surmise that Buddhist-Christian dialogue primarily exists as a dialogue of religious professionals.

2

ISSUES FOR DIALOGUE

HAVING EXAMINED THE HISTORY of dialogue, it is now time for us to turn to that task for which we need to lay out some parameters or markers, things to avoid, and things of which we need be cognizant.

BUDDHISM IS NOT A "SECULAR PHILOSOPHICAL" ALTERNATIVE

As seen, many in the increasingly secularized West are attracted to Buddhism, understanding it more as a non-theistic philosophy lacking metaphysical systems, having no need of divinity. As such Buddhism is often perceived as an alternate non-religious wisdom teaching. This opposition between religion and a philosophy, however, cannot be sustained, for in the East philosophy and religion are not compartmentalized. Distinct from Western philosophy, with its speculative roots in the Hellenic tradition, there is no Eastern philosophical tradition which is purely theoretical or speculative. All Eastern philosophy has an existential concern, making those often asked questions as to whether Buddhism is a philosophy or a religion nonsensical. Thus, while many in the West, guided by Western concepts, may wish to separate the two, perceiving Buddhism as a philosophy rather than faith, in the lands of Southeast Asia from which it comes, Buddhism is always understood and practiced as a vibrant faith.

This is distinct from the Western tradition which has held philosophy and theology separate, with philosophy, especially in the still largely dominant Thomist tradition, understood as a preparation and basis for theology. In the East this distinction does not hold. One understands, not by philosophical detachment but rather by immersion through experience. Christians, from their time of engagement with Hellenic religions, and on through their dealings with pagan faiths, have judged analytically using tools of philosophical analysis, from outside. That is not the practice in the East. For its Asian adherents Buddhism represents not a dispassionate philosophy but a powerful force with a social dynamism.

Indeed Buddha specifically rejected speculative philosophical metaphysics. For him if the question didn't result in objectively measurable effects it ought not be asked.

That we cannot understand Buddhism to be a type of philosophy, akin to secular speculation as to meaning, contrasting it with a religious or metaphysical Christianity, is the first parameter we must lay in the task before us.

BEWARE OF ORIENTALISM

In dialoguing with the East those on the West need to be particularly aware of Orientalism, a term, as we have seen, coined by Edward Said, denoting a romanticism held in many quarters in the West concerning "the mysterious East," often categorized as "fascinating and exotic." That idealization precludes the East from being seen and from speaking for itself. Such figures as Giuseppe Verdi, Lord Byron, Helena "Madame" Blavatsky, and the Beatles, among many others, have each helped perpetuate this type of image. Projected on to the East are all those things which the West feels it has lost, among them mystery, deep spirituality, compassion, and communion with nature. The wisdom of the East is also held to be attractive in how it regards human beings to be repositories of wisdom, with an ability to possess profound spiritual insight. That contrasts with the Western view, understanding humanity as "fallen," possessing a sense of depravity, severely limiting—if not making impossible—the quest for spiritual wisdom.

Cautioning against a simplistic fascination with the East, Carl Jung believed that so to temper this often-naïve fascination with the East, the West had a desperate need to rediscover its own gnostic roots. To his call we shall return. From an Eastern and Buddhist perspective, the Dalai Lama has likewise called for Westerners to explore their own roots.

This caution with regards to Orientalism shall stand as our second parameter for dialogue.

THE TWO FAITHS ARE NOT THE SAME

Next, in pursuing dialogue, we need to understand that some sort of homogenizing of the two faiths, so as to remove the distinctiveness from each of them, will not suffice for dialogue. This sort of understanding is popularity expressed in the oft-used statement that "all religions are the same."

Buddhism and Christianity are profoundly different in many ways, as would be expected, given they spring from vastly different cultural and religious backgrounds. Religions represent cultural and linguistic traditions, so that which makes sense in one of them will not in the other—or may, but only when interpreted in a different way. Ludwig Wittgenstein reminds us that concerning language, that what makes sense may only do so within a particular language game and cannot necessarily be extrapolated to make sense in another.

Both Christianity and Buddhism represent distinct faith traditions, the language of each making coherent sense within but unable to be forced on the other. Such is a temptation I have had to constantly consider in this writing. "Each religion is not only profoundly shaped by the culture in which it emerges but also becomes a culture with its own language (including images, myths, stories, and the rituals and practices which embody them). Buddhism and Christianity are thus as different as the cultural and linguistic traditions in which they are embedded."[1] We need to highly cognizant of this when we ask such questions as whether Buddhists are theists, for the concept of theism is very different between Christianity and Buddhism. Likewise, the goal in each, ego extinguishment into nibbana and eternal life, are very different.

Avoiding homogenization will represent the third of our parameters in dialogue.

NOT AS SIMPLE AS EAST/WEST

We often draw a division between the so-called Western religions of Judaism, Christianity, and Islam, and those in the East, normally understood as Hinduism, Buddhism, Confucianism, and Taoism. This distinction is, however, erroneous in that all the "great religions" come from the East. Those called Western all have their actual roots firmly in the East, specifically that part of the world often named the Ancient Near East. Only later did they take on Western forms. It was of course in its Western form in

---

1. Borg, *Jesus and Buddha*, 110.

which Christianity primarily interacted with Buddhism, especially during the colonial period.

Turning to the East, the Indian religions of Hinduism, Jainism and Buddhism all have stronger affinities with the much of Hellenic and Roman thought of the West, than they do with systems of thought located further east, including that which became the fountainhead of the "Western" faiths, the Semitic. Like the Greeks they seek wisdom and insight. Further, in Christianity particularly, the agapeic (love) component, rather than being Western, is Semitic in origin, having Eastern roots, while gnostic forms, more amenable to Buddhism, having Hellenic/Roman roots, are a product of the West.

Rather than contrasting faiths by their supposed geographical location, East and West, a better distinction is to speak of the agapaeic and gnostic aspects of faith, regardless of geographical location. Gnosis represents saving knowledge, while agape represents redemptive love. While different faith traditions and individual adherents of them may center more on one than the other, they ought not to be seen as being mutually exclusive. Rather, "They are two mystical moods that can alternate according to the spiritual fluctuations of individuals, groups, and even of entire cultures, without either of them allowing itself to be totally submerged by the other."[2] There needs to be a dialectical interplay of wisdom and love. For that to happen Christians need to overcome their long suspicion of gnosis, something persisting due to its early rejection of Gnosticism.

Within Buddhism, prajna, the Sanskrit word approximating Greek gnosis, and karuna, the Sanskrit approximating agape, are always held together. The Buddha's own life makes this evident. Likewise, in Christianity the two are held close, the life of the one at the heart of the faith, Jesus being the clearest example. While Christians most associate Jesus with love, even a cursory reading of the Gospels shows him to be a great wisdom teacher, speaking a wisdom which often confounded his opponents.

Simplistic divisions based around geography, the wisdom of the East contrasted with the agapeic West, represents another thing of which we need be cognizant.

EXAMINING THE NEGLECTED SIDE OF EACH FAITH

Rather than making the divide a geographical one between the so-called Western religions and those of the East, the difference is best seen as that of psychological types.

2. Pieris, *Love*, 9.

In terms of Buddhist-Christian dialogue Christianity represents a dynamism oriented primarily outward while Buddhism constitutes the inverse. Christianity is associated with such external values as human dignity, reason, freedom, action, science, techniques, wealth, and well-being. Values associated with Buddhism, on the other hand, are the internal values of human-heartedness, non-interference, selflessness, enlightenment, compassion, detachment, moderation, patience, and inner peace.

The Christian Sri Lankan theologian Aloysius Pieris charges Christians as having held too strongly to the first grouping of attributes at the expense of the other. "To put it in more precise terms, a genuine Christian experience of God-in-Christ grows by maintaining a dialectical tension between the poles: between action and non-action, between world and silence, between control of nature and harmony with nature, between self-affirmation and self-negation, between engagement and withdrawal, between love and knowledge, between karuna and prajna, between agape and gnosis . . . abuses of Gnostics have created a phobia in the West, which prevents theologians from approaching the question afresh."[3]

Each of these aspects forms a stimulating framework for dialogue.

The West needs to rediscover its gnostic tradition, and the best way to do this will be by entering into dialogue with faiths of the East such as Buddhism. That may help Christianity in its self-dialogue, as there is a rich mystic tradition, including that which is gnostic, reaching right back through its tradition. Such self-dialogue will serve to make Christianity more rounded. To facilitate this more work could be done on understanding the wisdom tradition in the Jewish Scriptures and on the Johannine understanding of Jesus as "logos" or the Word, understood as wisdom. This will involve massive theological change in that so much of Christianity has been premised on the idea of humans being essentially fallen, lacking wisdom, and being alienated from God. Given that premise, in Christian orthodoxy there is no way that the divine can be found analogous with humanity from within, the result being that the divine has been externalized, known only in a relational manner.

Having lost its early gnostic element, Christianity has become almost entirely "agapeic." This flight from the internal was a clear reaction to so much of Gnosticism in the early Christian communities being unworldly. Wishing to affirm the world, albeit a fallen world, Christians rejected Gnosticism as a whole in the name of love. Unfortunately the proverbial baby was thrown out with the bath water. A dialogue with Buddhism will help show that such contrast between wisdom and love is not necessary.

3. Pieris, *Love*, 27.

From the other side, Buddhism is not the "world denying" religion as so often characterized in the West but contains within it a profound emphasis on compassion and love—karuna.

Again, Pieris notes, it is true that "the Indian sage seated in serene contemplation under the Tree of Knowledge and the Hebrew prophet hanging painfully on the Tree of Love in a gesture of protest—here are the two contrasting images that clearly situate the Buddha (the Enlightened One) and the Christ (the Anointed one) in their respective paradigmatic contexts of gnosis and agape," before later concluding, "any valid spirituality, Buddhist or Christian, as the history of each religion attests, does retain both poles of religious experience—namely, the gnosis and the agapeic that moves as the spirit progresses through the dialectical interplay of wisdom and love."[4] People from both traditions need to acknowledge the reciprocity of these two poles, as both being legitimate languages of the human spirit. Dialogue between the two faiths will greatly assist in this.

In this dialogue Christians need also draw from the deep gnostic stream from within their tradition. Despite suppression the gnostic tradition survived as an important though minor tradition in Christianity. It extends from the Alexandrian school and the desert fathers to Christian monasticism, and informs the writings of the medieval mystics such as Hildegarde of Bingen, Saint John of the Cross, the anonymous writer of the *Cloud of Unknowing*, and Meister Eckhart, among others. It is present in the works of modern Christian mystics such as Thomas Merton, Bede Griffiths, and Dag Hammarskjöld, the last being a former Secretary-General of the United Nations.

In the Western medieval period knowledge "cogitio" was understood both as intellectual knowledge (scientia) and salvific knowledge (sapienta). Mysticism, rather than being understood as contrary to love, was defined in terms of both cogitio and amor, as evidenced in the medieval Thomist/ Franciscan creative tension. Both movements, from the same period, represent different responses to a holistic mysticism. Wisdom and love belong together rather than being viewed as in opposition. Buddhism, though it centers on vidyā (correct seeing), likewise holds compassion (karuna) very highly, with Buddha being known as "the compassionate one." That attribute, as we shall see, is strongly emphasized in the Bodhisattva concept. While the idea of the Bodhisattva is associated with compassion, etymologically the word is linked to wisdom (bodhi).

In entering this dialogue Christians will need to rid themselves of the idea that Buddhism promotes a type of detached passivity which excludes

4. Pieris, *Love*, 86, 111.

any interest in the world with its social domain. Such an understanding was most regrettably proclaimed by Pope John Paul II, who wrote concerning Buddhism:

> We do not free ourselves from evil through the good which comes from God, we liberate ourselves only through detachment from the world, which is bad. The fullness of such a detachment is not union with God, but what is called nirvana, a state of perfect indifference with regard to the world. To save oneself means, above all, to free oneself from evil by becoming indifferent to the world, which is the source of evil.[5]

As seen, however, Buddhism, does not lack an agapeic side. Indeed, it recognizes two of the three things which must be overcome, as being agapeic, with only one linked with wisdom. Those three are raga—erotic, selfish acquisitive love; dvesa or dosa—hatred and ill will; with only the third, avidya—delusion and slowness of mind—concerned with insight, panna. Nibbana consists of araga, adosa, and moksa, understood in turn as being non-selfish love, forgiving love, and liberating knowledge (of the dhamma). Within Buddhism then, knowledge is intimately linked with love. Bhakti, an affective knowledge, is rooted in love, a devotional love directed not only to Buddha but also to others.

Many Christians understand their Scriptures as rejecting knowledge in favor of love. They refer especially to Paul's writing, in what is probably his most famous passage, that knowledge without love is like a clanging bell (1 Cor 13). James in his epistle seemingly strongly concurs. There is not a rejection of knowledge, however, but rather a critique of it when poorly understood. Paul, as we shall see, has a strong gnostic dimension in his writings.

In both Buddhism and Christianity, the two attributes of which we are speaking belong together. The emphasis on love in Buddhism is particularly strong in the Mahayana tradition, most clearly in Buddha's refusal of the last temptation, presented by Mara, to pass immediately following his enlightenment into nirvana. Instead he chose, out of love, to remain upon the earth, to proclaim the liberating message. This episode is the basis for the Bodhisattva ideal. Following his rejection of this enticing temptation, Buddha spent the rest of his life, often under hardship as a result of this act of love and compassion. While prajna may be seen as the constitutive element in Buddhism, it is certainly not a religion without love. Of Buddha, Pieris writes,

---

5. John Paul II, *Crossing the Threshold*, 86.

Though the gnostic idiom in which he couched his message may give the wrong impression that he advocated a world-denying asceticism, his praxis clearly revealed it to be a world-transforming spirituality . . . An attempt was made to affirm a complementarity between prajna and karuna, the two constitutive dimensions of Buddhahood. The former denotes "salvific knowledge" implying disengagement from samsara, whereas the latter stands for "redeeming love" that engages the Buddha in a program of restructuring the psycho-social life of human society in tune with the supreme goal of nirvanic freedom. By gnosis a Buddha anticipates here and now the beyond, but by agape, so to say, he transfigures the here and now in terms of that beyond. Thus wisdom (prajna) is thought to have provided him with a vantage point to serve the world with loving-kindness (karuna). This then was his twofold posture toward the world: gnostic disengagement and agapeic involvement, wisdom and love: prajna and karuna.[6]

Such is common right across the range of Buddhism. Without doubt however prajna lies at the core of knowledge Buddhism for it alone liberates, but always in and through love. Karuna may make a Bodhisattva but only gnosis makes a Buddha, that even being the case in Mahayana.

For Christians dialogue with Buddhism will necessarily involve re-examination of their own gnostic roots, while also ridding themselves of ideas of Buddhist passivity to the world. On the other side, Buddhists will need to more deeply discover that other side of their faith, karuna, which calls them to social involvement and political action, something which is increasingly happening in forms of socially engaged Buddhism. They will also need acknowledge that Christianity has a deep internally directed spiritual dimension and also understand the wisdom dimension present in Jesus' teachings.

This examination of the neglected side of each faith will represent our fifth parameter framing dialogue.

SOME WORDS AND CONCEPTS DON'T CROSS OVER

A further difficulty for Christians and Buddhists in dialogue is that terms, so central to one's own faith understanding, find little resonance in the other or may be interpreted very differently. Words so core to Christian understanding and experience, such as "God" and "soul," may make little sense for

6. Pieris, *Love*, 75.

Buddhists. Ultimate truth for Buddhists cannot be understood in personalized terms. Instead, Buddhists use gnostic-style categories to express final
liberation. For a Christian to speak of being redeemed or to have found
salvation makes little sense to a Buddhist. From the other side, Buddhist
concepts of impermanence, anicca and anatta, along with nibbana, are at
absolute odds with Christian concepts.

It has been claimed that dialogue is essentially impossible, as the faiths
differ so strongly on the question of divinity, some charging that while
Christianity is clearly theistic, Buddhism is atheistic. This represents, however, an over-simplification. Buddhism never denies the gods, even in its
Theravada form, but more so relativizes them in that one must move past
them, given that they are also enmeshed in samsara. Later in Mahayana,
the significance of the gods return, with even Buddha himself being made
such. Certainly, Buddhism doesn't allow for a high divinity which, even if in
intimate relationship with creation, as in Christianity, is in essence separate
from us as personality, as implied in the term "relationship." For Buddhists
there is no personal God but rather an understanding of the Godhead as
being unborn, uncreated, undifferentiated, a formless source of all that is. It
does not greatly differ from how Christian mystics and increasing numbers
of theologians speak of God. One such theologian, Paul Tillich, is best-
known for speaking of, "the God beyond god."

Even the terms Buddha and Christ don't easily cross over. Buddha, signifying enlightened "wise one," a process arising from his turning inward,
means something very different to Christ, meaning "messiah," bringing an
externalized reign of peace. Associated with such is the exclusivity which
develops around each figure in their respective faiths, concerning their role
to the exclusion of all others. Again, this makes comparison of the terms
difficult.

It may be helpful to understand that it not the names themselves, Buddha and Christ which save, but rather the mediating reality that both show
forth. In different cultures that mediating reality receives different names
and is framed differently. The understandings of both Buddha and Christ
are framed by their faith backgrounds, Hinduism, and Judaism respectively,
even though each radically reworks those backgrounds. These distinct
backgrounds set how each figure is perceived by their followers, along with
how they understand their very distinct soteriological roles, one centering
on prajna/gnosis (wisdom), the other on karuna/agape (love).

Understanding the distinct ways in which each faith primarily understands the "divine," relationally as person, or internally as ground of being,
along with the response one makes to such difference, will represent the
sixth parameter by which we will establish our discussion.

THE NATURE OF TRUTH: 'THE' TRUTH IS NOT 'OUR' TRUTH

Another difficulty for our encounter is that both faiths, being missionary, make claims for truth at such depth, that their adherents wish to proclaim and spread their respective faiths. This is primarily because the truth they each claim is a higher order truth, exclusivist in nature, calling it therefore to be propagated. This is distinct from most other faiths and philosophies, which though holding themselves highly, do not subscribe to such exclusivist views. Such understanding is not found in other major world faiths such as Hinduism or Judaism, faiths, as noted, more identified with a people, having limited missionary stimulus. How then do Buddhists and Christians, having held, perhaps still holding, such high understanding of their respective faiths, enter dialogue?

For genuine dialogue to take place, two things are necessary, both to do with respect: respect for one's own faith and respect for the interlocutor's faith. Without these things genuine dialogue is impossible, being reduced rather to a polite discussion, in which only knowledge about the other faith is shared. There may be a strong tendency to perhaps avoid offense, to relativize both one's own faith and that of the other. There is nothing inherently wrong with this, but it does not represent genuine challenging dialogue. Only when someone perceives their own faith as an absolute entity are they able to encounter the absolute claims of another's faith. Faiths are not equivalent definitions of one absolute, unable to be reduced to each other. Neither are they all relative. They are alternative absolutes, excluding each other in any but a transcendental sense. Rather than being relativized, thereby losing their distinct claim, each faith needs to be held whole.

From the foothills to the mountain top there may be many paths. For those on all these paths the summit is its own distinctive summit, but from the summit it is clear that each path is but one path, distinct and different among many others. Each path allows those on it to have absolute confidence in where it is leading, meaning for them there is only one path, that path upon which they are treading. They fully commit themselves to this path, given it is impossible to be on two. One commits to a path, which to them is the only path, while acknowledging others have the same perception of the completeness of their path.

My path for me is an existential truth. It is true for me but this does not equate to absolute truth. Neither mine, or others existential truth equates to the absolute. All such "truths" are partial, existentially true, beyond which there is no need to go.

Being cognizant of the nature of the exclusivist claim each faith makes for itself and its founder will represent the seventh parameter for our examination.

THE PROBLEM OF EXCLUSIVE CATEGORIES: JESUS IS LORD/BUDDHA IS LORD

One of the greatest difficulties in Christian/Buddhist dialogue is the unique ontological status which each of these faiths give their founders. Both Buddha and Christ, though beginning as human beings, become ontologically elevated to an incredible degree, far beyond anyone we find in the other great faiths.

The elevation of both Jesus and Buddha began almost immediately, even in their lifetimes, and following their deaths, they continued to be lifted higher. That Buddha was called such during his ministry evidences that profound elevation while he still existed in biological human form. Jesus, within his lifetime, was recognized as a prophet, even the Messiah, both of these categories still human, but soon after that event central to the Jesus story, his death and resurrection, his elevation gathers pace. Just some twenty years later the apostle Paul is speaking of him as being ontologically different, counted equal with God, but emptying himself of divinity and taking low form suffering for us, that being redemptive (Phil 2:5–11). By the fourth century Christians come to formally understand Jesus as being the Son of God, divinity itself, the second part of the Trinity. Christians interestingly understood this of how Buddhists viewed Buddha, the second century Christian writer, Clement of Alexandria, as seen, noting that Buddhists understood him to be divine.

Within Buddhism, the one that begins as the wise teacher of the path to nibbana, becomes progressively elevated until he is beyond even divine. Even in Theravada he has a soteriological role as the one who uniquely discovered and preached the saving dhamma. Buddha is progressively elevated to be first a human teacher (sattha), then in turn, a saint (arahant), a great being (mahasatta), and finally Lord (bhagavan). We read in the Anguttara Nikaya that when Buddha is questioned by Brahma as to his being divine, he responds that he is neither human nor divine, but rather is Buddha, implying a state clearly meant to be higher than divinity.

In Mahayana, Buddha is raised progressively still further finally taking a three body form as nirmanakaya (the embodied Buddha), the sambhoghakaya (body of bliss) and the dharmakaya (the truth body knowing no limit).

So highly was Buddha regarded he became equated with the dhamma, the eternal truth undergirding all reality. The same is said of the Christ in the Christian tradition, wherein it is charged that he is the logos, the Word, the eternal principle of the universe, present from the very beginning, the one in whom all is held together and finds purpose (John 1:1-18; Col 1:17).

Not Moses nor Muhammad nor Confucius, or any human figure in Hinduism, holds such a place in those faiths as do Buddha and Christ in theirs. "This is what makes the Buddhist-Christian dialogue a dangerous exercise. Far from being a religious conversation about Jesus and Gautama, or a comparative study of their different historical and cultural backgrounds it can easily explode into a kerygmatic confrontation between the Jesus interpreted as the Christ and Gautama interpreted as the Buddha."[7] There is a uniqueness to each, as Christ, "the son of God," and Buddha, "the dharma tathagata."

Does this unique ontological status, however, of both figures given in each faith, need to be extended to all dimensions as a universal maxim, or can it be limited to within those faiths springing from each figure? In other words, does the Christian assertion "that no one comes to the Father except by me (Jesus) (John 14:6)" necessarily mean that such ontological specificity need be extended to non-Christians, so that they are unable ever to enter salvation? Does the Buddhist claim that the Buddha is the tathagata need be extended to non-Buddhists, so that they are excluded from reaching nibbana? I do not believe so. Neither need be viewed as the absolute or sole agency of salvation for all. If they were, then clearly any meaningful dialogue would be at best severely limited, if not curtailed.

The absolute claims made of each can be confined to the traditions in which they are made. I am reminded again of Wittgenstein with his idea of language games. Words may have totally different meanings in different contexts yet be totally true in each. The term "off-side" in sport is fully defined in the distinct languages associated with both cricket and football in vastly different ways, yet equally true in how each defines it. One is not true and the other false. It would make no sense to extend the cricket definition to football, or vice-versa. Equally so with Buddha and Christ. In each of the faiths named after them they represent fullness, but there is no need to extend claims made of Christ into Buddhism, nor Buddhist claims concerning Buddha into Christianity.

To put it another way, we are all unique, but does my uniqueness need exclude other's uniqueness? I am uniquely human, but that doesn't exclude others from being uniquely human. I may make the statement that my wife

7. Pieris, Love, 124.

is the most beautiful woman who has ever lived, but surely such a statement should not be pushed beyond the specificity of my claiming such. Such a statement, of course, is limited to being existentially true in that it has a truth to my existence but does not extend further. Indeed, by the nature of my relationship with my wife it cannot. Another man may make the same statement regarding his wife. Such differences as to who is the most beautiful woman in the world do not necessarily bring us into conflict. We can discuss those things, which make each uniquely beautiful to the beholder, without need to compete, to exclude the other's wife from the category "most beautiful woman." Each of us are speaking existential truths, rather than an impossible-to-prove absolute truth.

Buddhists can therefore hold that for them the way of the Buddha is the true way, without having to say to a Christian that their way of Christ is less, and of course vice versa. In the example above, if we were to swap wives, we may each find that the other's wife was incompatible with us. We have developed ways of being and doing things which wouldn't fit into the new relationship. There is something like that with faiths. There are things germane to them, along with their accretions, with which we are familiar, which are not part of the other faith. Our own faith fits us, but that need not mean we make any universal claim regarding its truth; rather we should limit our claim that for us it is truth. Our dialogue partner can likewise say that for them, their faith is their truth.

Between Buddha and Christ there may be a uniqueness about the names and the nature of the soteriological path they offer, but it isn't the names nor the paths that are crucial; rather it's the mediated reality they both show forth, however it be named. The names "Christ" and "Buddha" are only human categorizations framed by a given culture. What saves, as seen, is not the name but rather the mediating reality to which varying names are given.

Uniqueness doesn't necessarily include universality. Christ and Buddha were each recognized as unique in their own cultural traditions and were thus given high soteriological status. This doesn't mean, however, that this soteriological status reaches across all cultures. Returning again to the image of the mountain, there may be two paths—probably more than two—to the summit, each of them unique. It is the mountain summit which is important, rather than the path by which one travels to the peak. The path one picks will mostly be determined by the religio-cultural tradition from which they come. It has an exclusivity about it in that it is our path to the top, but it does not exclude other's exclusive paths. It is, however for us, starting from where we come from, the best path.

Of course, some of these issues are not as sharp when Christians are in dialogue with Theravada for Theravada does not ascribe high soteriological status to the Buddha as a type of savior but rather to the path he walks. This understanding, however, creates another problem in dialogue for Theravada presents a direct challenge to the Christian contention that there is a need for a savior figure. If the Theravada adherent does not see Buddha as a soteriological figure, then they certainly will be unable to agree with the central Christian contention of Christ being such a soteriological figure. The adherent of Theravada can only agree that Christ is a teacher of the dhamma, though at a lesser level than Buddha.

Though the high ontological status given by each faith to the person after which their faith is named makes dialogue extremely difficult, such status can not be lessened, ignored, or glossed over. Such a claim needs to be recognized however as an existential truth, without need to be extended to a universalist claim. Recognition of such will serve as our eighth parameter for dialogue.

OUR FAITH DOES NOT COMPLETE THE OTHER'S

Given that both Buddhism and Christianity have provided succor and a framework of meaning so very deep and complete for their adherents, it is hard for those of each faith not to feel an obligation to extend that experienced fullness to the other. Given this, it may be tempting for adherents of each, while holding the other highly, to understand their faith as something which would bring that other to completion.

While there can be hardly any more arrogant view than limiting salvation or enlightenment to one's own faith alone, there may be a more subtle temptation in that one may hold a position in which, while allowing the other to hold their faith, still believes there to be something in one's own faith, which if only the other would adopt, would bring a greater fullness to it. Such understanding from a Christian might see Buddhism as being better if only it would take, say, a protest toward injustice from Christianity, rather than possessing a perceived passivity. On the other side a Buddhist may see Christianity as being able to be bettered if Christians would take into their faith the meditative practices of Buddhism. This however, still represents some type of imperial type of arrogance in that it regards one's own faith as superior.

Both Buddhism and Christianity regard themselves as complete faiths, the adherents of each seeing no need for either to be bettered or completed by the other. From the Christian perspective that type of understanding of a faith being completed by another is something normally associated with Judaism. Christians often understand Judaism as being incomplete, super-seded finding its completion in Christianity. Such supercessionist views have no real validity given Jews find their own faith complete without need of anything being added to it. In like manner supercessionist views are not appropriate when held by Christians in relation to Buddhism, for Buddhists likewise find their own faith complete without need of completion by Chris-tianity. Christians after all don't believe their faith is incomplete, finding completion only in the later faith of Islam.

There is a similar temptation for Buddhists. Buddhists present the Buddha as being beyond the old Hindu gods, portraying them as paying homage to Buddha as their superior. Given that Buddhism calls one to move past the Hindu gods, understood, like humans, to be ensnared in samsara, Buddhism can easily present itself as a supercessionist faith from Hindu-ism, out of which it emerged, They could then apply such understanding to Christianity. Buddhists, however, must understand that Christians have found a wholeness in their faith, and that it has no need to be completed by their faith, which though chronologically earlier, comes later in most Chris-tian experience. Christian experience of their faith was whole before any experience of Buddhism in the West and remains so even after Buddhism has made its way there.

In dialoguing then we need to have respect for both our own faith, complete in itself, while similarly holding deep respect for the other's faith, likewise for them complete. It need hardly be said then that we ought not be dialoguing with the covert aim of converting the other to our faith. This may not be as easy as it sounds, when we are called to have such deep com-mitment to, and confidence in our faith, and with each of the faiths we are discussing making exclusivist claims of themselves.

This acknowledgement of the deep missional impulse of each faith, and rejection of supersessionist ideas will be our ninth parameter in dialoguing.

DON'T CO-OPT THE OTHER INTO OUR OWN

A similar temptation is to relativize the other's faith by fitting it into one's own faith categories Thus, a Christian, unable to accept Buddha in the terms that Buddhists hold him, may wish to make of him as being one of the great prophets, understood as showing the way to the Christ. In like manner, a Buddhist may relativize Christianity by reducing Christ as being just an-other bodhisattva, holy, but not of the same order as the Buddha, using the concept Pacceka Buddha, one achieving enlightenment without explicit knowledge of the Buddha or his teachings.

Such understandings link to the Karl Rahner's idea of the "anonymous Christian," in which he held that those not explicitly Christian could nonetheless be saved through the sacrificing atoning death of Jesus, even when not acknowledging, or even having knowledge of it. By such the adherent is categorizing the other's faith in a manner framed by their own, so not really allowing the other's faith to stand in its own right. By using one's own categories to make sense of the other's faith, there is an assertion that their own faith is superior. Considering what we have said as to the necessity of holding firm to one's faith in dialogue we need genuinely acknowledge how difficult it is to find a way out of this conundrum.

Paradoxically this type of tolerance becomes a type of intolerance as the other's faith is understood as having inherent value not in itself but only in light of one's own faith. Such understanding strips the other religion of its right to proclaim itself on its own terms. The Indian Christian theologian Raimundo Panikkar calls this "intolerant tolerance." One wonders how a Christian would react to a Muslim dialoguing with them saying that Jesus was merely preparation for the one chronologically after him, Muhammad. The Muslim may be very tolerant pointing out their high regard for Jesus, something indeed true in Islam, but the Christian in such dialogue is highly likely to be offended to hear that Jesus is but a preparatory prophet, even more so if such is followed by the statement, that the graciousness of Allah "the compassionate" will extend to saving them as being "anonymous Muslims."

We must allow each faith its right to the absolute claim it makes and not reduce it so to fit into our own faith framework. If we understand our own faith as an absolute, containing fullness, we need allow the other to experience their faith in like manner. We would not like our own faith being relativized and ought not relativize that of our dialogue partner.

Each religion understands itself as the center, self-sufficient to itself. Using again our mountain paths analogy, each path is complete in itself leading all the way to the summit, not just being preparatory for another.

Not relativizing the other's faith in terms of our own will stand as our tenth parameter.

DIALOGUE IS MORE THAN DISPASSIONATE CONVERSATION

While holding confidently to our own, we must not be afraid to plunge into the other's faith. Initially in dialogue we encounter the concrete form of a faith, never the indescribable experience which lies behind those forms. We first meet the philosophically, culturally, and ideologically interpreted forms of the other's religion and probably communicate our faith in like manner. It is easy to remain at this level, in a type of dry objective discussion without moving to the deeper experiential dimension. These things, however, are not the heart of our nor another's faith, so in limiting ourselves to this level, we are left with a dialogue which precludes us from touching the heart level of each other's faith. At this secondary level, we are safe from that deeper response, which challenges us when we enter experientially into the other's faith. To truly enter another's faith we need to move to a deeper experiential dimension, through joining in such activities of the other faith as worship, prayer, and meditation.

A Christian may choose to participate in a Buddhist puja, while a Buddhist could join Christian worship. Ideally an experience of the seminal high festivals is optimum, a Christian attending Vesak, a Buddhist sharing in Easter. This level, beyond mere communication of the external, calls us to a deeper domain of understanding in an experiential presence with the other. Of course, the deepest level of dialogue is the attempt to appreciate the unique soteriological role that both Buddha and Christ have in their respective religions.

Buddhists themselves differentiate in how one may know their faith distinguishing that knowledge as obtained though intellectual mastery—paryapti—from that gained through practice—prattipati—or that achieved through gnosis, or deeper knowledge of enlightenment—prativedha. This distinction picks up those differences in knowing theoretically, by participation, and through deep experience. Within Christianity the same range of knowing exists. Christians of their own faith are called to move beyond knowing their faith just theoretically to a deeper level of transformative knowledge. Two of the most famous instances are Saint Augustine, who while intellectually knowing the gospel very well, and therefore its ramifications if he accepted it, cried "not yet" to its challenge before later fully dedicating himself to it, and John Wesley who moved from a formal Christianity to something far deeper when he "felt his heart strangely warmed."

There may be a few reasons for staying with a safe, second-level response. One may be unsure of one's own faith and out of uncertainty may feel intimidated by the other's faith immersion, or conversely the adherent may feel great certainty about their faith in a narrow exclusivist manner which then claims that there is something inherently wrong in the other's faith. In either case one will be hesitant about getting too close to the other's faith.

A preparedness to encounter the existential or lived experience of the other's faith will serve as our eleventh parameter of dialogue.

WHEN IMAGES MAKE BLIND

The iconography associated with each of Buddha and Christ can represent another barrier to dialogue. The image nearly always associated with the Buddha is his sitting in one of the classic poses of meditation. Sitting passively, he is clearly centered in the act of seeking prajna. In Christianity, on the other hand, the core image is Christ in an agonized crucifixion posture. Here clearly is an act centered on agape: "no greater love has a person than that they lay down their life for a friend" (John 15:13).

Such assumptions could easily have us understand that Buddhism lacks political involvement and that Christianity lacks a long meditative, contemplative tradition. That, however, is not the case, there being several modern-day examples. As we have seen, Buddhism has acted as a force against colonial oppression in Southeast Asia and China and later in Tibet. Political involvement from Buddhists can be seen for both good and bad, as we have examined. Whether it has acted for what we would judge as good, or for evil, it can be seen in just these few instances that Buddhism is certainly not a passive faith without a political dimension.

Buddhists will of course be quick to point out that they know too well that Christianity has a political dimension, one, in their experience, not for the good, using as evidence, its justification of the colonial occupation of the Buddhist lands of Southeast Asia.

They would be wrong, however, to charge that Christianity lacks the inner aspect of meditation. To do so would be to ignore a long tradition extending from the desert fathers through the Christian monastic tradition, including the powerful mystical tradition typified in such figures of whom we have already spoken.

We shall need to move past the common images, as signified in the iconography associated with each. This shall be our twelfth parameter guiding our discussion.

POLITICAL ENGAGEMENT

As we have already seen Christianity is a faith encompassing politics. The place of the political dimension of Christianity has been radically re-emphasized in a recent powerful and necessary movement within Christianity, liberation theology. The option for the poor lies at the heart of this theology, with it speaking of the love exemplified by the crucified Jesus, a love grounded in his concern for justice. It understands God making an option for the poor and calls the church to likewise choose. Many, especially in the more oppressive situations in the world, find in this movement great succor.

This movement raises problems, however, when it comes to dialogue due to both its choice of interlocutor and also due to its Christocentric nature.

Traditionally Christian theology had as interlocutor, philosophy, in an attempt to be sensical to the world (apologetics). Liberation theology has as its prime interlocutor not philosophy but rather sociology, often Marxist, not to make sense of, but rather to change the world. It claims the world, with its current societal and political order, to be unjust, the goal of faith being then not to become sensical in such a world but rather to call that world to radical change. At the heart of this theology of protest lies a high Christology, in that Christ is understood as standing opposed, dialectical to the existing order, including the religious realm. Liberation theology had its genesis in Latin America, a highly Christianized continent. Though vibrant indigenous faiths remain in such places as Bolivia and Peru, and syncretistic faiths are present in Brazil, the other major world religions are scarcely represented. Outside that continent, when faced with a faith as deeply acculturated as Buddhism, with its deep religious ethos penetrating right through society, there are problems in dialoguing both, from such a perspective dialectic to the culture, and in doing so using such a high Christology.

Liberation theology is but a modern movement within Christianity, its roots extending back some fifty years. Historically it represents a rejection of the Constantinian accommodation between church and state. Buddhism, though never having the same radical response to power as did Jesus and the earliest church (Buddha had numerous wealthy patrons), had its own "Constantinian compromise" when it was similarly co-opted to the civil order under the Mauryan king Ashoka during the 3rd century BCE. As with Christianity, Buddhism became the religion of the state. It has yet to experience the radical attempts present in liberation theology, though similar movements are emerging in Buddhist nations, with a growing number of Buddhists rejecting the essential nexus between the societal order and faith.

A political Buddhism with a concern for justice and the social order is increasingly evident. Along with the instances just mentioned, throughout Southeast Asia numerous sanghas have been involved in actions to conserve the forest against encroaching economic development, while historically, Buddhism also served as a strong cultural force opposing the Western colonial domination of the nineteenth and twentieth centuries. Increasingly evident is a "socially engaged" Buddhism.

Buddha of course made a radical protest against his society, something mostly not acknowledged, in the political dimension. The protest he made has often become directed toward an otherworldliness, in the sense of being anti-world, rather than being about an anti-worldliness calling for a transformed or alternative society. That is understandable given that he was radically anti-material in that he believed material things to be mere illusion (maya), with our thirst to have them being the cause of our suffering. Again, this understanding of the material as illusionary opens up the possibility of protest against the materialism of our world, where the thirst for material things socially has caused such inequality and oppression.

Buddha's withdrawal can be seen much more as a rejection of worldliness than a rejection of the world. His rejection is of a worldliness which abrogates the bounty of the world to a few, rather than the many, actually represents a deep concern for the world.

As Christian liberation theologians have moved to break the connection between faith and sanctification of the existing order, Buddhist scholars may likewise follow, with Buddha increasingly becoming understood as one protesting against his social order, as Christ has become for many. That Buddha came from a place of prestige in that order can make his protest against it even more radical.

Again, Buddha, rejecting the caste system, established the sangha as an alternative societal model, radically distinct to that around him. To the surrounding sociopolitical order the sangha offered a radical critique. This is comparable to the early church, whose members understood themselves as people of "the way" (the earliest name by which Christians identified), standing as an alternative to the Roman Empire's order.

The sociopolitical dimension present in both Buddhism and Christianity, expressed in their rejection of caste and their belief therefore in the essential equality of all believers, has found a current commonality in India where there is a movement of those traditionally called outcasts, the Dalits, to embrace either Buddhism or Christianity as means of both protesting and escaping the oppressive order imposed upon them in the name of religion.

The choice of interlocutor for Buddhists in choosing a political option is problematic. That chosen by Christian political theology has often been Marxism. Much of the Buddhist world, China, Vietnam, and Laos, exist within Communist nations, clearly making necessary dialogue with Marxism. However, in these lands Marxism, rather than representing an alternative to the order, is instead the prevailing order.

Liberation is wider of course than just sociopolitical realm, though it can never leave that dimension behind. Speaking from his Asian context, but having wider application I believe, Piernis notes, "For the evolution of the new society and the emergence of the new person constitute one indivisible process; which is to say that Marxist class analysis and gnostic self-analysis form a pincer movement in the liberation of Asian peoples living in the context of religion and poverty."[8] The sharpest critique of a social order and action to take to change it will come from one radically self-aware.

Mostly both Buddhism and Christianity have comfortably accommodated themselves with the various political orders in which they find themselves. The British monarch is crowned by the Archbishop of Canterbury, US Christian evangelicals mostly believe the state and God are essentially synonymous, Thai royalty is intimately linked with Buddhism, and Sri Lankan and Burmese leaders are very clear in looking to Buddhism as justification for their policies.

The political dimension must be part of any contemporary discussion of faith. We need be cognizant of it while noting that the political dimension makes a fertile field for dialogue. This will serve as our thirteenth parameter in our dialogue.

A WHOLE EARTH ECOLOGICAL PERSPECTIVE

An essential part of any dialogue today, whether religious or other, is responding to ecological questions. The earth, with its intricate ecological web, is metaphorically screaming due to the intense harm being done to it. "One does not need to look far to see that the Tree of Life is dying, and Mother Earth has cancer of the womb."[9] While Christianity liberated people from an often fraught, fearful relationship with nature and the cosmic forces understood to lie behind it, it has done so at great cost. The resultant desacralized world has been laid open for an exploitation, which has become increasingly rapacious with advances in technology. Though communion with nature has been suppressed in the West, it has not been squashed. It is evident in the words of the mystics, most clearly in the one, known often as "the saint of the natural world," Saint Francis of Assisi (1181–1226) and

8. Pieris, *Love*, 40
9. Shearer, *Intelligent Heart*, 31

still manifests itself in peace, anti-nuclear, and ecological movements. These modern movements, however, usually have a tenuous if not non-existent relationship with the churches, indeed with Christianity itself, which is often viewed as an enemy. Even the architecture of churches is telling, built upward, steeples aspiring to the heavens, leading our eyes away from the earth.

The tension between Christianity and ecology was raised by Lynn White in his seminal essay, "The Historical Roots of our Ecologic Crisis" (1967).[10] Though a devout Christian, White claimed that much of Christian thought was responsible as the source of western environmental degradation. He linked this to the desacralizing of the world which the Christian gospel had brought, charging that Christianity's ideological victory over paganism had radically changed our relationship with nature. Whereas under animistic paganism humans were part of nature, Christianity understood humans as being over nature. Scripturally the book of Genesis gave humans dominion over all animals and nature, thereby establishing a dualism between humanity and nature. By desacralizing nature Christianity made its exploitation and destruction ideologically justifiable. Not only did Christianity provide the philosophical basis for this ecological destruction, but through its teleological understanding it gave rise to the science and technology which made such possible. White found a possible solution in line with his own professed Christian faith advocating a radical rethinking of Christianity along the lines of Saint Francis.

White's thesis was criticized for his assertion that a change of thinking, philosophically or theologically, would bring about a change in our attitude to the cosmos, in that he ignored the economic and political causes of the ecological crisis.

Though Buddhism hasn't always exhibited a high ecological concern, its record is less destructive than that of Christianity. From early on monks and nuns were instructed not to travel in the rainy season, lest they kill or injure other animal forms, while from within pancasila is found the prohibition against killing fellow creatures. Much of this is premised on the idea of reincarnation and the possibility that which one kills or harms may after many lifetimes become a Buddha. Again, environmental sensitivity is seen in that Buddhist sanghas are built in forested areas away from the bustle of the urban environment, even when placed amid a major modern metropolis. Of course, it could be said that Christian monasteries are likewise built, but we need remember that the sangha plays a far more central place in Buddhism than does the monastery in Christianity. Zen Buddhism manifests the beauty of creation in some of the most beautiful gardens possible

10. White, *Historical Roots*

to imagine. Just the appearance of these intricate gardens is a celebration of beauty.

In passing it should be noted that though the garden plays an important part in the Judeo-Christian myth, particularly in connection to Babylon with its hanging gardens, the beauty of a garden is not something widely celebrated in either Judaism or Christianity, though it does find expression in the faith which springs from them, Islam. For evidence of that one only need think of the beautiful gardens right through Islamic cultures from Spain to India.

Ecological issues must serve as our fourteenth parameter.

THE ROLE AND STATUS OF WOMEN

Dialogue need also engage with the place of women. The track record of both faiths is hardly edifying, with neither giving women equal place, a practice which still continues. A desire to flee the world and flesh has led to both faiths viewing that which is most clearly of the flesh, sexuality, as sinful. The lust for indulgence in sexual pleasure is viewed as the most powerful force turning our minds away from spiritual practice to the indulgences of the world. Given the strongly patriarchal nature of both faiths that sexual temptation appears as in the guise of women.

In the Buddhist story one of the temptations faced by Buddha at his enlightenment is a bevy of young women sent to tempt him away from the spiritual path. The acceptance of women to the sangha comes, as we shall see, only after Ananda is able to convince Buddha, who even then only grudgingly accepts women, making them a second-class part of the sangha, subject to extra conditions and strictures.

Jesus seems more open to accepting women, Mary and Martha and Mary Magdalene, the latter being a prominent figure, all being part of his original circle. Women, we are informed, are the initial witnesses to the event central to Christianity, Jesus' resurrection. In the earliest church women seem to play an important place, with several, named by Paul in his letters to various churches, acting as leaders within those communities. That soon changed, however, as a patriarchal understanding soon asserted itself. Women were forbidden church roles and given second-order status. The denigration of women is seen even as early as the Christian Scriptures. Finally, in the sixth century, Pope Gregory proclaimed, with no evidence, that Mary Magdalene had been a prostitute, an occupation which most ascribe to her until this very day. Her "fall" from significant early leader was complete.[11]

From early times until now women have had a secondary role in Christianity. Only recently, in a small segment of the church, have they been declared to possess equal status with men.

In the West feminist theology has brought a change in theological emphasis, a renewed attention to sophia as wisdom, understood as a necessary corrective to the predominant masculine categories present in traditional gospel presentations.

We may note a similar phenomenon is also present in indigenous theologies where it is held that the spirit of the divine was long present as sophia before Christianity was present.

Again, this more sympathetic wisdom understanding allows Christians to better engage with other faith traditions, in contrast to the heavily Christocentric understanding lying at the heart of the mainstream Christian tradition, something clearly serving as a major barrier to genuine interfaith dialogue. The usual understanding of Christ centers on his soteriological role in which he, being ontologically distinct from us, saves us. Of course, Christianity must take the one after which the faith is named seriously, but it can do so without that name becoming a hindrance to dialogue. Christ, understood more as wisdom rather than savior, can best facilitate that dialogue so crucial, and clearly unavoidable, for our contemporary world. The Christ who calls and shows us the path to divine wisdom, is far more attractive and understandable to those outside the Christian tradition than that who transacts atonement between us and God by means which not only seem increasingly nonsensical, but also ethically unsustainable. To this I shall return.

On turning to Buddhism we are faced with a very ambiguous record. Texts provide us with widely different evaluations on the status of women. Within the Pali Canon (the scriptures of the earlier Theravada tradition), we

---

11. Mary Magdalene has almost become synonymous with prostitution. Initially the process involved her being associated with a "woman of ill-repute" who washes Jesus' feet, drying them with her hair (Luke 7:36–50), she in turn becoming associated with a Mary of Bethany (sister of Martha) who sits at Jesus' feet (Luke 10:39), that Mary in turn being identified with Mary Magdalene, meaning Magdalene is linked with the first woman. The tarnishing of Mary Magdalene's reputation was completed by the sixth-century pope Pope Gregory I who in 591 CE declared her to have been a prostitute. In actuality, Magdalene, we are told, traveled with Jesus offering financial support (Luke 8:2–3), being mentioned twelve times in the Gospels, more than most of the apostles. The Gospels tell us she witnessed Jesus' trial and was present at his crucifixion and resurrection. She is highly regarded in the several gnostic writings, being even called "the apostle of the apostle

have several examples of women becoming arahants, thereby attaining nibbana. It ought be noted that in Theravada the achievement of Buddhahood
is extremely rare, making such even more telling. The record is, however,
ambiguous. Early Buddhist texts within the Vinaya Pitaka in the Pali Canon
such as the Cullavagga have Buddha say that a woman can attain enlightenment, although such would only be in a transfigured male body form.[12] In
the Bahudhātuka-suttait it is clearly stated that there can never be a female
Buddha. However, from the Theravada canon in the Jataka tales (stories of
the Buddha's past lives as a bodhisattva), in the Sutta Pitaka, we are told that
Buddha spent one of his past lives as a princess, while Yasodhara, the wife of
Gotama, is said to have become an arahant.

In Mahayana a woman can become enlightened, but usually understood
not in female form. Dating from the fourth century the Bodhisattvabhūmi
states that a woman about to attain enlightenment will be reborn as a male.
Thus, of the Dragon King's daughter, upon her achieving perfect enlightenment, the Lotus Sutra declares, "Her female organs vanished, the male
organs became visible, then she appeared as a bodhisattva." In that same
Sutra we do read, however, that "a woman who embraces this sutra not only
surpasses all other women but surpasses all men."

Female Buddhas appear in Vajrayana. In the tantric iconography of
that school they sometimes appear as consorts, but other times as Buddhas
in their own right, examples being Vajrayogini, Tara, and Simhamukha.

An important indicator within a faith concerning the acceptance of
female equality is ordination. Ordination has been barred to women in
Christianity until very recently and is still only practiced in a few traditions.
In Buddhism, the ordination of women, though at a lesser level, has always
been practiced in some regions, such as East Asia, though not in Thailand,
and is currently being revived in some countries such as Sri Lanka.

As in Christianity, the emergence of women from secondary roles
traditionally assigned to them, is in Buddhism bringing bringing a renewal
to that faith. While we are speaking of gender it is likely that the issue of
gender preference will grow in importance. Certainly within Christianity
this is increasingly viewed as important. The role and status of women will
serve as our fifteenth and final parameter.

I have outlined, I believe, questions and issues which must frame our
dialogue between these two faiths.

Before we more fully enter that dialogue, however, we need be more
familiar with the faiths. In order to do that I want to begin by examining

12. Gos. Thom. 114 has Jesus saying the same to Peter, that women must be turned
to become men so to achieve salvation.

the wide differences in Buddhism, particularly between Theravada and Mahayana. I do so because dialogue between Christianity and Buddhism will be quite distinct depending on which school of Buddhism with which Christians are engaging.

I center on Buddhism for two reasons. First, the distinction between the schools within Buddhism is profound, far wider than that found in Christianity, and second, I am assuming most of my readers will be coming from a Western or Christian perspective, thus the need to center and more deeply examine Buddhism.

3

TO SWIM OR CATCH THE FERRY?
The Buddhist Schools

WHEN SPEAKING OF BUDDHISM, we need continually keep in mind just how varied are both practice and belief, that distinguishing it from Christianity, where differences are largely confined to practice, doctrine being largely uniform.

If we were to observe a Thai Theravada ritual followed a Vajrayana puja from Tibet, we would immediately note great differences. The same can be said of the differences within Christianity, between say Free Presbyterian worship and that of Russian Orthodoxy. Christian differences, however, are largely limited to ritual, a doctrinal conformity largely existing. Christianity is marked by a concern for orthodoxy in belief, something extending right across its different denominations. Councils of churches, such as the World Council of Churches and corresponding national bodies, include churches whose practices and ecclesiology range from that found in the Orthodox churches to those very Protestant in practice, but where doctrine varies by anything more than a small degree from that considered orthodox, the result is exclusion. Thus, Unitarians, with their non-acceptance of the doctrine of the Trinity, are excluded by Christians from the definition of Christianity, as in like manner are the Church of Jesus Christ and Latter Day Saints (Mormons), with their additional scriptures and beliefs. Such exclusion by doctrinal difference is not the case within Buddhism, there being a far greater doctrinal differences between schools.

Buddhists basically can be divided into two major schools: Theravada and Mahayana. There is another grouping of which we have already spoken, Vajrayana, though others categorize them as being part of Mahayana.

Given that Buddha neither selected a successor nor instituted a hierarchical order, the possibility of division was always greater. This is contrary to Christianity, where not long after Christ, an increasingly rigid hierarchical order was instituted, one progressively enforcing a narrowing doctrinal conformity. Such was the concern for a unified order within Christianity, the idea of an appointed successor to Jesus was written into the Scriptures, even placed on to the lips of Jesus, with Peter, "the rock upon which the church would be built," anachronistically claimed to be the first pope, a universal leader for the church, though there is no proof that he was so recognized during his lifetime. Within the later books of the Christian Scriptures, the so-called Pastoral Epistles (1 and 2 Tim and Titus), we find a strong concern for proper authority as means of guaranteeing right doctrine in the church. There were many other expressions of Christianity in the infant church, but it was to be this more narrowly defined group which would win out, their rigid delineation of faith probably serving as the main cause for this triumph.

Thus, when division came to Christianity, first between the church in the West, which became the Roman Catholic Church, and the Eastern or Orthodox Churches, and then again with the later split in the Western church which gave rise to the Protestant traditions, those splits were sharp and deep with bitter wars fought over them. Such was the feeling, following the split between the Western and Eastern Churches in 1054 each mutually excommunicated the other, this being the greatest anathema they could hurl upon each other for by such they were each condemning the other to eternal damnation. Later, in 1204 Western Christians on the Fourth Crusade would sack the seat of Eastern Christianity, Constantinople. Certainly there were organizational and political issues behind these divisions, but the emphasis was placed on doctrinal differences concerning orthodox belief. Christians take doctrine very seriously!

The divisions within Buddhism are much less acidic, due largely to a lesser concern for doctrine. The bitter anathemas seen in Christian history are mostly absent. While it is belief in Christianity which engenders the sharpest divisions, Buddhism is different. Certainly, there are divisions around doctrine, but there exists a coexistence between the schools, something present from the beginning. Thus the Lotus Sutra (Saddharma Pundarika) speaks of how the different vehicles or yanas represent one path to the same goal.

Let us turn then to examine Buddhist divergence.

The first schism in Buddhism came as early as the 4th century BCE, just 100 years after the life of Buddha. By that time, the sangha had established what became known as the Doctrine of the Elders (Theravada).

Varying understandings of this tradition, however, led to division, from which eighteen strands developed, though of these only Theravada survives. Having no texts from these other schools, we are reliant on those of Theravada, which are unlikely to be objective, concerning their doctrines. The split seems primarily to do with the status of the Buddha vis-à-vis others achieving enlightenment through his teachings, whether the arahant had, like Buddha, totally extinguished craving, and possessed his all-knowing omniscience. The schools were also split by different monastic practices. While these groups, apart from Theravada, did not last the distance, they left a legacy which later led to the formation of a radically different school of Buddhism, Mahayana in the first century CE. The strongest roots for this radically new school are found in the Mahasanghika (the Great Assembly), a school noted for its more democratic rule and new doctrines.

The division between Theravada and Mahayana represents the main split in current-day Buddhism. It has been put that the difference between the two schools, using an image common to Buddhism, is that the former calls us to ford the river through our own effort, while the latter calls us to board the ferry, captained by Buddha, already crossing.

The relationship, though lacking the acrimony found in Christianity, is not always amicable, followers of Mahayana believing in the superiority of their school, often reinforcing their point by derogatorily calling Theravada "Hinayana" (lesser vehicle). They claim this to be merely factual as Theravada, by making the journey to nibbana/nirvana far more difficult, is therefore a lesser vehicle in that fewer can use it.

Theravada is found mainly in Southeast Asia (Thailand, Cambodia, and Laos) and on the island nation of Sri Lanka, while Mahayana mainly exists in China, Vietnam, Japan, Mongolia, and Tibet where, taking a quite distinct form, it would be known as Vajrayana. This variance is often due to the Buddhism of those lands drawing upon the older indigenous faiths, Confucianism in China, Bon in Tibet, and Shinto in Japan. Buddhism lives far more comfortably with the older preexisting faiths with which it came into contact than does Christianity.

The languages in which their respective scriptures are composed further serves to divide the schools. Those of Theravada are composed in Pali, the language of the earliest Buddhist communities, while the Mahayana Scriptures are composed in Sanskrit, a related though distinct language, the sacred ancient language of the Hindu Vedas.

Theravada, "the doctrine of the elders," is the more conservative of the two schools, its followers strictly adhering to the teachings of the Buddha, gathered in the earliest tradition, refusing to accept any doctrine which they judge as not emanating directly from Buddha. They view the doctrines coming directly from Buddha as being largely recorded in authoritative texts called the Tripitaka (three baskets) dating from the first century BCE.

Theravada is understood to have originated in India at the time of that first schism, of which we spoke, of the eighteen schools in the fourth century BCE. It was brought to Ceylon (Sri Lanka) in the third century BCE and later became the dominant faith in that land. The Pali canon is believed to have been completed and compiled at Anuradhapura, and it is the only complete text to have been preserved in this archaic Indian language.

By the fifth century CE, Theravada had been established throughout southern India, Sri Lanka, and various parts of Southeast Asia, though the classical Theravada Buddhism we recognize today was not developed until between the fifth and tenth centuries CE under the tutelage of such teachers as Buddhagosa and Dhammapala.

By its emphasis on the Tripitaka, Theravada has a commonality with Christian Protestantism, though Protestantism understands itself as cleaning out the accumulated detritus of the Christian tradition by making a return to the Scriptures, whereas Theravada views itself as the original pure form of scriptural Buddhism. Mahayana has a wider scriptural tradition containing introduced new texts outside the narrower Pali tradition. These Mahayana sutras, however, are not accepted within Theravada as being canonical.

In Theravada, unlike Mahayana, there is no divine assistance in the journey to nibbana, it being instead wholly the responsibility of the individual. In this, Theravada believes itself as holding strictly to the teaching of Buddha, who made clear that the path to nibbana was extremely arduous, requiring absolute devotion and sacrifice, achieved only by a select few, who must follow the rigorous path laid out by him, with arrival at the path's destination taking perhaps thousands of lifetimes. With rare exceptions final deliverance can only be achieved by one in a monastery, as only from within the sangha, free from worldly concerns, can a person be sufficiently unencumbered and concentrated to complete the path. Within Theravada there are no Bodhisattvas to assist on the journey, and ultimately a person walks the path alone, although encouragement and support is available from within the sangha, part of the reason for its centrality within Theravada.

Another difference is the original Theravada discouragement of icons and relics of Buddha. Again, in this, Theravada stands closer to Christian Protestantism. The original sign of Buddha within Theravada was a footprint of Buddha or the Dhammachakra (Buddhist wheel) for that was all that was left of the Tathāgata, the "thus gone."

Nowhere in Christianity is the believer left, as they are in Theravada, without divine grace to seek their salvation, assistance always being available from the saints, comparable to the Bodhisattvas in Mahayana, the Blessed Virgin Mary, and of course from Christ himself. Protestantism excludes this divine grace being extended from any but the latter. Certainly there are Christian practices of discipline, but distinct from Theravada, they never of themselves are responsible for liberation, which always must come as God's graceful gift. This extension of divine grace always lies at the heart of Christianity.

Mahayana, meaning "greater vehicle," as it offers a wider and more simplified way to nirvana, commenced around the period 100 BCE to 100 CE, becoming the dominant Buddhist school between 300 and 500 CE.

It is claimed that the roots of the Theravada/Mahayana division can be traced back to the Council of Pataliputra in 340 BCE, where a rift occurred between those adhering to the traditional teachings, the Sthaviras, and the Mahasanghikas, "those representing the majority." The latter gave rise to numerous groups, who later would be called Mahayana.

Mahayana brought several new emphases to the faith. Of Buddha it made him to be a supernatural being, representing the essence of all natural phenomena, extolled the salvation ideal inherent in the Bodhisattva tradition and further advocated the philosophy of nothing having an essential or intrinsic nature, which it called sunyata. In Mahayana, nirvana is said to flow through all things, illuminating and transforming them. Not only is one's own nature experienced as infinite, but also all things, with the boundaries between them subsumed into an all-embracing unity, possessing "Buddha nature."

While Theravada had understood Buddha as a teacher-saint, guiding those who choose the path, in Mahayana he becomes savior. In Theravada, Buddha's direct influence ceased with his death and entry into nibbana, his teaching becoming prime; in Mahayana his direct presence continues after his death as a source of grace.

Monastic codes were loosened so that Mahayana disciples could travel more freely than monks of the older schools, that greatly facilitating the rapid expansion of the school. Being more open to the different religions and cultures it experienced also assisted in its expansion. Not only was Mahayana able to coexist with, it was even able to draw from, strong indigenous religious traditions, as seen in such places as China, with its preexisting Taoism and Confucianism, Tibet's Bon faith, and Japan's Shinto tradition.

There is no firm evidence of any link between Mahayana and the newly emergent Christianity of the same epoch (first century CE), but there are numerous similarities.

Before examining these, we need again remind ourselves that historical links certainly existed between the geographical locales, though what is more likely is that while the cultures were not in close contact they did experience a common "spirit of the times," extending across the Eurasian landmass, causing broadly similar responses.

The first similarity between Mahayana Buddhism and Christianity is the concept of a savior. In Mahayana, the idea of finding refuge in the Buddha, dhamma and sangha, the three central cores of Theravada, began to be turned into the belief that the Buddha had a salvific role in that he was able to bring one to nirvana. This is similar to the savior role assigned to Christ within Christianity. As in Christianity this salvific role is linked to sacrifice, and is in the Jatakas Buddha is depicted as sacrificing himself for others. In that giving, we find the genesis of the Bodhisattva concept. In one case, in a previous incarnation, we are told he even throws himself onto a fire to provide food for a man starving in the forest.

Such sacrifice comes from a deep compassion. Within Mahayana the idea of compassion (karuna) for others has a core role, largely replacing the earlier Theravada emphasis on striving for wisdom—pañña (Sanskrit: prajñā) so as to achieve one's own enlightenment—bodhi. This earlier emphasis, dismissed as selfish, was replaced by the idea of becoming a Bodhisattva, one who, eschewing their own salvation or entry into nirvana, chooses instead to work tirelessly and unselfishly to assist others reach that goal. Technically all who take the path of Mahayana are bodhisattvas.

Thus, within Mahayana, love becomes more predominant, karuna becoming as central as that same attribute—agape—within Christianity. The wisdom concept however is in no way absent from Mahayana. This is most clearly seen in that those figures epitomizing love are called by the term noting wisdom, Bodhisattvas (literally "one with wisdom seeking awakening"). In Mahayana, however, the deepest wisdom lies in serving others in the love extended to them. As such Mahayana understands itself as a belief bringing both wisdom and love together. One seeks to develop generosity, ethical behavior, patience, effort, concentration and wisdom, the last attribute guiding the others.

The compassionate Bodhisvatta, working for the benefit of all beings, replaces the arahant, striving for their own liberation.

While preexisting in Theravada, wherein it was believed that Buddha had to strive for many lifetimes before his enlightenment, the Bodhisattva ideal became so central to Mahayana it was originally known as Boddhisattva-yana, the vehicle of the Bodhisattvas.

This love/compassion dimension is closer to the Christian tradition. Paul in his epistle to the Corinthians makes it clear that there is no wisdom without love, charging that so called wisdom bereft of love, as being a mere "clanging gong" (1 Cor 13). He makes this strong statement reacting to other streams of Christianity, influenced by Gnosticism, which being more concerned with wisdom had little reference to love. While here Paul uses love as a corrective to a one-sided emphasis on so-called wisdom, he does so, as we shall see, have great appreciation of the place of wisdom.

Buddha himself was understood as the inspiration for this Boddhisattva ideal, having rejected the idea of passing straight to nirvana at the point of his enlightenment, choosing instead to remain to teach the saving doctrine. It is likely that the stories concerning this rejection, as found in the Lalitavistara, find their final form in the Mahayana canon. Christianity, built around the example of Christ, who lays down his life for others, is full of this call to help others, to even self-sacrifice for them. "Greater love has no one than they lay down their life for a friend" (John 15:13). Bodhisattvas are not able, with the exception of Pure Land schools, to redeem others, as Christ does in Christianity, but rather by helping, encouraging, and teaching, assist them in finding nirvana. They are more matched in this role by the saints in much of the Christian tradition.

With the role of the Bodhisattva growing in Mahayana, Buddha was progressively elevated as a revered and exalted figure. Becoming ever more associated with miraculous deeds and occurrences to do with his life, he increasingly became viewed as a semi-divine being. While earlier Buddhism held that Buddha, having passed into nibbana, no longer existed, Mahayana believed that as a semi-divine being, he still had existence in a transcendent realm, where given his compassion, he continued to assist others, from whom he could never have cut himself off. As Bodhisattvas took an analogous role to Christ in Mahayana, so Buddha himself often came to take a role somewhat similar with God in Christianity, a benevolent supernatural being, not present in this world, existing in a transcendent realm, dispensing grace.

This ontological elevation of Buddha within Mahayana led to a Buddhology, wherein the Buddha was conceived as having three bodies (Trikaya), existing simultaneously in three dimensions: earthly, heavenly, and transcendent. The Buddha's earthly body, nirmanakaya, was that in which he had been manifested on earth, while his heavenly body, sambhogakaya, dwelt in a blissful realm, somewhat akin to the Christian idea of heaven, from where came grace and the heavenly creations. Last, Buddha's transcendent body, dharmakaya, the body of the void, represented his being identical with ultimate truth, in a manner like how some Christian mystics speak of God as ultimate truth or reality. That we gain vision of Buddha as such indicates that we are all potential Buddhas.

This idea of the divine present in three persons has parallels to the Christian Trinity, a similar attempt to understand the divine in different guises as transcendent ultimate, incarnate in Christ, and present in the on-going immanent presence as the Holy Spirit. In such schema Buddha in his bodily form, nirmanakaya, has similarities to the divine in Christianity taking human form in Jesus as Christ.

The role of individual effort vis-a-vis the acceptance of grace is another area where the division within Buddhism between Theravada and Mahaya-na is somewhat analogous to that found in Christianity, between the catho-lic tradition, present in the Roman Catholic and Orthodox Churches, and that found in the Protestant Churches, though the distinction is greater in Buddhism. Theravada Buddhism and Protestantism share the idea of each being responsible for their own salvation, though that responsibility is exer-cised in different ways, by acceptance of grace and confession of faith within Protestantism, and by rigorous self-discipline within Theravada. Both, as we have already seen, hold more strictly to a set scriptural tradition. On the other hand, Mahayana Buddhism and Catholic forms of Christianity share the idea that help and intercession are available through the agency of the holy, Bodhisattvas within Mahayana, the Blessed Virgin Mary or the saints within Catholic forms of Christianity.

The new Mahayana developments are picked up in their Scriptures, dating roughly from the period of the Christian Scriptures. Whereas the old Pali texts of the Theravada tradition could be understood as being the words, or at least as having some connection with the historical Buddha, these new Scriptures clearly are later and bear the marks of the work of many hands. Still within Mahayana they came to have great status, under-stood as visionary and inspired. Given the cosmology of Mahayana, that seemed logical for it was the elevated Buddha who acted as the source of revelation for them. This is not unlike how Christians popularly (incor-rectly) view their Scriptures, the Gospels, supposedly being the words and actions of the historical Jesus, while the other Scriptures are understood to be revealed by the elevated Christ or indeed God through such figures as Paul, Timothy, and James. Scriptural study, both within the Buddhist and Christian tradition shows such to be far too simple.

Many new Mahayana Scriptures enter Buddhism: the Lotus Sutra, the Vimalakirti-nirdesha, the Prajna-paramita, the Lankavatra, and the Gan-davyuha the most popular. The more conservative Theravada rejected these additions.

Some of the Mahayana sutras radically rework Buddhism, with the Lotus Sutra (c. 200 CE) totally reimagining Buddha. According to this sutra, though Buddha appeared to live and die an ordinary man, this was not really the case. Actually he was an enlightened one from time immemorial, who had preached a simplified dharma to people ill-equipped to understand the more profound nature of his knowledge. That fullness of knowledge was only now being revealed in the Mahayana scriptures, to a people further along the cyclical incline of the eon, more capable of understanding. This became known as upaya, the capacity to teach at a level commensurate to one's listeners.

In Mahayana, the early Pali scriptures are held to be not false but rather just incomplete, that incompleteness even leading some in that tradition to sometimes derisively make light of them. Thus we find in the Mahayana text the Teachings of Vimalakirti (c. 400 CE), Theravada monks being baffled by a mere layman schooled in the ways of the Mahayana.

Christian gnostics, in similar manner, understood Jesus as only appearing to have human form, teaching a simpler provisional message to those unable to comprehend the depth teachings, which were imparted to them by an elevated Christ, as those possessing gnosis or knowledge.

Both gnostic Christians, believing their Scriptures to hold a deeper revelation of a transcended Christ, and the adherents of Mahayana, claiming likewise their Scriptures to be a deeper revelation, operate in like manner.

In Mahayana there exist many Bodhisattvas from whom grace may be drawn for one's own enlightenment. In this there is a similarity with the Roman Catholic idea of supererogation, whereby certain saints have achieved a righteousness beyond that needed, this excess representing a type of credit which may be drawn upon by others to assist them in their path to salvation.

Mahayana developed a detailed pathway leading to enlightenment. That path begins with the "thought of enlightenment" or Bodhicitta, a type of conversion experience wherein a person commits themselves to save others. Having made this commitment, a vow is sworn—pranidhana—by which one commits to save all beings by bringing them to nirvana, no matter how long the task may take. To do this one must develop loving-kindness, compassion, sympathetic joy, and equanimity.

This Bodhisattva ideal within Mahayana contrasts with the Theravada idea of the arahant. These different ideals manifest themselves in the way the clergy are perceived. In Theravada, Bhikkhus, and Bhikkhunis are understood through the lens of seclusion in a sangha pursuing nibbana, whereas in Mahayana they and the sangha are in a much more reciprocal relationship, the clergy and laity offering alternate forms of service to each other. With greater concentration on grace, lay as well as the ordained have the real possibility of reaching nirvana.

Within Mahayana the historical Buddha, rather than being unique, is but one of the manifestations of the Buddhahood principle existing throughout the universe. Followers could thus direct their devotion toward an infinite series of Buddhas and Bodhisattvas.

Well-advanced Bodhisattvas were highly revered, seen to be virtually indistinguishable from Buddha in his heavenly form. The most important and beneficial of these celestial Bodhisattvas are Avalokitesvara (the one who looks down in compassion) and Manjusri (the one of noble gentle glory). They each pick up one of the core Buddhist atributes, the former emphasizing karuna or love, the latter prajna or wisdom. Both are often found at the entrance to temples, Avalokitesvara, pictured as one with many arms, always ready to use to help those suffering, while Manjusri carries a burning sword, ready to cut through ignorance, so to find wisdom. It is claimed, Avalokitesvara has amassed boundless treasures of grace to give to those who call on him, that complementing and filling the contribution made by the petitioner. The deep devotion given to such Bodhisattvas has often resulted in their being transformed into gods. This divine status, however, in contrast to the older gods, is beneficial to the believer.

The concept of an end or eschaton represents both a contrast and a similarity between Mahayana and Christianity. Distinct from Christianity, in Mahayana each end is the end but of an eon, following which another Buddha will return to the earth bringing again the seed of enlightenment, thereby opening the possibility of those in that cycle attaining nirvana. Gautama is but the most recent in a line extending back to the beginning of the cosmos. Following this current cycle it will be Maitreya, the Benevolent One, (the name is possibly derived from mitra—friend), the great future Buddha, who will inaugurate a time when vast multitudes achieve enlightenment. As found in Christianity this eschatological concern has led to the formation of messianic cults, some of which, as in Christianity, have achieved significant popularity. Buddhism, however, in line with its Eastern origins, moves in great cycles, each eon representing a cyclic rise followed by decline until a new Buddha comes to turn the cycle upward again. Christianity, in accord with all Western faiths is teleological, moving in a singular linear manner from a beginning to an end point, whereupon the Messiah Jesus returns to the earth.

Maitreya is particularly important for many Buddhists, who realizing they cannot complete the spiritual path in their present lifetime, pray to be reborn as one of his inner circle of disciples. Tibetan Buddhists invoke him in the Red Crown Ceremony to appear before his time.

Much of the information on the Buddha's previous lives is found in the Jatakanidana, a text from the fifth century CE, though stories of the Buddha's previous lives can be found as far back as the birth stories in the Jatakas in the Pali Scriptures. Reference to the past incarnations is made via the present in that each chapter commences with discussion of a current issue, to which Buddha responds by speaking of a like event in a previous incarnation, this serving to clarify the topic under discussion.

Some of these Buddhas are understood to be divine beings, while others, such as Gautama Buddha, are known as Manusibuddhas or human Buddhas. The Manusubuddhas are recognized right across the Buddhist spectrum, even in Theravada. They are, in turn Dipankara—"bringer of light," Bhaisajyaguru—"supreme physician" (understood in Vajrayana as sMan-bla to be the first of a series of medicine Buddhas), Kasyapa, then the current Buddha, with the fifth being Maitreya. While Theravada recognizes only the five Manusibuddhas, there are up to twenty-five Buddhas recognized in some schools of Mahayana.

There were five spiritual mediation Buddhas or Dhyanibuddhas, this term in Mahayana increasingly replacing the older Tathagata. All of these emanate from the primeval divinity, Adibuddha, envisaged as "sunya" (void), sometimes referred to as Vajradhara, from which comes the name of the school, Vajrayana.

Distinct from the more conservative Theravada, Mahayana was marked by a flexibility assisting it to expand into new forms such as the Chinese schools Ti'en Tai and Ch'an, which became respectively Tendai and Zen in Japan. So radical was the change effected in Mahayana within Tibet, the resultant school, Vajrayana, is often held to be a third distinct stream within Buddhism. The flexibility of Mahayana, along with its ability to absorb and be changed by these faiths, means that in each of those lands the older faith traditions survive, sitting comfortably with their later Buddhist arrival, sometimes almost indistinguishable from it. This is sharply different to Christian missionary expansion which, while incorporating aspects of older religions such as dates for ceremonies, and even the gods translated to be saints, violently suppressed the faiths into which they came into contact. Such open flexibility assisted in Buddhist propagation.

Mahayana expansion was also facilitated by the creative ongoing study of the sutras and their commentary by such prominent thinkers as Nagarjuna (second century CE) and Asanga (fifth century CE), with their scholarship assisting in the investigation, comprehension, and contextualization of the Buddhist Scriptures.

Mahayana was particularly attractive in that it made nirvana accessible. In the older Theravada tradition, as we have seen, nibbana could only be viewed from a very long way off for the vast majority, taking likely hundreds, perhaps even thousands, of lifetimes to achieve, usually only from within the sangha. For a layperson the only realistic hope was to be reborn into a better place, a slight movement along that extremely long road of samsara. Mahayana on the other hand opened the possibility of nirvana to all. Mahayana expresses it thus: "Just as the most beautiful flower, the lotus, grows in muddy water, so the lay practitioner can find clarity and compassion in the turmoil of daily life."[1]

Pure Land, a particular form of Mahayana, popular in East Asia, made nirvana most easily acceptable. It is focused on Amitabha, the Buddha of infinite light, said to be a transcendent being existing beyond the limits of space and time, dwelling in the western paradise of Sukhavati (blessed with happiness). This paradise of pure bliss came into being due to a series of vows made by Amitabha, while he was still a Bodhisattva, Dharamakara. Before his teacher he had made forty-eight vows, the most important being that he would bring forth this sacred realm, sparkling with gems, beautiful rivers, and all manner of delights, often pictured as a garden. Not only was existence in such a place beautiful, it was the most propitious place from which to attain nirvana. Rather than relying on the efficacy of one's own practice, one relied instead on the great practice and grace of Amida Buddha to bring them to enlightenment. This paradisiacal existence is given the devotee out of pure grace, and once born into this realm enlightenment is guaranteed.

In Pure Land, Buddhist practices are followed not in order to purify the mind, but rather to show that one is already swimming in the ocean of purity and compassion. Pure Land became popular in Japan with the Jodoshu, Jodo Shinshu, and Nichiren schools. In the latter the Lotus Sutra was so central that the mere recitation of its name with faith meant one's wishes would all be fulfilled. From this school comes the currently very popular Soka Gakkai.

With its emphasis on grace given by mere calling upon the name, this Pure Land school of Buddhism is very similar to the Christian invocation, 'call upon the name of the Christ and be saved' (Rom 10:13). The 'solo fides' (by faith alone) of Martin Luther has a Buddhist precedent. Clearly this is far removed from the original Buddhist precept, wherein each person was responsible for finding their own salvation. It should be noted, however, that one reborn in the Western Pure Land has not achieved nirvana, though that final goal is guaranteed. Rebirth in the Pure Land is best understood as a long and highly advantageous ladder in the cosmic game of "snakes and ladders" associated with samsara.

Ch'an, originating in China, though better known in the West by its Japanese appellation, Zen, represents a quite distinct Mahayana school. This often iconoclastic school is built around meditation, centered on the present moment, a practice held to allow radical insight into reality. It finds

1. When speaking specifically of Mahayana I will use the Sanskrit term.

it roots in Buddha's Flower Sermon, where, refraining from speaking, he simply held a flower, a golden lotus. Only Mahakasyapa understood the significance, thus being understood as a precursor of the deeper way represented by this school. In response Buddha says, "Reality is formless; the subtle teaching doesn't depend on written words but is separately transmitted apart from doctrine."

Insight comes in this school, without the conceptual constraints of words. Such may come gradually, or as sudden insight (though usually after long years of preparation). The variance is picked up in the two schools of Rinzai and Soto. The former centers on the use of koans, paradoxical conundrums making no sense to the conceptual mind, the best known being "what is the sound of one hand clapping?" These are designed to demonstrate the limits of language and intellectual concepts. Soto is more concerned with highly disciplined sitting meditation shikantaza, or zazen.

Zen has at its heart a radical non-duality, the goal being to realize the inherent Buddha nature in oneself and all things, which are united in this nature. This radical non-duality may lead to a brave embracing of death, something clearly associated with Japanese Zen. Such non-duality is imaged in the famous ten ox herding pictures. One searches for the ox, finds it, tames it, and rides it home, before first the ox and then the herder (oneself) both disappear, all differences, and even being, dissolved.

The adept is challenged to have a direct experience of truth, beyond the mind, beyond the Scriptures, and even the Buddha himself. In Zen we thus find the most iconoclastic of all statements: "if you meet Buddha on the road, kill him." Knowledge must be direct, not mediated, even through Buddha.

Beyond rationality and thought lies an understanding, known as satori, which comes like a flash of lightning. At such a moment a person directly experiences their own Buddha nature. The master or Roshi is especially important as only they can confirm whether satori has taken place.

Drawing from the social concern of its Chinese Ch'an roots, the enlightened one chooses not to retire into solo bliss but rather remain in the world, now seen as profoundly beautiful (hence the beauty of Zen monasteries), so to share the truth they have found. All actions, even the most mundane, henceforth are imbued with the spirit of Zen. Again, we find a parallel with the Thomas tradition in Christianity where Jesus says, "Split a piece of wood and I am there. Lift a stone and you will find me" (Gos. Thom. 77). For the enlightened the divine is present in the utterly mundane.

Zen has great appeal to the post-structuralist West as it is not built around acceptance of doctrine but rather offers direct experience.

TO SWIM OR CATCH THE FERRY? 63

Mahayana Buddhism understands itself as not rejecting the earlier tradition but rather as fulfilling it, sometimes as reclaiming things "lost" or "not understood" by those who came before them. Much found in Mahayana represents a re-emphasis but in a different manner, of that which lay at the core of earlier practice. Compassion, being central to the Buddha's own practice, had always been at the heart of Buddhism. Within Mahayana this, however, is refashioned and strengthened by the idea of the Bodhisattva. In similar manner Mahayana in the Madhyamaka school reemphasized "emptiness," again something present in early Buddhism, in the teachings of anatta (impermanence) and anicca (no self), while the Idealism (citta-matra) of Mahayana is likewise anticipated by the earlier meditative practices, built on developing the enlightened mind. Such meditation foreshadows the idea that the mind contains the only reality.

The greatest change between Theravada and Mahayana Buddhism is in the development of Buddhology, the devotional cults which developed around the different Buddhas and Bodhisattvas. Given that Northwest India was the locale where much Mahayana devotion came, there is speculation that Zoroastrian, even Hellenic, ideas could be a source of such developments. As we have found, such contacts between these disparate cultures were already in place. However the source of such devotion is more likely to be found in India, Hinduism having developed devotional cults, particularly those linked with Shiva and Krishna. Also, again, early Buddhism itself contained the seed of devotion to the Buddha.

In that Mahayana views itself as the completion and fulfillment of an older tradition, there are again parallels with Christianity. As Mahayana understands itself as a completion of the Theravada tradition, so too does Christianity see itself as fulfilling and completing Judaism. Indeed, the earliest followers of Christ understood themselves not as a new faith, but rather as being in continuity with and part of the old. Such an understanding may have indeed continued, but for a shattering event which changed everything: the Jewish rebellion against Rome and subsequent violent Roman response. This seminal event, which we will examine, caused Christianity to become a predominantly gentile and a separate faith. That cataclysm led to Christianity understanding itself apart from Judaism, with the two faiths growing apart. Even after such division Christians still saw themselves as the successors of Judaism, viewing their faith as a completion and perfection of Judaism. Such supersessionist ideas continue to this day, Jews understandably being offended by such. Likewise there is resentment from Theravada toward those in Mahayana understanding their faith as superseding Theravada.

Over time, from within Mahayana, a whole series of new sutras were composed, many of them deeply complex philosophical tractates, setting forth the ideas of this radically re-worked Buddhism. The most famous author was Nararjuna, c. 150 CE, founder of a new school, the Madhyamaka or "middle school." Using this traditional concept of "the middle way," he developed the idea of "origination in dependence," which claimed that nothing existed essentially in itself but rather was a constant changing mixture of compounds, these compounds being dependent on that dharma giving rise to their formation. This idea had previously posited the compounds to be real elements, but Nararjuna extended the idea in a more radical direction, charging things were not just impermanent but lacked any real being. This form of philosophical idealism—citta-matra—claimed that ultimate reality lay within the mind rather than being exterior to the person. Consciousness is the sole reality, things having no objective existence outside the mind's perception of them. "Nothing in the whole universe is comparable to the mind or can take its place. Everything is mind-made."[2] This is a type of philosophical idealism. Given the centrality of the mind, yogic practice sat at the core of this school's life, for only rigorous yoga would enable practitioners of the school to develop the sharpness of mind necessary to understand a reality, which lay so contrary to the "common sense" perceived by the ordinary person. This was not nihilistic, for it did not charge things had no existence but rather that they have no essential existence in the manner that we commonly think of them as independent realities. Rather, things lay somewhere between having existence and being non-existent, hence the identification of the school as a middle way.

That nothing had essential being took away the difference between nirvana and samsara. What after all could be the difference between these things, neither of which had any real existence? With no difference between the things themselves the only distinction could be in how we perceived them. Nararjuna provides an example of the difference of a person, who in the twilight misperceives a rope for being a snake and therefore panics, with the one who truly perceives the actuality. A person's vision must be purified, allowing them to see the same perceived things in the true light. What is seen by the ignorant as samsara will be truly seen by the enlightened one as nirvana. Nirvana is here and now but present only for those who have eyes to see. The parallel is strong with Jesus who charges of God's reign, "nor will they say, 'Look, here it is!' or 'there!' for behold, the kingdom of God is in the midst of you" (Luke 17:21). Paradise is perceived by those having eyes to see.

2. Khema, *Being Nobody*, 10

As found, from Mahayana comes another form of Buddhism known as Vajrayana or the "diamond vehicle." As the "diamond vehicle," it is believed to possess the hard sharpness of a diamond, so that through its practice, an adept is able to cut through, to reach nirvana in a single lifetime. To use the ferry analogy, here is the fast boat. This breakthrough could be achieved by using powerful, often frenetic, tantric energies, even making use of things normally prohibited, alcohol and sexuality, including coitus, in which it was held that the opposites were transcended. The power lies in the transcendence of these opposites.

The school takes its name from Vajra, the thunder god in the Indian pantheon. The term has distinctly phallic connotations, for while being translated "thunderbolt," it also is a term used for the male genitalia. As such the vajra is worn as a symbol of the creative power of the Buddha. These sexual connotations, which may extend to forms of orgiastic worship, are not well-viewed within much of mainstream Buddhism. Though sexual license, used as a method of cutting through and uniting opposites, is still not unknown in Vajrayana, its prevalence diminished from the eleventh century when the Indian scholar Atisha imposed a strict celibacy rule within the sangha.

First practiced in India in the fifth to sixth century CE, Vajrayana passed to China and Japan, where it is known as Shingon. This style of Buddhism, however, is most associated with Tibet, Nepal, and Mongolia.

Exponents of Vajrayana believe that Buddha gave many teachings, most of which were too powerful for ordinary followers. These were passed to a select few, whose descendants only later transmitted them.

Enlightenment in the Vajrayana tradition, along with leading to a deeper recognition of the nature of mind, leads to such things as intense clarity, tranquility, and fearlessness. It is also accompanied by magical powers.

Being so distinct, Vajrayana is said to represent a third string of Buddhism. Built around secret knowledge, truth in Vajrayana is only accessible through initiation—ahiseka—given by a teacher or guru (rinpoche), usually communicated through complex rituals built around mantras, mandalas, and mudras. While these are present right through Buddhist schools, they are especially associated with Vajrayana, where they acquire special power.

Mantras, already present in Vedic Hinduism, are sacred syllables or words, possessing special power. 'Spoken repetitively, usually in a mechanical manner, and transcending rational reasoning, mantras are a simple, though powerful mystical sound device by which a person can be greatly helped in achieving their goal of nirvana.' Often associated with magic, the words uttered may not even be intelligible, though that is not always the case. As we shall see, this use of magical and occult powers has roots in Buddha's own practice.

Tantra, being so strongly associated with mantras, was originally known as the mantrayana (way of the mantras).

Especially in written form a mantra can operate as a type of charm. Often placed inside an image, the mantra empowers the image to become the manifestation of the deity to whom the mantra refers.

Mantras are usually inserted into a longer form of Buddhist prayer known as dharani, a type of prayer believed to generate immense power. These prayers often consist of an apparently meaningless juxtaposition of syllables, usually at the beginning or the end of the prayer. There are various methods of utterance with the mantra either being voiced aloud, "throated" with a deep sound in a method known as kanthika, or uttered silently—ajapa.

There are many types of mantras, those using the "om" or "aum" sylla-ble being best known. In the older Hindu tradition, these three letters were meant to represent the three principal deities, Brahma, Vishnu, and Shiva, while in Buddhism they are understood to represent the triatna, the "three jewels" of the faith: Buddha, the dharma, and the sangha. Being simply one syllable, it along with others of the same type is called a bijamantra. Another common form of mantra is "om mani padme hum," associated with the wor-ship of Avalokitesvara (Tibetan Chenrezig), of whom the Dalai Lama is held to be the living incarnation. Although technically linguistically meaning-less, the phrase is usually interpreted to mean "Hail the jewel (mani) in the lotus (padma)." Mani represents the Buddha while the padma is believed to represent the world, or the flower from which Avalokitesvara was born. It may be also linked also to the male-female union, sexual or otherwise.

Mantras are somewhat analogous to what is found in Christianity with the novena or prayers to the saints in Roman Catholicism, the Jesus Prayer in Orthodoxy, and Pentecostal "speaking in tongues," the latter also being usually unintelligible, although in Buddhism, while the mantra may be meaningless, it is formulaic.

In Christian popular practice, while there is a strong disavowal of such, these forms often operate in a manner similar to magic. Prayer likewise may be understood as being analogous to magic, but it provides the petitioner with an "out" if the prayer is unanswered, in that it can be said, "that asked is not in accord with the will of God." Magic is much more automatic in that it is judged objectively by its effectiveness.

Though the occult is usually strictly forbidden in Christianity, such prohibition having arisen from Judaism, we find it present in the scriptural account of something as central as the drawing of lots to find a replacement for Judas among the disciples. While Jesus is less prepared than Buddha to use miraculous or magical powers, his ministry is still marked by his use of what the Gospels call "powers and wonders."

Along with speech utilized as mantras, other bodily uses are made in Vajrayana. Vision is employed in the perception of mandalas, and hands in forming mudras. These, likewise, are each held to possess magical effect.

Used in many types of Buddhist meditation and practice, mandalas are sacred images possessing special powers, fully understood only by those initiated into their deep secret meanings. The word can be translated literally as "center and circumference." Originating in India thousands of years ago, mandalas are used as an aid for certain advanced Hindu and Buddhist meditation practices. In the early twentieth century, the Swiss psychoanalyst Carl Jung introduced them into Western thought as a therapeutic tool for exploring the psychic unconscious, believing them to represent a universal archetype we all possess.

Mandalas are especially important in Vajrayana, where their meaning is passed on from a master or rinpoche to student. Central to this is the identification with a meditation deity, known as "yidam," imaged in the mandala. The geometric patterns of a mandala contain great magic and power. A simple one may be made by grains of rice being spread on the ground, while more complicated mandalas, often using colored sands, include precise patterns of figures, syllables (bijas), and shapes. These beautiful intricate mandalas, over which much care and time has been spent, are then destroyed, in accord with the Buddhist understanding of impermanence.

Buddhas, it is held, live in perfectly pure worlds known as mandalas, referring both to the environment of that world, and to the beings who inhabit it. The mandala represents an offering of this idealized vision of the universe, imaged as Pure Land. Each of these worlds, and therefore mandalas, are slightly different but generally include an ornate square palace situated in the middle of a beautiful landscape, surrounded by a round protective barrier claimed to ward off interferences to the meditation practice. The main figure can be male or female, on their own, or as a couple, sitting or standing in the middle of the palace, often surrounded by an array of other figures, usually presented in a fantastic style, possessing multiple faces, arms, and legs, while holding a variety of hand implements. Mandalas may inform the design of a temple.

The practitioner develops their Buddha nature by participating in the mandala, imagining that they are present in each of the figures inside and outside the palace, but also in the palace itself, with the different architectural features of the mandala palace representing various aspects of meditation practice. The four walls often represent the four noble truths, while the palace, being square with equal-length sides, indicates the emptiness of the void.

The third of these M-words is mudra (Sanskrit for seal or sign). These are various gestures made with the hands, having symbolic and magical meaning. Buddhas and bodhisattvas are nearly always depicted in Buddhist art with these stylized hand gestures, each mudra having a specific meaning. These are:

- The dhyana or meditation mudra symbolizing a path of compassion for all living beings. In this the right hand is placed on top of the left hand, palms face up and thumbs lightly touching. This mudra symbolizes the union of opposites.

- Bhumisparsha, the earth-touching mudra, one of the most well-known mudras. The historical Buddha is often presented thus, the mudra having its origin in the moment Mara was trying to seduce Buddha. On his touching the earth, it quaked violently causing the demonic hordes to flee in terror while giving testimony to Buddha.

- The vitarka, the teaching or discussion mudra, symbolizing the transmission of the dharma, or the truth teachings of the Buddha. Here, the thumb and index finger meet to form a circle, a form of hand gesture seen across many religions, including Christianity. The circle represents completeness and wholeness.

- The abhaya, a symbol of fearlessness and protection. The left hand is as in the dhyana mudra with the right hand held upright, the palm facing outward.

- Anjali, representing "suchness" (tathata)—the true nature of all things, beyond distinction. The hands are held in a manner Westerners associate with prayer.

- Vajrapradama symbolizes unshakable confidence. In this the fingertips of the hands are crossed.

- The varada, where the right hand is held open with fingers pointing down representing compassion and wish-granting.

Practitioners use these mudras to evoke a particular state of mind. In the Vajrayana school, mudras assume an esoteric significance, usually combined with mantras and tantric visualization. Containing secret magic powers these mudras are passed to the adept by their rinpoche. Every mudra has both an outer/symbolic and an inner/experiential function, communicating aspects of the enlightened mind to both, the person who performs them and also to the observer.

Mantras, mandalas, and mudras are of essential importance in Vajrayana as the school while holding the understanding, along with all Buddhism, that the appearance of things is illusionary as "maya," then adds that beyond the physical plane, it is possible to directly identify the individual with the absolute. This involves a transcendence of the intellect, achieved by following certain techniques centered around the use of these, utilizing the magical qualities found in them. The importance of secret knowledge imparted by wise or initiated teachers has led some to again compare Vajrayana Buddhism to gnostic Christianity, where likewise deeper knowledge could be passed to adepts by their teachers.

Within Vajrayana are found mystical, magical forms of Buddhism known as Tantrism. Tantra has as one of its roots the word "extension," it being held that these new teachings were being added to those preexisting in Buddhism. The other root of the term is "weaving," these new ideas understood as being woven into Buddhism. Often these extended teachings came from the older faiths, already present in the lands to which this form of Buddhism came, this particularly being the case with the Bon faith in Tibet. These new streams or strands emphasized means of using the subconscious mind to access the spiritual and mystical powers, which lie latent within.

The Tantric school, as it is built around magical manifestations, is sometimes known as "the magical vehicle." It possesses a series of ritual and magical texts, claimed to originate from Buddha, for the evocation of deities, the use of which enabled development of occult powers, the best known being the Fire Sacrifice. The repetitive use of these as a mantra, along with other meditative practices, it is claimed facilitates the direct contact of the Buddha and Bodhisattvas.

Other texts, called termas, were composed and hidden by Tantric masters with the intention that they would be discovered at an appropriate time by other masters.

Tantrism may be divided into right-handed tantrism involving the male deities, or left-handed Tantrism, centering on Shaktism, the worship of the female deities, imaged as standing to the left of the god. It is left-handed tantrism, also known as vamacana, which dominates both Vajrayana and Lamaism. Based on a series of Tantric texts, not generally recognized by other schools, this Buddhist form is similar to the older Shaktism found within Hinduism, in that devotees pursue worship of the goddess. Known as Tara, meaning "star," this goddess is most often the Shakti, or female aspect of Avalokitesvara, but may also be that of various dhanyibuddhas such as Adibuddha or Amoghasiddhi. Within Lamaism one of the most celebrated is Sitatara (the white tara), claimed to be an incarnation of the Chinese Tang princess Wencheng, one of the wives of Sron-bysan-sgam-po, the ruler responsible, against strong opposition, for bringing Buddhism to Tibet in the mid-seventh century CE, following his conversion to Vajrayana by monks from north India.

An important text from the tradition is the Bardo Tholdo, popularly known as the Tibetan Book of the Dead. This charts the death, and after-death experience, read to the dying person to facilitate their transition to after-death bardo (immediate) state. This assists in a more auspicious re-birth by following a series of steps in a forty-nine-day period.

The fusion of Tantric practice with the Bon faith, a faith based on a hi-erarchy of magician priests and complicated rituals, gave birth to Lamaism, the main form of Buddhism in Tibet and Nepal and then later, Mongolia.

The term lama originally referred to gurus of great veneration, often called tulkus, held to be conscious reincarnations of their predecessors but was later extended generally to include all teachers and members of Tibetan monastic orders.

The two faiths, Bon and Buddhism, came to live together harmoni-ously, due largely to the eighth-century scholar Padmasambhava. A yogi of the Tantric school and a master of the occult, Padmasambhava founded the first Tibetan Buddhist monastery at Sam-yay. Two of his successors were believed to be reincarnations of the Buddha Amitabha and the Bodhisat-tva Avalokitesvara (known in Tibet as Chenrezi), from whom respectively developed the separate roles of the Panchen Lama, representative of the spiritual domain of Tibetan Buddhism, and the Dalai Lama, who in succes-sive incarnations is understood as the temporal leader. In the seventeenth century the Mongol emperor installed the fifth Dalai Lama as absolute mon-arch, a position held until the fourteenth Dalai Lama fled into exile in 1959. The Chinese Communist rulers replaced the Dalai Lama with the Panchen Lama, who in turn was stripped from his position for refusing to denounce his compatriot.

Tibetan Buddhism is divided into four main traditions, the Nyingma, the Kagyu, headed by the Karmapa, the Sakya, and the Gelugpa founded in the fourteenth century, identified with the Dalai Lama and the Panchen Lama. Only one of the schools is strictly celibate, though that does not mean there is widespread sexual license. Again, we have a connection with Gnosticism in which some, viewing the material body as having no intrin-sic worth, indulged in libertine sexual practices, though most, as in Tantra, took the ascetic line.

The Tibetan Buddhist canon was completed in the fourteenth century, and with the almost total demise of Buddhism in northern India, this canon became very important in preserving the tradition.

In conclusion, of Buddhism we may say the differences in the faith are massive, to the extent that they make different wings of the faith hardly recognizable as the same religion. These include, as in Christianity, differences in religious forms seen especially in worship but distinct from Christianity, include also the realms of doctrine and scripture. Theravada, Mahayana, and Vajrayana represent very different Buddhist responses, and even within those distinct forms there are schools which are sharply different. Each of these schools, while sharing core scriptures, also has others germane to itself. Scriptures are not only translated into but are composed in different languages over an exceptionally long period. As such there is a continuing fluidity about the developing tradition within Buddhism, almost entirely absent from Christianity. In Christianity, once scriptures and orthodoxy were established, the former essentially by the third century, the latter in the fourth and fifth centuries, fluidity disappeared, and a set tradition was established.

We now turn to the Scriptures, first examining how they vary, particularly in Buddhism according to school in telling the story of their founder's life, and in the doctrines they expound, before turning to examine the Christian Scriptures, wherein we will find a much greater uniformity.

4

THE SCRIPTURES

FOLLOWING THE DEMISE OF their founders, both Buddhism and Christianity were faced with the problem of how to preserve their founder's teachings. Initially these were kept in developing oral traditions, and we must never forget the phenomenal capacity of those in antiquity to faithfully keep oral traditions, before finally being set into written traditions.

Again, we turn first to the faith chronologically prior, Buddhism.

With Buddha having died, refusing to nominate a successor, it was necessary to develop an authority structure within the sangha. With this in mind three sources of authority were established. The first was Buddha's teachings, the second, the discourses of the Buddha contained in the Sutta Pitaka, with the final being the monastic discipline contained within the Vinaya Pitaka. Kept initially in oral forms these pitakas later developed into a large and varied written collections in different languages.

In their written form, the Buddhist scriptures come long after the time of Buddha, probably from the first century BCE and then continued to expand over an exceedingly long period. We do not find in Buddhism the tight canonical tradition found within Christianity, this resulting in a far greater variation in scriptures between different Buddhist schools, with each of these schools attaching greater importance to varying scriptures. In this there is an elasticity absent from Christianity with its narrow, strongly defined canonical tradition. New schools within Buddhism did not discard writings, though they did rearrange them, while also adding new writings. This is far different than that found in Christianity, where we find a near complete uniformity of Scripture.

Within Buddhism there are important differences in the canons of different schools, some texts being only accepted by Mahayana and/or Vajrayana, while others are more universally accepted across all traditions. The later traditions, Mahayana and Vajrayana, claim their scriptures, despite their late compilation, being truly the words of Buddha, or "Buddhavacana," holding them to contain deeper teachings, designed for people with a more profound understanding of Buddha's ideas, those on the Bodhisattva path. These Mahayana texts all come from at least the first century CE and are not recognized by Theravada as having authoritative scriptural status.

The Buddhist scriptures are far more extensive than those in Christianity, sufficiently voluminous to take up several library shelves. The early Pali version alone extends to forty-five volumes, around eleven times the length of the Christian Scriptures, that representing but the first stage in the expansion. Some Buddhist canons are truly massive. The Chinese tradition extends to 55 volumes containing 2,184 texts, while the Tibetan canon is even larger expanding to 325 volumes holding 1,108 texts, believed to have all Buddhavacana, along with another 3,461 texts spoken by revered scholars. Along with the massive Buddhist Scriptures there are huge numbers of commentaries, and even sub-commentaries known as "tikka."

Buddhist scriptures are written in several different Asian languages, whereas those in the Christian canon are nearly all written either in Hebrew (those from the Jewish tradition, often called the Old Testament), or Greek (those peculiar to Christianity, usually called the New Testament).[1] If this lack of tight coherence and delineation, understood through Western eyes, is viewed as problematic, it does not disturb the Buddhist, for Buddhists, as we shall see, understand their scriptures in a different manner than do Christians.

Within Buddhism attitudes to the scriptures vary. In Theravada and in Tibet they are held to have great importance, and textual study is important, while contrastingly, Zen places little emphasis on them. In any case the types of literalism, associated with some Christian understandings of their Scriptures, is rarely present. This is likely because for Buddhists the life of the Buddha lacks the foundational importance of that of Christ for Christians. For a Buddhist truth is found in Buddha's teaching, whereas for a Christian the Christ event, his living, dying, and resurrection, as presented in the Scriptures, is of prime importance. Following the precepts of the Buddha himself, both the authority and veracity of the Buddhist Scriptures lie in

1. It has increasingly become the custom to speak of the Jewish or Hebrew Scriptures and the Christian or Greek Scriptures, thereby avoiding the pejorative term, "Old Testament," understood by those of the Jewish faith as meaning their Scriptures have been superseded by another.

how they work inwardly, the experiential being prime, whereas the Christian Scriptures, making reference to a foundational event, one external to the reader, are understood to have greater importance being revelatory of necessary truth.

In surveying the Buddhist scriptures, we need first to remember the very distinct main traditions; Theravada and Mahayana, each with their own scriptures, reflecting the differences between the schools. Even within these main schools, as well as in the divergent tradition of Vajrayana, there may be a significant variation in inclusion, importance, and level of acceptance attributed to different scriptures. Such is the variance, it is probable scriptures from the Vajrayana tradition with their distinct doctrines would be quite unrecognizable to a strict Theravada observer.

The differences between these Buddhist scriptural traditions are far greater than the minor differences found within the Christian tradition between Roman Catholics, Orthodox, and Protestants. Despite the great differences in devotional practice in Christian traditions, in their scriptures there is an overwhelming commonality. It is true that Roman Catholics include the Apocrypha (essentially those Jewish scriptures written in Greek rather than Hebrew), though at a second level, along with some churches like the Ethiopian Orthodox having an extended canon, but essentially in the Christian tradition there is a uniformity of scriptures.

Christians have set a limit on the size of the Christian Scriptures, a barely changed canon having been long delineated from as long ago as the late second century, found in the Muratorian fragment, giving a list of accepted Christian writings, very like we have today. A clear delineation is placed around what is accepted as Scripture within Christianity, something quite distinct from that found in Buddhism, where the tradition is far wider, varied, and ongoing.

The process of trying to establish a norm in Buddhist teachings probably began with the First Council, which the Pali texts inform us occurred, held at Rajgir, the capital of the kingdom of Magadha, some fifty years after the death of Buddha. At this council, over which Mahakashyapa presided, Buddha's followers began to establish a method of assessing the various doctrines and practices in circulation. It is claimed that a monk named Upali recited the Buddha's rules for monks and nuns from memory, while Buddha's cousin and attendant, Ananda, rendered the Buddha's sermons. It is more likely the compilation was more collaborative. The teachings were probably set into verses, as possibly even Buddha himself had done, to be sung or chanted in a formulaic manner, a style still present in the texts. This assisted in the retention of the teachings orally. Such skill, maintained by methods, built around repetition, communal recitation, and mnemonic devices, was one of the yogic disciplines.

The Christian Scriptures likewise share an oral tradition prior to the written text, though in Buddhism that tradition is far longer, extending almost half a millennium.

Due to this long oral tradition it is impossible in Buddhism to find an initial early layer of tradition, distinct from its ongoing development. While within Christianity, there may be problems in differentiating the earliest layers of the Gospels, the proto-Gospels, from that of the final redaction, we can easily distinguish between the scriptures and the later tradition found in church fathers and the councils of the church. This is not the case, however, with Buddhism given the long length of the oral tradition. It is possible with a reasonable amount of certainty to see how a written tradition develops, but with an oral tradition such is clearly impossible for we only have the final redacted form before us.

About sixty to one hundred years after Buddha's death, a Second Council was held at Vaishali, at which the monks divided the oral tradition into three sections or Tripitaka, literally meaning three baskets. The Tripitaka contained, in turn, the Sutta Pitaka (the teachings of the Buddha), the Vinaya Pitaka (codes of disciplines for monks), and new teachings, probably dating from this council, which formed the Abhidhamma (special or more esoteric philosophical teachings). The last shows us that Buddhism is more accepting of secret or more advanced teachings, with these being presented in a range of versions, than Christianity which would expunge such secret teachings contained in the gnostic traditions.

During, or not long after, the Second Council, the sangha began to separate into different schools as the Elders, Thera (Pali), or Sthaviras (Sanskrit), viewing themselves as keepers of the tradition, split from the reforming Mahassamghikas. As we have seen, there are known to have been eighteen schools with only Theravada surviving. Only one of the Tripitakas, from this time, that of the Theravada, originating from Sri Lanka, is extant, though not all in its original later written form in Pali, we being reliant then on translations preserved in Chinese and Tibetan scriptures for much.

When finally committed to writing, these earliest Theravada Scriptures were written in Pali, a north Indian language believed to approximate Magadhan, the language probably spoken by Gotama. Recording the teachings of the Buddha, these works are known as Suttas (later called Sutras in Sanskrit), the term meaning "to read." Preserved by the Theravada monks in Sri Lanka, Burma, and Thailand, these also have much commentary and tikka (sub-commentary).

There exist numerous versions of the Tripitaka, held by the different schools, including six Vinayas, all distinct, written in various languages, extant in Pali, Sanskrit, Mandarin, and Tibetan.

Within the first of the "three baskets," the Sutta Pitaka, there are five collections—nikayas—of teachings, numbering some 10,000, all claimed to be Buddhavacana (Buddha spoken), even when many clearly are not. Parts of the Sutta Pitaka in their oral form reach as far back as the First Council, though mostly they were expanded over the following century, that expansion seen particularly in the last two nikayas.

This Sutta includes suttas (prose), gatha (verse), udana (inspired speech), jataka (previous lives), and abhutadharma (concerning wonders and miraculous events).

The first nikaya, the Digha Nikaya, contains thirty-four of Buddha's longest discourses, focused on the fruits of the contemplative life, particularly mindfulness. It is directed toward both the spiritual training of the monks and the duties of the laity, while also including an account on the Buddha's qualities—sampasadaniya—along with a description of his last days in the mahaparinibba. This is followed by the Majjhima Nikaya, a collection of 152 of Buddha's mid-length sermons. In this nikaya there are numerous stories about Buddha, detailing his enlightenment and early preaching, as well as some core doctrines, particularly concerning kamma. The third collection, the Samyutta Nikaya, contains thousands of suttas in five sections or vaggas, divided by subjects such as the eightfold path, causation, and an analysis of the human personality, particularly the senses. This is followed by the Anguttara Nikaya, again with thousands of suttas but this time divided into eleven divisions grouped in numerical patterns, mostly found elsewhere in the scriptures. The last of these five collections, the Khuddaka Nikaya, is a collection of sermons, doctrines, and poetry, including probably the best known of all Buddhist texts, the Dhammapada, literally meaning "path of the dhamma," dhamma being both the teaching of the Buddha and the cosmic order of all things.

Just as the Gospels represent the heart of the Christian Scriptures, so does the Dhammapada within the Buddhist scriptures. Consisting of twenty-six chapters with 423 verses, it is claimed to be a concise expression of the Buddha's teaching. It has three primary aims; human welfare in the here and now, favorable rebirth into the next life, and the attainment of the ultimate good, though these aims could be said to be reflective of all Buddhist teaching. Contained in the Khuddaka Nikaya also are stories of the previous lives of the Buddha and his companions in the Jataka.

The second basket, the Vinaya Pitaka, the book of monastic disciplines, contains the rules of the sangha. It has three parts. The first, the Sutta

Vibhanga, includes the pattimokka, listing the 227 offenses to be confessed by monks at the fortnightly monastic chapter, with an explanation of how each rule came to be, along with the seventy-five rules of decorum for monks. This is followed by the Khandhakkas, divided into two parts, the Mahavagga (the great series) and the Cullavagga (lesser series), giving rules for admission to the sangha, the way of life within the order, and details of various ceremonies and their origin. The commentaries introducing each rule have preserved important legends concerning Buddha, especially those to do with the birth cycle (Jatakas). Finally, the third section of this basket, the Parivara, summarizes and classifies the rules.

The final basket, the Adhidhamma Pitaka, meaning further dhamma, deals with philosophical and doctrinal aspects pertaining to Buddhism. Much of this is presented in an academic manner, dry and arcane for most believers. It is traditionally believed to have been preached by the Buddha to the devas (non-human angelic figures) so they could preach it to others, including his departed mother.

Within the Theravada canon there are layers of importance between those Suttas understood to be Buddhavacana, and others not so regarded. One early, well-known text, however, generally not regarded as Budhava-cana, though still held to be important, is the aforementioned Milinda Panha (Questions of Milinda). Though not Buddhavacana this is included in versions of the Pali, and later Mahayana, canon.

The variance in the Scriptures held by the differing schools follow-ing the Second Council was originally confined to the variations in the Vi-naya, but as differences expanded from different monastic disciplines into the realm of doctrine, various schools began to hold different Tripitakas as a whole. The greatest difference, as would be expected, given increasing differences in doctrine, was within the third basket, the Abhidharmas, the Mahayana version, called the Sarvastivada Abidharma being quite distinct from that of Theravada. Given growing monastic differences Mahayana also follows a different Vinaya, the second component of the Tripitaka, called by them the Dharmaguptaka Vinaya, while within Tibetan Buddhism a third version, the Mulasavastivada Vinaya, is followed.

Despite the prodigious memory of the monks, material in an oral tradition would have been inevitably lost, perhaps intentionally, when it was less confirmatory of the traditions of a monk's particular school. Thus, while it is claimed that monks had no editorial input into the writings, the scriptures inevitably reflect what they believed. Despite protestations to the contrary, the same holds for the Christian Scriptures.

The Mahayana canon retains the scriptures of Theravada, translated into Sanskrit, but adds its own, originating from the first century C.E.

forward, composed in Sanskrit, though for most of these we have only Chinese translations. The most common Mahayana canon is the Chinese Taisho Tripitaka, believed widely in Mahayana to have been spoken by either Buddha, a disciple of the Buddha, a deva (a non-human being having some divine characteristics), or a rsi (an arahant or Bodhisattva). It is therefore held to be Buddhavacana, though only in Mahayana. We have also translations of the Mahayana canon in Tibetan as the Kangyur, of which there are varying editions, and again later Japanese editions, such as the Taisho Shinshu Tripitaka. The Chinese and Tibetan texts provide us with the earliest collection of Sanskrit texts, and though these translations come from the fifth and sixth centuries CE, some one thousand years after the life of the Buddha, parts possess antiquity finding agreement with early Pali texts. The Chinese and Tibetan texts function as the two existing canons within Mahayana, though some Sanskrit texts are extant.

Within Buddhism textual criticism is beginning to find a place, though the rigorous critical textual study which has marked Christianity for over two centuries is only a recent phenomenon. Thus a text, highly popular within Buddhism, the Asvaghusa, an epic style poem coming from the second century CE, more than half a millennium after the life of Buddha, is still widely accepted as Buddhavacana, though clearly not spoken by him. As stated, this uncritical acceptance is largely necessary due to the extremely long period between the lie of Buddha and written accounts concerning him, making textual criticism highly speculative, if not impossible.

The search for "the Jesus of history" is an important part of modern Christian study with whole groupings of scholars such as The Jesus Seminar being devoted to it. This rigorous search for the historical Jesus finds, however, no equivalent in Buddhism, largely because it would present those trying with an impossible task. The life and teachings of Buddha, as variously given in the Scriptures, are mostly by Buddhists uncritically accepted, even when clearly legendary.

New writings were added in each of the Mahayana canons claiming to tell the life and words of Buddha, believed by them to be spoken by him in a transcendent state, having therefore a deeper symbolic truth, and as such considered Buddhavacana. Such Mahayana Sutras include the Avatamsaka (Flower Garland), the Brahmajala (Brahma Net), Shurangama (Heroic Valour), Ratnakuta (Jewel Heap), Lankavatara (the Entering into Sri Lanka), Suddharma Pundarika (Lotus Sutra, literally "sutra of the wonderful law"), the Pure Land Sutras, along with the Mahaparinirvana Prajnaparamita (the Perfection of Wisdom). The last is claimed to be the final teachings of Buddha as he was dying. In total there are some six hundred Mahayana Sutras in the Chinese and Tibetan canons. It is clearly difficult to date the composition of these sutras as for the most part we only have translations.

Varying Mahayana schools understand Buddhavacana differently. Shingon divides the Buddhavacana into those words spoken by the physical manifestation of the Buddha present in Gautama, those held to have come from the Buddha in his Sambhoghakaya (Body of Bliss) known as the Ekayana, and those emanating from the Buddha as Dharmakaya (the Truth Body knowing no limit), known as the Vajrayana. The last becomes central in the school bearing that name. In Tibetan Buddhism the Buddhavacana collected in the Kangyur are believed to have been revealed either through supernatural beings known as nagas or though other Buddhas or Bodhisattvas.

From the seventh century CE another class of scriptures, which we have already examined, called Tantras, was composed. These are found primarily in the school of Buddhism, Vajrayāna, resident in Tibet, Nepal and Mongolia. As we have found these outline ritual and yogic practices which may be employed to assist in achieving nirvana.

Along with the scriptures there are other Buddhist writings, systematic treatises, written by later canonical experts, the shastras.

The golden age for Buddhist scripture creation is widely held to be from the first century to the fourth century CE, the latter being some eight hundred years after the life of the Buddha.

There are no Buddhist equivalents of the four evangelists of the Christian tradition, who clearly and intentionally have an input in how they each distinctly present Christ. We can, by studying each Gospel, make suppositions about each writer, their personal interest and understanding of Christ, something clearly present in their writings. In the epistles, the majority composed by Paul, we find even more the personality of the writer. Rather than being disinterested objective figures, simply recording events, the evangelists fashion a figure of Jesus reflective of their own theologies. This enables us, though speculatively, to get in behind these presentations to make informed conjectures the human Jesus. We thus have a much more rounded figure of Jesus, seen from differing angles, than we have of the Buddha presented in Buddhist Scriptures. The Buddhist authors, from such a long period after his life, present largely legendary accounts of the life and teaching of Buddha, resulting in us seeing little if anything of them as authors, nor of the human Buddha. Legend having overwhelmed the account, we have flatly presented, without personal interpretation or understanding, what each writer proclaims to be Buddhavacana. This clearly adds to the impossibility of finding any early layer of tradition, of which it could be argued as being most representative of the actual Buddha.

This, however, again does not greatly bother Buddhists, who believe as an issue of faith that the transcendent Buddha, resident in nirvana, is speaking through the scriptures, seeing less need for scriptural criticism with its goal of finding "the historical figure." For a Christian, that Christ lived and died is a necessary article of faith, therefore the fascination in knowing his life. For a Buddhist, faith can survive without such examination of Buddha for it is the teaching, and the effectiveness of its inner working in the recipient, rather than the person who gave it, which is prime. As we have found, radical traditions within Buddhism adjure even killing the Buddha if he is a hindrance on the path to this goal! The veracity of Buddhism is found in its effectiveness, not in the external.

The lack of concern for a delineation of the actual words and deeds of the historical Buddha is evidenced further in that as Buddhism spread, new scriptures, written in the local language, were composed to meet the new contexts. It is highly unlikely that these new compositions, so removed from the time and context of Buddha, would contain any of the actual words of the historical Buddha.

As the Theravada canon had served to confirm Theravada belief, new emerging schools likewise wrote and collected new material, claiming it to be revelation, in accord with their beliefs. While this also occurs in the Christian scripture it happens over a far shorter period, with the censor's cut being far more severe on those texts claiming to be revelation from the transcendent Christ. Closed early the Christian canon excised those scriptures, mainly gnostic, claiming to be from the transcendent resurrected Christ.

That the Buddhist scriptures operate as legendary accounts of the life of the Buddha does not, however, empty them of all historical veracity. From them we learn much of fifth century BCE India, this corroborated by other oral traditions contemporary with Buddhism, along with later Jain texts. The early Buddhist texts demonstrate an accurate understanding of the Vedic faith at time of the Buddha, something absent in later writings. We even learn about historical figures such as King Bimbisara of Magadha, along with the substantial social changes of the period, such as the growth of urban life and the changing political, economic, and social institutions. Archaeological evidence also largely supports the Buddhist writings. We need remember however that, as has been said elsewhere of the Christian scriptures, the presence of historical events and personages no more turns these legendary accounts into history than does the presence of the historical figures of King John and the Sheriff of Nottingham turn the legendary accounts of Robin Hood into history.[2]

---

2. John Dominic Crossan, Unpublished private notes from a lecture.

Let us turn now to the Christian Scriptures. Those used by Christians include both the Hebrew or Jewish Scriptures, which Christians call the Old Testament, and those composed by Christians, peculiar to their faith, the Christian or Greek Scriptures, believed by Christians to represent a New Testament. By such terminology we can see that, though they still hold the Jewish Scriptures sacred, Christians view them through the lens of their own Scriptures, seen as fulfillment of them. This effectively places the Jewish Scriptures at a lower level, in that their meaning is derivative of the Christian Scripture, rather than standing by themselves. Thus, in the Christian lectionary (cycle of readings) the Hebrew Scriptures used are selected by the criteria of how they reflect the main gospel reading.

The Jewish Scriptures, almost exclusively composed in Hebrew, are divided into three sections, called in Hebrew the Torah, sometimes known as the Pentateuch, given it consists of the first five books of the Scripture, held to be of prime importance; the Nevi'im or prophets; and the Ketuvim or writings. For that reason, it is often known by Jews as the Tanakh, a word combining the first letter of each of the three names. These Scriptures were composed around an eight hundred year period.

The specifically Christian Scriptures consist of the Gospels, epistles, primarily composed by Paul, but also including the pastoral epistles, along with two distinct books, the Acts of the Apostles, a clearly biased presentation of the expansion of the earliest church, and finally Revelation, an apocalyptic vision of the end, with the triumph of Christ and his followers. All these writings were composed in koine (common) Greek, the lingua franca of the Roman world, a simplified form of Greek intelligible to those for whom it was not their first language.

Along with these writings are others known as the Apocrypha, held to be of second level authority or deutero-canonical. These consist of writings from the Jewish tradition, primarily composed in Greek rather than Hebrew, which the Jewish Council of Jamnia, just after the time of Christ, judged to be non-canonical. These are recognized as Scripture by the Roman Catholic and Orthodox Churches, though at a second level, but not by Protestants. The best known are the books of Maccabees and Tobit.

All parts of the Scripture are held to be authoritative by Christians, though the importance placed on different sections varies. Of prime importance for Christians are the Gospels, segments of which are set for reading each week in the church's lectionary, which cycles through the Gospels in a three-year period (the Gospel of John is interspersed with the other Gospels, which each have their distinct year). The Christian lectionary almost always includes readings from the Jewish Scriptures, though as just seen, it is the Gospel reading which determines the theme.

There are also many other early Christian writings not included as part of the canonical Scriptures. Some of these have always been long used in Christian devotion such as the Didache, the Epistle of Barnabas, the Gospel of the Hebrews, and I Clement, but others, viewed as a threat to a narrowing orthodoxy, were either destroyed by those opposing them or conversely hidden by those holding them in regard. We have long known the contents of many of these destroyed and lost books through the writings, of their orthodox adversaries, in which they were selectively quoted. Others, however, have now been recovered, the best-known cache being the Gnostic Gospels found at Nag Hammadi in Egypt in 1945. As the name implies these writings, fifty-two texts in thirteen codices, were gnostic in content, with the majority claiming Christian origins, though some do not.

We ought note, Gnosticism is a very broad term covering a range of schools: Sethians, Valentinians, and Marcionites, among others, each of them quite distinct. This Nag Hammadi cache included the Gospel of Thomas, which some scholars date among the earliest of Christian documents, though there is sharp disagreement on this. This Gospel, called gnostic by association with the other writings with which it was found, is only partly so. It has a distinct theology, to which we will return. Many of these gnostic texts claim to contain secret teachings of Jesus only meant for advanced initiates capable of understanding that deeper knowledge (gnosis).

Christians, as we have noted, usually hold the truth of their Scriptures more rigorously, hence, distinct from Buddhists, their use of censorship to excise documents not in accord with that truth. This is largely due to Christians largely establishing the veracity of their faith as defined by their Scriptures. This is a circular exercise of course, truth found through the Scriptures, in turn determining which books will be accepted as scriptural.

Christians popularly understand their Scriptures as accounts of recordable events, though a range of views are held as to how strictly. God, as external, is revealed through divine actions, so these actions need to be truthfully recorded, particularly those appertaining to Jesus. Thus, little allowance is made by many Christians for the categories of myth and legend, whereas Buddhists are much more accommodating of these. As found, Buddhists experience the veracity of their faith through its internally verifiable effects, truth being found in wisdom within. Christians, with the divine external to them, are in need of revelation, therefore a need for truth concerning that revelation, that believed to be given in their Scriptures.

In Buddhism meaning and wisdom are found by turning to an inward rather than through the testimony of external events, so scriptures, and their recording of events, do not need to hold such high status. In one the truth of the faith is found by inner evidence measurable subjectively by its positive effect. For the other the veracity of the faith is found externally in relationship to the divine, that relationship being laid out in the scriptures; therefore the greater concern by Christians to see their scriptures as external truth, revelatory especially of Jesus.

So keen are Christians to find the "real Jesus" that we find in popular Christianity versions of the Scriptures with every word purported to have been spoken by Jesus printed in red, accepted without question as to its providence. This only really exists at the popular level of faith, distinct from even conservative Christian scholarship. However, scholarship, as we have seen, is also keen, even if in a more sophisticated manner, to find the historical Jesus.

Christian scriptural studies in the past century have been marked by three major "Jesus of history" periods of studies. The first, taking place in the late nineteenth century, was quite uncritical, finding a Jesus confirmatory of the scholars own social and cultural norms. Another flowered, as critical methodologies further developed, in the mid-twentieth century, until sophisticated high-level studies carried out in the present epoch by those in the Jesus Seminar, among others, have given further insight.

This concern for finding the historical Jesus is largely due to the prior Jewish understanding wherein God was understood as being revealed in history, that being recorded in the Scriptures.

The pivotal account for the Hebraic historicist understanding of the divine is found in the exodus (Exod 3), believed by Jews to be an historical event through which God had delivered them from slavery in Egypt to the promised land. The story commences with Moses standing before the bush, burning but not consumed. Intuiting that God is present in the bush, Moses enquires concerning the divine name. Rather than being given an understandable epithet he is instead told, "I am who I am," or "I will be who I will be." Contrary to other gods of the surrounding nations, who had given names, the Hebraic God carries no intelligible name.

In the Ancient Near East names carried great importance, defining the nature of the one who held them. We find such later in the Gospel accounts of the giving of names to both John the Baptist and Jesus. By no definable name been given, we are being told that the divine is beyond any definition which would accrue with such. For like reason graven images of the divine were also forbidden. Instead, we are told, as echoed through the divine voice coming from the burning bush, God will be known through divine actions within history, specifically the Exodus, which Moses is being commissioned to lead. God is the God found not in static categories of name and image, but in the flow of history, particularly in the freeing and liberation of the oppressed. "I have observed you and what has been done to you in Egypt, and

I promise that I will bring you up out of the affliction of Egypt" (Exod 3:16-17). This revelation of God in history, rather than in the internal mystical or spiritual, is what primarily shapes both the Jewish and Christian (and later Muslim) understanding of the divine. Though the mystical and experiential are present in the Western faiths they stand as a minor key to revelation taking place in historical events.

In the Judeo-Christian tradition the understanding of the divine is externalized in relationship, in events, while in Buddhism it is internalized, found in inner wisdom.

Given such need to find this externalized truth in the Scriptures, many Christians, despite Western critical scholarship being over two hundred years old, either hold little appreciation or knowledge of its findings or very deliberately reject it, clinging doggedly to a literal understanding, perceiving the only alternative is to concede the Scriptures as being false and therefore to have no standing. In such a case faith itself collapses.

Core to this is the popular understanding of truth. It is usually equated to factuality, with little understanding, if any, of myth, metaphor, and symbol. Either something is literally true, or it is false, with little or no grey in between. Given that it is through divine actions that God is known, with these being recorded in the Scriptures, these Scriptures must be factually true. While, as we have noted, in some parts of the Christian tradition the concern for literalism has been carried to extreme conclusions, it is fair to say that what informs it, God known by divine actions in history, shapes overall the Christian (and Jewish) tradition. When scholarship makes clear that such inerrancy is not the case, many Christians struggle.

Much of the literalism we find particularly in more conservative streams of Christianity, but also in general, paradoxically comes from the triumph of the scientific mindset in the West, the very science which much of this conservative Christianity opposes. Science is popularly (incorrectly) understood as viewing things in a binary manner, either factually true or false. Such understanding is so dominant it has relegated all other understandings to being equated with falsehood or to be non-understandable. Myth particularly becomes non-intelligible, relegated to falsehood. Without the nuances of myth we are left to understand the historicist Scriptures as either true or false.

This is problematic as critical scholarship has uncovered many things in the Scriptures not literally true, things as central to the Christian tradition as the birth of Christ and his trial and resurrection. Such discoveries are clearly extremely challenging for many Christians caught in mindset. Within such a framework the varying accounts of the same event in the different Gospels should mean one must be right at the expense of the others.

This however is rarely the case in the literalist's mind as such differences are ignored or glossed over, becoming invisible.

The same mindset causes others to reject Christianity on the basis that if the scriptures are not literally true, then the only option remaining is that they, and therefore Christianity, must be false. If we are unable to believe that creation came about in seven days, or that it is possible by holding up one's hand to control the hour of sunset (Exod 17:8-13), or that Jonah survived in the "belly of the whale" for three days, then the Scriptures, and the faith they represent, have as a whole no veracity. Each side having been inculcated in this literal factual understanding, wherein truth equates to fact, is unable to appreciate those things which actually shape the Jewish and Christian Scriptures, particularly myth, often presented as metaphor and symbol, being alternative forms of truth. For each the accounts of say, Jesus walking on the water, or his dividing a small amount of bread, so there is sufficient for thousands to consume, are caught up in this web of literalism, meaning these things must factually be true or false. One will defend their historical reality, the other dismiss them as meaningless. As such these accounts are unable to be appreciated for what they really are.

Many of these supposed historical accounts are better understood as being what is known as midrash, a Jewish method of paralleling a current event or person to one in the past, to show that God, understood as having been present in that past person or event, in like manner is now present in the current person or event. In these two just referred accounts concerning Jesus, what is being claimed by his actions only proper to God, the control of water, and the miraculous provision of bread, is that in Jesus, divinity is present. As such Jesus' actions operate as a type of myth in that the truth of the event is found not in whether or how it literally occurred, but rather in that which they signify.

Common use of midrash is made through the scriptures in both their Jewish and Christian parts. The clearest example concerns this division of water. Moses is the first to divide the waters (Exod 14:21) with the question as to Joshua being his true successor settled by his likewise doing (Josh 3:16). What of Elijah? He also is presented as one used by God for he in similar manner divides water (2 Kgs 2:8). Is Elisha truly one who inherits the prophetic mantle of Elijah? He must be for he also is able to divide the waters (2 Kgs 2:14). Again, Jesus trumps them all for he not only divides the waters in his baptism but also the vault of the sky, above and behind which the ancients believed lay the primeval waters. Jesus' status is verified in that from this now opened domain the Spirit descends proclaiming Jesus as God's beloved son (Mark 1:10). Again using midrash we find in this event nothing less is being said than that in Jesus a new creation is being inaugurated, for at the advent of creation the spirit had likewise moved over the waters. (Gen 1:2). Jesus, we are informed, can also still the waters (Mark 4:37-41) and even walk upon them (Matt 14:25-26).

This control of waters is highly significant, for it was believed as powerful myth that the chaotic primeval waters were ever threatening to overwhelm the order of creation, only able to be controlled by God. While the others named invoke the name of God for their feats with water, Jesus does these things without reference to God, in his own power. In such, we are being told that Jesus is to be understood as having great divine favor, or even as being divine himself. This is classic midrash whereby Jesus is shown to stand firmly within the holy tradition, while being able to extend it.

The "history" given in the Scriptures is always shaped and subsumed by the concern to show that God, understood external to the believer, is known through the events which the divine executes in the historical domain. Even those things which never happened, such as fantastic events in the infancy narratives of Jesus, are thus presented in a manner which appears historical. This is not to say that there is not history to be found in the Scriptures but rather that the telling of history is always subservient to, and shaped by, the goal of it showing the revelation of the divine.

Thus, the Gospels are not biographies nor histories telling us Jesus' life but rather missionary tracts, revealing the divine in Jesus. They do not seek so much to give us a life of Jesus as to change the life of the reader, opening them to this divine revelation. The means of doing this is to present not a Jesus framed by actual history but rather a Jesus who, though presented historically, is understood in the light of the already resurrected Christ of faith. The events given to us in the Gospels of Jesus' life are all shaped by the faith of those remembering him from a post-resurrection perspective and as such are the work of the writers writing as theologians, attempting to make sense of Jesus' life within their own context, rather than presenting a factual account of his actual life. Thus, we have four Gospel accounts with each Gospel writer understanding the significance of Jesus' life in a different manner. This is not to say that the Gospels are fictions, creating a life of Jesus having no connection to his actual life but that theology, rather than history, is the writer's main concern. The actual things Jesus did shape part of what they record but are all understood and presented through eyes of faith, the aim being to engage those reading, calling them to a commitment to follow Jesus. For us moderns, shaped by the discipline of history, this will likely appear to be illegitimate, but it was a common practice in antiquity.

This concern particularly informs how they present Jesus in relation to his own faith tradition, Judaism. While the Jesus of the Gospels is presented as being in opposition to his parent faith, in reality he lived and died a Jew, rather than as one intent on forming a new religion. Having said that though, he seems to have been a radical contentious teacher, to the point that finally the authorities within his own faith tradition were happy to collaborate with the secular Roman officials to be rid of him. That Jesus both lived and died a Jew is something on which few Christians consciously reflect. He is simply unconsciously thought of as "one of ours, not theirs."

The actual Jesus and the Jesus presented in the Gospels are quite distinct. The changing reflection on Jesus' meaning and significance was shaped by several things.

First, his sudden violent death had come as a shock. His followers had entered Jerusalem with him, confident that the reign of God, standing at the heart of his teachings, and on which his ministry centered, was about to be inaugurated. Yet suddenly he was taken from them and executed in a perfunctory and brutal manner. As the expected Messiah, Jesus had clearly failed. A few days later, however, we are told that those who had cowered in fear were now fearlessly pronouncing his triumph, claiming him as risen from the dead. As to the nature of that resurrection, I have examined that elsewhere.[3] Here let its nature not concern us, but rather let us note that belief in it was soon widespread among Jesus' followers, radically transforming their thinking concerning him. For his followers it clearly represented something profoundly real. For them this represents a radical change in the meaning of Jesus. He is turned from (failed) Jewish messiah to something else.

No doubt their reflection on Jesus was also affected by their knowledge that those at the center of their own faith had collaborated with the Romans in having him executed, that likely to cause Jesus' followers, all of them Jewish at this early stage, to begin to think on their relationship with their parent faith. This reflection by the initial Jewish followers concerning their parent faith, and what it now meant to be following Jesus, who had failed to carry out the expected Jewish Messiah role, represents the first step in reflection on the significance of Jesus. This happened very quickly, built around this significant event, resurrection. We thus find, just twenty years after Jesus, in the writings of Paul, "a Hebrew of the Hebrews" as he calls himself, a radically reoriented Jesus, particularly in his relationship to both his and Paul's parent faith.

Along with this reflection by the earliest followers of Jesus as to his meaning came a cataclysmic historical event which would profoundly shape the telling of the gospel story. In 66 CE the Jewish nation, sorely oppressed under the Roman heel rose, at first successfully, driving the Romans out,

3. Queripel, *On the Third Day.*

before their return under the future emperor Vespasian, whereupon they exacted terrible revenge, ruthlessly sacking Jerusalem, including that which lay at the heart of Jewish belief and identity, the temple. The subjection was completed at the famous siege and mass suicide of the Jewish defenders at Masada.

This had a major effect, further separating the grouping of those, still mainly Jews, following Jesus, from the mother faith, Judaism. It was alleged that many of the Jewish followers of Jesus, due to conflicting loyalties, had not been sufficiently involved in the resistance to Rome, retreating instead out of Jerusalem. Their allegiance was therefore viewed as questionable, seemingly being more directed toward their teacher than to the nation.

Following the failed rebellion, the prevailing Judaism was radically different from that of the time of Jesus. That, which had consisted of Sadducees, Pharisees, Zealots, and the Essenes, along with numerous charismatic teachers such as Jesus himself, was no more. By the time of the writing of the Gospels this, due to the rebellion and subsequent Roman reconquest, had all changed.

Linked to the temple and governance in the Jewish nation, the Sadducees had been eliminated, something equally true for that group, associated with an alternate temple ritual, the Essenes. In the Dead Sea Scrolls they portrayed themselves under "the Teacher of Righteousness" in mortal combat with "the Evil Priest" and "the Kittim," understood to be Rome. It is understandable then that the Romans didn't spare them the sword. The rebellious Zealots of course had been decimated, leaving only the popular teachers, the Pharisees. It was from them that a revived, radically changed form of Judaism, which we know as rabbinic, would spring. The failed rebellion and destruction of the temple meant Judaism had changed from being a faith built on the temple cult to one centered on the book, that book being the Scriptures, the Tanakh. The interpreters of these Scriptures were the rabbis, the inheritors of the Pharisaic movement. Under such rabbinic leaders as Johanan ben Zakkai at Jamnia, in particular, Judaism took a radically new structure. By the time of the writing of the Gospels, all written after this cataclysmic event, the Jewish faith was very much a dramatically changed religion from that of the time of Jesus.

This represented a massive change, a change as great (and similar) as that in Hinduism when the external Vedic sacrifices were replaced by a much more interior faith found in the Upanishads.

Likewise, the faith of those following Jesus had become very distinct from that which Jesus had taught. That change had been necessary due to his not fulfilling the expectations of being messiah. His significance had to be made different.

After intense debate the followers of Jesus had begun accepting gentiles into their grouping, such action, following the failed revolt, one in which they were accused in taking little part, caused them to be increasingly estranged from their parent faith. This acceptance of gentiles, the destroyers of the city and temple, into their movement was viewed as traitorous, while the growing centrality in which they held Jesus also led them to be more and more viewed by the Jewish community as heterodox, viewed with askance by those who in such a catastrophic context following the disastrous rebellion were trying to redefine and re-establish their faith and identity. In face of the catastrophe which had befallen them, radically redefining their faith, they understandably would view it necessary to exclude others more extreme.

Given the massive innovations and changes in both groupings, each were forced to strenuously assert that they, despite the huge changes they were embracing, not the other, were the true inheritors of the Jewish sacred tradition, one so different from what either were now practicing. Each had become people of the book, but what they were reading from the book was increasingly different as the followers of Jesus began to develop new scriptures.

Inevitably this led to a growing invective between the groups. These differences were then extrapolated back to the time of Jesus, leading him to be turned into one rejecting his faith tradition. A critical reading of the Gospels will show that this certainly was not the case. Instead, we find Jesus clearly observing the Jewish festivals, visiting both synagogue and the temple, while preaching a classically Jewish message of the coming reign of God.

Central to this turning of Jesus against his tradition was his supposed opposition to the Pharisees, from which had come the rabbis, the opposing group to the followers of Jesus at the time of writing. Jesus was turned from one who in his lifetime was probably identified as a Pharisee into one pictured as being fiercely opposed to them. We know of the actual Jesus' close affinity to the Pharisees from the practices he shares with them, such as his teaching style, his gathering of a group of disciples, and his sharing in table fellowship.

Thus, the pictures we have of Jesus painted in the Gospels are not historically accurate. They were never intended to be. Again, we find that while the Judeo-Christian Scriptures appear as giving a dispassionate history, they represent a very interested or biased account. We need repeat, rather than giving us history the Gospels are bending it to their real interest, making clear the revelation of the divine through Jesus, with an intent to change us.

In light of the above Jesus is radically changed. No longer is he the Messiah preaching and enacting the "kingdom of God" (an era of peace and justice), instead becoming a cosmic savior enabling followers access to an otherworldly salvation. This radical turning of Jesus enabled his followers to understand his failure as Messiah, while making sense of the growing opposition of his Jewish faith tradition to him. It also supports their acceptance of gentiles and the movement away from their parent faith. Jesus the Jewish Messiah is turned into a cosmic savior. We have given to us not the historical Jesus but rather one who makes sense to the gospel writers in light of events between his actual life and their own context.

Frequently to support their case as to the veracity of the specifically Christian Scriptures, Christians will argue the relative proximity of their composition to the events they describe. As seen, the earliest part, the letters of Paul, were composed just over two decades after the life of Jesus, with the writing of the Scriptures continuing for another 125 years until the composition of the final writing, almost universally held to be 2 Peter.

There is however, a significant variation within these Scriptures with Paul's understanding of how a person is reconciled with God, grace alone through faith, strongly countered by James's "faith without works is dead." In similar manner, Matthew's view of Jesus' tightening the Jewish Law is far removed from Paul's understanding of Jesus abrogating it.

Despite this variety the Christian Scriptures are significantly narrower than what they once were, due to the censors' hands. The earliest church had a wide diversity of views. There were a range of gnostic schools, holding in common the idea that Christ was the revealer of a sacred truth, the knowledge of which enabled one to find salvation, along with others, known as Judaizers, understanding him as being much more aligned with his Jewish faith, claiming therefore that his followers had to keep to the precepts of the Torah.

We can see this range from just reading the Pauline letters, wherein he interacts, debating with the numerous different theologies, held by his interlocutors. Of course, we only have in the Scriptures one side of the argument; the views of the other side are not present.

The Pauline epistles represent an early attempt to enforce a certain orthodoxy, something ever more successful as permissible views within the church narrowed, until uniformity became enforced following Christianity becoming the official religion of the Roman Empire in the early fourth century. However, long before the empire enforced a conformity the church had chosen that direction with lists of accepted scripture compiled, most notably, as found, in the Muratorian canon from the late 2nd century. Along with an officially recognized canon of Scripture, Christian uniformity was also progressively enforced by the recognition of orthodox lineages of church leaders, "bishops," and the development of set creeds establishing orthodox belief.

Orthodoxy having determined what went into the scriptures was then increasingly defined by those Scriptures, so that a reciprocal relationship, operating by a circular "logic" was established, whereby Christian orthodoxy and the Scriptures shaped each other in an increasingly narrow manner. Both writings and understandings which moved outside that narrow constraint were rejected, especially those Christian traditions which wanted to add new Scriptures.

This concern for doctrinal orthodoxy has, as we have seen, no equivalent concern in Buddhism within which there are numerous widely different schools of thought. Thus, something as crucial to a faith as soteriology, varies greatly, as we have seen, in the various schools of Buddhism. The soteriology of Theravada with its self-dependence, guided by teachings from Buddha, is a long way removed from that of Mahayana schools such as Pure Land, with their understanding of Buddha as gracious savior. Similarly, the Theravada Buddhist will probably find completely non-understandable the belief in the magical qualities of the mudras, mandalas, and mantras found in Vajrayana. There is less concern for what is "normative" within the Buddhist scriptures, schools possessing distinct compilations, along with emphases within those compilations. This open scriptural tradition operates reciprocally, leading to a more open acceptance within Buddhism of new schools such as Mahayana and Vajrayana, though there is a residual conservatism within Theravada which rejects, or only grudgingly accepts both, these new schools with their new scriptures.

CONCLUSION

In conclusion, while we can conclude that though both faiths hold their Scriptures highly as sacred writings, they differ in the range, flexibility, and number of Scriptures (and therefore size), they admit to their canonical traditions.

The Buddhist tradition developed over a far longer time, first as oral tradition and again in written form. New writings were still being composed, in varying languages, more than a millennium after Buddha's life. That contrasts sharply with that found in Christianity with its far shorter oral and then written traditions, the final canonical writing coming from only around 120 years after the life of Jesus.

Given the externality of the divine within Christianity, therefore need for revelation, believed to come through the Scriptures, Scriptures are held to be more integral to the veracity of Christian belief than in Buddhism. Christianity objectifies the divine, the Scriptures being revelatory of that. In Buddhism "the divine" is found by turning inward to find wisdom, as did Gotama, rather than in adherence to external authority as in a scriptural tradition. The scriptures inform the Buddhist of how that turning inward is done, their importance being derivative of that. Though important they lack therefore the centrality they have in Christianity where they make known the external transcendent, otherwise unknowable, God.

5

THE LIVES
PREFACE

LET US NOW TURN to look at the lives of Gotama and Jesus, as presented in scriptures and tradition, while also taking a more critical look at the lives of each.

Getting at the lives of either, in the sense of being able to construct a coherent biography, presents us with many problems. Historical biographies having a goal of being accurate and unbiased are a modern concept. Even then they are often unsuccessful in that endeavor. In the ancient world depictions of great figures were deliberately mixed with myth, metaphor, and legend, often with some magic thrown in as well. Those categories, rather than being peripheral, lay at very heart of such accounts. That means with such figures as Buddha and Christ it is not as simple as believing we can remove myth and legend as accretions so to find an historic kernel. Rather, dismissing the miraculous to leave the mundane as the supposed "historical," whether it be with Buddha or Christ, is to distort the accounts. Instead of excising it, we must seek rather to understand what the miraculous, mythological and non-historical, is trying to say.

As we have seen with one of our faiths, Buddhism, it is not generally the life of Buddha but rather his teachings which are crucial. Getting to the historical Buddha is not then so important, and Buddhists are content to live with what for the most part are legendary accounts of his life.

Of Buddha's life there is little biography in the earlier Pali texts, and for what follows we are largely reliant on the later Sanskrit tradition. The clearly legendary nature of that account will become abundantly clear as we read through it.

Given the length of the oral tradition and the lateness of the written tradition it is far more difficult to find "the Buddha of history" than it is to find "the Jesus of history," as difficult and controversial as that latter quest has been. The life of Buddha we can surmise has been almost totally merged with myth and legend.

As expressed in the foreword to this work, in surveying the lives of each the first difficulty we face is that the nomenclature of each has clear contrast. Gotama becomes the Buddha within his lifetime and then continues for many years in that high status given him by his followers, whereas Jesus only becomes the Christ in Christian belief following his death and resurrection, an event understood as the pivotal redemptive act in the Christian tradition. It is extremely unlikely that Jesus ever was viewed as Christ in his lifetime. Indeed, the Gospels, written when he was already well on the path of elevation to such status, still predominantly name him as Jesus up to the end of his life. On those occasions in the Gospels he is named Christ, it is clear the term is a post-resurrection projection of that status back to his temporal existence. This is different to Gotama, who is presented as Buddha within his temporal existence. Even if historically Gotama was not necessarily known as Buddha during his lifetime, within the faith story he is elevated to be the Buddha during his temporal life, and it is the faith story which determines the nomenclature which I will use. When either are referred to as objects of faith statements by adherents, I will use the elevated honorific form.

I have chosen therefore to call each by what I judge to be the appropriate name by the context in which I am speaking of them. Thus, before his enlightenment I have called the one who was to become the Buddha "Gotama," choosing to use the older Pali form of his family name. With the one who was to be known as the Christ, I will call him Jesus, until the point of his death. Only in the post-resurrection period do I call him Christ, for it is that moment which is transformative.

We need of course to remember that neither the terms Buddha or Christ represent names but rather titles, markers of the ontological status in which each was held by their followers. As seen, Buddha means "one awoken to perfect enlightenment, therefore in nibbana," while Christ is the Greek form of the Hebrew "Mashiach" or Messiah signifying "the anointed one," expected to bring the divine reign.

Having established these parameters let's examine the life of each, beginning with the one chronologically prior, Gotama, who comes to be known as Buddha.

THE LIVES: GOTAMA

In giving an account of the Buddha's life we need again remember that it was not until some five hundred years after his life that any full chronological account is given, with only partial accounts existing prior. It is from that time also that we find the earliest images of Buddha in paintings and statues, whereas previously representation had been through symbols such as the dharmachakra, the Buddhist wheel, bodhi tree, or footprint. While this primarily picks up on the idea that the "Tathagata" is indeed the "thus gone" and therefore cannot be imaged, it may also be further evidence of the lack of concern for the historical Buddha. Again, it is not the life but rather the teaching of Buddha which is prime. To tell his life in a sense is to hold onto him who, like all else, has no permanency.

The earliest Theravada tradition gives us little biographical information, so we are reliant on later Sanskrit texts such as the Buddhacharita, or "Acts of the Buddha" composed by Asvaghosa in the first century CE, the Agamasutras from the second century CE and to a lesser extent on the Lotus Sutra (first to second centuries CE). Even then we are given little systematic information on the forty-five years of Buddha's teaching mission. Thus, the Lalita-Vistara from the Mahayana school (first to second centuries CE) concludes with Buddha preaching his first sermon, while another later scripture, the Nidana Katha (fifth century CE), ends with the formation of the first Buddhist settlement in Sāvatthī near the beginning of his mission. From those writings we have no information at all for twenty years of his life.

Only extremely late do we get extended biographies, the Tibetan Lalita-Vistara (third century CE) and the just mentioned Pali Nidana Katha. There are also the Pali commentaries on the canon by the fifth century CE scholar Buddhaghosa, which purportedly place in chronological order the unordered events narrated in the Pali canon. It is that detailed in these later texts which has become the accepted life of Buddha, accounts coming from nearly a millennium after the events they describe. Given this there are, as we would expect, all kinds of accretions, that explaining the often legendary rather than historical life we possess. Such can be seen in the account I give following. While it is asserted that these chronologies are based on far earlier oral accounts of Buddha's life going back to the Second Council, this can only be conjecture as oral memory leaves no historical record.

The lack of concern for Buddha's life is understandable given that he always claimed his teachings and path were his own insight not dependent on others, adjuring his followers to likewise not just blindly follow him. For a Buddhist it is foolish to waste time on pinning down the Buddha of history, rather than to more profitably spend time on learning and applying the teachings he gave. The Christian, however, needs Christ to have lived, though that life may be essentially reduced, as it is for the apostle Paul, to just his death and resurrection. The teachings of Jesus are held by his followers to be less important than those of Buddha for the Buddhist. Buddhist teachings are held to be the key to liberation, while for the Christian, it is not Jesus' teachings which offer salvation but rather the action of Christ in death and resurrection.

Such is the low regard to history in the Buddhist accounts, we cannot even be certain as to which century the Buddha lived. Traditionally he is thought to have lived c. 566 to c. 483 BCE, though some Chinese sources place his death as late as 368 BCE. Recent research suggests the likely time of his death as being c. 410 BCE.

Like Jesus, Gotama was born into a very volatile and violent age, a time when a series of feudal kings, the Magadhas and Kosalas, were waging ongoing wars against neighboring republican (more so oligarchical) tribes, including that to which Gotama belonged, the Sakya. This is the reason Buddha is often called Sakyamuni or "sage of the Sakyas." Gotama's father, Suddhōdana, was a member of the old governing assembly of aristocratic oligarchs, the sangha, the name Buddha was to later give to his followers. The wars marking the time of Gotama were being made worse by the advancing technology with bronze weaponry being replaced by that of iron. The efficiency of these royal kingdoms was particularly attractive to a rising merchant class, grown tired of the infighting among the tribal republics. This rapidly changing political and social context, with the breakdown of the old aristocratic order, and replacement by one built around mercantilism, provided a favorable space for reform movements like Buddhism to grow.

One ideal, in the context of this increasingly violent period, became powerfully influential, the way of "ahimsa" (the avoidance of harm to any living being), something strictly held in that faith born contemporary with Buddhism, Jainism, yet also influential in Buddhism itself. Much later ahimsa would be core to the thought of Mahatma Gandhi. In this concern for non-violence there is a parallel with Christ who, likewise coming from a violent epoch, shared it.

Due to the rise of this mercantile society, the Sakya, once isolated, were no longer so, with the tribal capital Kapilavatthu being on a main trading route, making it attractive proposition for the major nearby kingdoms.

In the religious realm there were also major changes, centered around a growing discontent with the formal ritualism of the existing cultic Brahminic religion. In the low status he held the efficacy of sacrifice offered to the gods, Buddha was not unique, that judgment also present in Jainism, while within Hinduism itself there was like weariness with the old forms built around Brahminic cult and ritual, with its claimed automatic efficacy, guaranteed to bring one to moksha. This weariness and discontent gave rise to the Upanishads (derived from the Sanskrit api-ni-sad, "to sit near"). These laid out a more personalized, less automatic path for the pilgrim to tread. The contention of the Upanishad was that the inner essence of any individual thing, the atman, was identical with that unchanging, all-pervading Brahman, which had created and was sustaining the universe. It was this spiritual realization, rather than the sacrifices of the Brahmins, which was held to be efficacious. This search for the inner Self was to motivate Gotama through his rigorous search, though he was to come to a radically opposed conclusion concerning the existence of the atman.

This time of the emergence of new ideas and new religious forms has led many scholars to call this era between the eighth and fifth centuries BCE "the axial age," given that many new faiths came into being, or old faiths took an axial turn. Much of this change right across the world was represented by an internalization of religious forms, and the Indian religious tradition was no exemption. The Jewish tradition was to find the same thing, particularly in the writings of Jeremiah. "I will put my law within them, and I will write it upon their hearts; and I will be their God, and they shall be my people" (Jer 31:33).

Contemporary with Buddha there was also a rise in sramanic movements, a term meaning "one who strives." As such, these demanded a more active personal response than the passivity associated with the Brahminic tradition. One such movement was the Aranyaka movement, which may be thought anachronistically as a hippie new age movement, in which one searched for a more personal experience by way of paññā, often sought by seeking sanctuary and freedom in the forest.

These movements represented a discontent with the Brahminic liturgical emphasis (karma marga) and a desire for a more personal experience and way of knowledge (jnana marga).

Buddha's teaching and philosophy were very clearly shaped by this context, both religious and wider, in which he found himself.

Over time the accounts of Buddha become ever more elaborate, increasingly emphasizing myth, legend, and miracle, as he was progressively changed from a human being into one beyond even divine. This elevation, though present in the Theravada texts, became such that it led to a whole different school, the Mahayana, the most popular in Buddhism, who deified the Buddha, making of him an object of worship.

We are told that the Buddha was born Siddhattha (meaning "he whose aim is accomplished") Gotama of Queen Maya, a consort of King Sud-dhodana, though the birth was through no human agency, Buddha having descended from Tusita, one of the heavens. He then enters the womb of the queen at a propitious time, in the form of a white elephant, which either places a white lotus in Maya's womb or enters through her side. The birth is above the realm of the carnal or sexual, coming instead from the higher chakras. Further, Queen Maya, like Mary the mother of Jesus, was a virgin. Jesus is born likewise not out of sexual union but of the Spirit. These non-sexual means of the births of the figures central to them are indicative of both faiths having a long and difficult relationship with human sexuality.

We are informed that on the night of her conception Maya dreamed that a Boddhisatva would enter her body. Propitious births are often associ-ated with visions and dreams, and again we find a parallel in the birth of Jesus, with the vision to Mary by the archangel Gabriel in the Annunciation, and in the thrice-dreaming "father," Joseph. The greatness of both figures is extrapolated back on to their births, for neither carried that fame at birth. I have examined that of Jesus in a previous work.[1]

As was the custom when a pregnancy neared term, Maya journeyed from Kapilavatthu, where she was resident, to her hometown to give birth, this journeying again paralleling the birth story of Jesus. Gotama's birth occurs in Lumbini, labor commencing while Maya walking in the gardens reaches out to touch the blossoms of a plaksa tree. The birth takes place from the propitious right side, and it is said that the Hindu Gods, Indra and Brahma, among other deities, descend to pay homage. This last aspect of the story is intended to show Buddhism as being superior to the older Vedic Hindu tradition, Buddha understood to be superior to even Brahma, the highest of all in the Hindu pantheon of gods. Brahma may believe he is the creator, but this is only an illusion (maya) in which he, unlike Buddha, is mired. Likewise, to make that same point on the day following the birth we are told sixty-four Brahmins, those most highly regarded in Hinduism, inform Maya that she has given birth to the future Buddha. The status of Gotama is confirmed by his bearing thirty-two marks of a "great man." Such testimony concerning unique status is likewise found in the birth of Jesus with the wise men, later to become the "three kings." Again, in like parallel, in the Christian tradition Jesus is viewed as being greater than Moses, the one who stands supreme in Judaism, the tradition from which Christianity sprung.

1. Queripel, *Christmas Myth, Magic and Legend.*

Following Buddha's birth, we are told the infant stood up, taking seven steps in each quarter with his right hand raised in the gesture of abhayamudrā (fearlessness) and his left turned down in varadamudrā (granting wishes). With one hand up and the other down the implication also is that he will be honored, both in heaven and upon the earth. He then announces that this will be his final birth. Seven days after she had given birth Gotama's mother, Maya, died, meaning he was brought up by his aunt, known as Mahapajapati or Pajapati, who would become Suddhodana's second wife.

It is possible that the royal couple Suddhodana and Maya never existed as they are pictured. The queen's name, meaning illusion, provides us a clue, while the clan of the Shakyas as a small republic, would have been governed by a council rather than by royalty. Suddhodana would have been an important figure, among others in government, rather than a king. That title is given to him so to fit a later time when kings did rule. While the title and prestige of Suddhodana is clearly inflated, in the Jesus story there is like doubt concerning Joseph's existence.

The pomp and power of the court into which Buddha was born becomes increasingly exaggerated in the later Scriptures, we being told there were even three palaces, one for each season of the Indian year. This noble birth of Buddha became an important feature in later art.

Gotama's family belonged not to the priestly brahmin caste in Indian society but rather to the second of the four main castes: the khattiyas (Sanskrit "ksatriyas"), the aristocratic warrior and administrative class. There is, however, no evidence that the caste system was practiced among the Sakyas; perhaps this been part of the reason for Buddha's later rejection of that system in the sangha.

As found often with figures who achieve greatness, incredible stories develop around their childhood years, and that of Buddha is no exception. We are told that on one occasion Gotama was taken to the temple by Pajapati to pay homage to the gods, whereupon he informs her the gods already acknowledge him as their superior, upon which the divine icons take life, descend from their shrines, and give their respect. There is a parallel with Jesus in that as a child he also was taken to the temple by his parents, who upon realizing he is missing on the homeward journey, return to the temple to find him debating with, and even teaching, the priests.

Gotama grew up in Kapilavasthu, near the modern-day border with Nepal. Before his birth, his father had a dream wherein he was told that his son would grow to either be a great king, a cakkavatti, conquering with military power, or a great religious figure conquering by other means. The cakkavatti he could become was not an evil figure but rather one who in power would turn the wheel of justice for good. In this appealing temptation to the "good" we again find a parallel with Jesus who, taken in a vision to a high mountain, is offered all the kingdoms of the world so to do good. Throughout their lives and ministries both Buddha and Jesus would continually be confronted by the highly tempting alternative path of bringing the good by force of suasion or power.

Determined that his son would take the former rather than the latter path Suddhodana had him kept secluded, his goal being that Gotama would never realize the transitory and therefore ultimately meaninglessness of wealth, power, and honor. To this end Suddhodana arranged to have all old, infirm, and sick people removed from anywhere Gotama went. Being raised in total bliss, hidden in his father's palace, we are told that Gotama had no clue suffering existed until reaching the age of twenty-nine! Clearly in these narratives we are moving in the realm of legend and metaphor, calling us to suspend all critical thinking. In truth we know from elsewhere in the tradition that Gotama was aware of pain and suffering. Suffering was present with him from the very beginning, his mother dying while giving birth to him, something which later must have grieved him. Another time we are told, as a child, he feels distress when his cousin, Devadatta, a dark figure in the Buddhist tradition, shoots dead a swan, while on yet another occasion we learn he was upset while at a ploughing ceremony by the myriads of worms and insects killed and thus sneaks away from the crowd. To the important clearly mythological meaning of this account of Suddhodana's shielding of his son from reality we shall return.

We clearly are not to take this story literally, for to do so is to turn Gotama into one unbelievably naive about life. Instead, we need understand it mythologically and metaphorically. In such we are meant to learn from the significance and meaning of the event, rather than believing the event as being objectively true.

The episode of the ploughing ceremony becomes central to the story of Buddha's enlightenment. Taking Gotama, his father had left him with nurses, while he took part in the ceremony. Gotama fell asleep under a rose apple tree, and the nurses, becoming bored, left to observe the ceremony leaving the child alone. On awaking Gotama became quite distressed, but then in his empathy with all the creatures being harmed in the ceremony, felt in his solitude, a sudden touch of deep inner peace. It was selfless empathy which had brought him such intense feeling. Many years later, when seeking enlightenment Gotama remembered this powerful experience, it becoming pivotal to his enlightenment.

In what clearly are legendary additions to the story we are told that though the sun moved during the day, miraculously the tree under which

Gotama lay continued to shade him. When the nurses returned, amazed by such, they fetched Suddhodana, who then paid homage to his son.

We are clearly in the realm of the legendary for much of this narrative. The style of Maya's conception is clearly legendary, and moving into Gotama's life it is hardly possible, indeed one would hope not, that he remained in such naive ignorance of pain and suffering until well into his adulthood. These stories are mythological in that they demonstrate something beyond, and indeed deeper, than objective or literal truth. We find such also in the accounts of the birth and life of Jesus.

Around sixteen years of age Gotama was wedded to Yasodhara, his cousin, who bore him a son, Rāhula (meaning fetter). It seemed that Gotama would settle down to carry out the role his father wished for him.

In the legendary elevation of Gotama's birth status and subsequent luxurious upbringing, the story understood as myth is informing us that not all the pleasures nor prestige of the world can bring happiness and meaning, instead only bringing suffering. That realization causes Gotama to grow restless and inquisitive until one night he leaves the confines of the palace world. This same realization of the folly of earthly pursuits such as luxury, represents the beginning point for any who wish to pursue the way of Buddha.

Gotama absconds with a charioteer, Channa, a name meaning "charming," a later tradition telling us that it was the gods who were involved in making sure that Gotama did not remain secluded in the palace. Knowing that his destiny was to be Buddha, and being caught like everything else in the endless cycle of samsara, they had a self-interest in Gotama completing his true destiny and thus conspired to make the escape happen that they might be free of their entrapment.

On either one or four different excursions with Channa, Gotama observes four different things, each serving to have him understand the folly of the path for which he is being trained. Successively, he observes old age, disease, death, and a samana, a begging ascetic. Out of total ignorance of each of these states, he must ask Channa as to their meaning. On his being informed, it was clear that the first three of these states showed the shallowness of living a luxurious life, indeed how transitory all life was, while the fourth, the samana, suggested there must be a spiritual solution to the human condition.

His eyes opened to the reality of existence, Gotama, no longer content, determines to begin a quest for meaning. Fleeing his privileged but cocooned existence within the palace, he commences his search that very night, we are told in the later tradition. Escaping the palace confines in the dead of night he leaves Yasodhara and Rāhula sleeping, sneaking one last look at them as he stealthily exits their lives without so much as a goodbye. No longer will he be fettered (rāhula) to the mundane. This pabbajja or "going forth," leaving behind society to seek spiritual knowledge as a samana, sannyasin, or as a wandering bhikkhu was then, and still is, widely practiced in India. However, these mendicants, having first carried out familial responsibilities, are usually much older than Gotama. Even today they are held in high regard due to their exploration of the spirit, understood as an important contribution to society.

The observation of suffering by Gotama comes to lie at the heart of Buddhism, an acknowledgement that life is full of suffering or dukkha. This is not some type of pessimism but rather an honest recognition and radical engagement with reality. Life begins with the trauma of birth, associated in past times, as those of Gotama, with the much higher probability either of stillbirth, or the mother dying during childbirth, as in the case of Maya. We then move through all the vicissitudes of life, including accident, illness, and misfortune, again all more prevalent in the ancient world, until death, with its brutal universality, succeeds in taking our treasured life from us. Mortality is especially hard to bear, for perhaps only human beings are forced to reflect upon it. The world, which I can only see through my ego, one day, and that day is not far off, even extremely close in terms of cosmology, will not have me as center, nor indeed as any part of it. When truly contemplated this is a shocking, even brutal assault on the ego! Still, despite this, we aspire to find contentment in human life, by foolish denial of its tenuous reality. We bury our heads in the sand, satiate our appetites, or take refuge in any number of things, from drugs and alcohol, to sport and the arts, constructing our own palace walls in an attempt to shield us from this brutal truth of suffering. Being then so ill-equipped to deal with tragedy, we are devastated when it inevitably comes, for the harsh truth is there is no cocoon such as Suddhodana's palace to shield us from the reality of suffering.

Gotama, however, does not resign himself to this seemingly universal fate of suffering. There had to be "something else," with that something not being just confined to the other world of the gods but accessible here. Indeed, the gods he asserted, like human beings, being caught in the cycle of samsara, could offer no help. The journey would need be made by himself in his own strength.

Later tradition tells us that Buddha in his escape had ridden forth on his horse Kanthaka with the charioteer Channa, holding the horse's tail in a desperate attempt to preclude his leaving. To Channa's plea to remain with his kin and not leave, Gotama responds, "I have not left because I do not love them. It is because I do love them. It is because I love them all that I must find a way to overcome the sufferings of sickness, of old age, and death.

If I am successful I shall return. If I am not, then death would have parted us anyway." The gods open the city gates so to assist his escape. He then is faced with a final barrier to his fleeing. Mara, the evil figure in Buddhism, appears, telling him that in just one week he would become cakkavatti, and to think of all the good he could do in the world if he would remain and take that role. Gotama refuses the temptation, resulting in Mara charging that he will shadow him, just waiting for a single failing to snare him. Again, we have a parallel, eerily like that of Jesus' temptation in the desert, where the devil in the same manner offers subtle appealing temptations, including that to kingly power, and then following these temptations being resisted, leaves Jesus but "for a while."

For nearly all this crucial story of Gotama's leaving home the Pali texts give us little, so we are reliant of later texts, primarily the Nidana Katha, as we have seen coming from a millennium after the events described. Such late composition makes sense of the clearly legendary nature of the account.

Of course, Mara in the Buddhist tradition, like Satan in the Christian tradition, has no real existence, representing rather the shadow side, possessing special danger when that tempts in subtle ways.

Again, in Buddha's rejection of family we see a parallel with Jesus who likewise holds familial obligations in low regard. On one occasion Jesus, being told that his mother and siblings are waiting outside for him, says to the crowd he is teaching, "who is my mother, who are my siblings?" On other occasions he charges that anyone being his disciple, must leave wives, children, and aged relatives to follow him. In passing we can note it is a strange thing that religion is so often used as justifying traditional values, including sexuality, associated with the family!

This leaving behind the mundane, to seek the spiritual in the manner of Gotama and Jesus is archetypal of great religious figures.

These fantastic stories, we need again be reminded, are mythological, not to be understood literally, as being history. They tell us that one of such esteem as Buddha or Christ cannot be born of normal means, needing instead to be born in a miraculous manner. Later Gotama needs to make a dramatic choice that will cost everything, while the total ignorance he carries until his eyes are opened to seek nibbana, represents the ignorance we all share while we are so caught up in the mundane world, with no regard for the essence of the spiritual journey. Until we do so we are as unbelievably, naively, blind as is Gotama in that fantastic account. In like manner, that we cannot seriously believe Gotama was so blind, so we ought not be able to believe that we are that blind. That the story is beyond belief, is deliberate so to make clear our foolishness, which likewise is beyond belief.

Reading these mythological aspects of the Buddha's life we have found several parallels with the life of the Jesus, who likewise must be born of miraculous means, and who while born not to the elite as was the Gotama, has the elite concerned about his birth for either good (the wise man), or nefarious (Herod) reasons. Jesus, like Buddha, also must make a life choice of momentous import such that he needs forty days meditating in the desert as preparation, jousting with the same type of appealing temptations as Gotama, cast by the evil shadow figure.

Having escaped from luxury, Gotama determines to choose a path its very opposite, the holy life, (brahmacariya). As the first sign of this Gotama exchanges his clothes with a beggar.

This journey of Gotama in Buddhist understanding is entirely natural, in accord with fundamental structure of the cosmos, as is its goal, nibbana. While it may appear that the structure of the world affirms the power, and even violence, of the cakkavatti, ultimately the cosmos affirms the compassionate way based on the true understanding of Buddha. That affirmation by the cosmos will be powerfully evidenced at Buddha's enlightenment.

Rather than being supernatural, needing the aid of the gods, the path Buddha takes is accessible to any person putting their mind to it. It demands however, total dedication and commitment as it runs diametrically opposite to all our natural inclinations. As Buddha, Gotama would later teach his disciples that the same was necessary for them, and that they must not rely on him, for the journey must be walked, each for themselves. Each person must find their own enlightenment, the only advantage Buddha's followers having, being that he had already laid out the signposts of the path on which to travel.

The goal of nibbana is, in a sense, the very opposite of the Christian heaven. In Indian thought a person, faced with eternity, seeks release by extinguishment of their individual personhood to enter into moksha. In the West, on the other hand, faced with extinguishment, one seeks eternity. The two goals are diametrically opposed. In the Indian tradition the goal is not to live forever as a personal autonomous being, as that is a given, a person being born and reborn in the endless cycle of samsara (literally meaning "keeping going, flowing around") with dukkha or suffering always present. Such rebirth is due to the accumulation of kamma, bad kamma causing one to be reborn into a lesser situation, a slave, an animal or even a plant, while good kamma leads to rebirth into a better place, perhaps a higher caste, maybe even as a king or even a god. The latter has little advantage however, for one reborn even in such a prestigious place, even as a god, is still subject to dukkha and samsara, along with the accumulation of kamma, and liable therefore be reborn in a lower domain. The only way to escape dukkha was to be not reborn, instead achieving moksha or release. The meaning of nib-bana, as we have seen, is "extinguish" or "go out." The goal therefore is for an individual to no longer exist due to their destruction of kamma.

This schema represents an attempt in Indian thought in general to deal with the issue of suffering. Why does a person draw such bad or good fortune in their life? Kamma explains this as being due to their accumulated actions, perhaps over many lifetimes. The question of suffering is central to the Judeo-Christian tradition also, but is dealt with in a distinctly different manner.

Among those pondering these issues, the genesis of kamma increas-ingly had come to be understood as being desire, tanha. While ever desire was present there would be suffering, yet desire was absolutely a natural part of living. Indeed, life was not possible without it, for desire was necessary to cause procreation itself. One's family's well-being was sustained by the desire for material things. A ruler needed to have desire, prepared to fight for his kingdom, or he would not be able to guarantee the well-being of his subjects. For anyone in civil society desire was a necessary part of life, and as such created kamma, binding them to the ceaseless realm of samsara. They may live a good life, creating good kamma, and by such could rise to a higher place, perhaps even be reborn as a god, but while possessing kamma, could never gain release into nibbana.

There seemed to be only one way out of desire and the accumulation of kamma: to become a monk. The monk, freed from needs and therefore the desires associated with needs, had the potential to create no kamma, thus to enter nibbana. But of course, even for the monk there were many pitfalls, as taking monkish robes did not automatically extinguish desire. To eliminate tanha a monk needed to follow a highly rigorous disciplined path. Numerous schools under different teachers developed, each giving different teachings or dhamma to assist in this journey. Around these teachers, some-times known as "buddhas" (enlightened ones) by their disciples, formed different communities called sanghas or ganas. We know that Gotama in his search fell in with some of these, listening to and experimenting with different teachings.

There were several schools.

The Ajivakas, followers of Makkali Gosala and Purana Kassapa, held that all would reach nibbana but only after a set series of lives. With that guarantee there was no need to worry about the accumulation of kamma, for all were predestined eventually for moksa.

Another group, the materialists, led by Ajita, understood human be-ings as nothing more than material, corporeal creatures, who simply re-turned to the elements after death. Given this end, again there was no need to be concerned about kamma, for all shared the same fate, though they held it was probably best to create good kamma for the welfare of oneself and others.

The Skeptics, led by Sanjaya, rejected the possibility of any ultimate final truth or release, believing that a person's goal should be to create good kamma as this would lead to social harmony and peace.

Another school, the Jains led by Vardhamana Jnatrputra, known to them as the Mahavira or "great hero," believed that kamma covered the soul with a thin layer of dust, which weighed it down. They made their goal therefore the complete elimination of all activity, particularly that which harmed any other creature. In attempting this some Jains remained immobile, believing only by such would they not create kamma, as unnecessary movement heightened the chance of injuring something, another creature, maybe as small as an ant, or even the spilling of water, for all things contained living souls, trapped by kamma. Thus so, some Jains could starve themselves, refuse to drink or wash, or expose themselves to the elements. Some, the Digambara or "sky-clad," refused even to wear clothing.

It is interesting to parallel these religious and philosophical movements, many of them very similar, to those developing in Greece during the same period.

Gotama first chose to join a sangha led by Alara Kalama, a teacher of a form of Samkhya. This school believed that ignorance, rather than desire, was the core of the human problem, our suffering resulting from a lack of knowledge of our true Self. The Self, which we mistakenly confuse with our ego-centered involvement and concern with the transitory, was eternal, identical with the Absolute Spirit or parusa, lying at the core of all things. It is however, concealed by the material or praktri. The adherent, through meditation, needed to learn to discriminate between the two, living above the confusions of the temporal, while developing the intellect which reflected the parusa. When one achieved this difficult realization they would be liberated. This idea of misconception is remarkably similar to that held by both Plato, and later the gnostics.

Gotama did well in this school and Alara promised him that he would soon find enlightenment, even inviting him to join him in leading the school, yet he was not satisfied. Being a man of practical mind, Gotama believed that nibbana must be something directly experienced and so found this school, built around metaphysics, too theoretical. Further, he realized that the meditative state he was able to enter with such proficiency was something merely "manufactured" by yogic disciplines, temporary only in its effect. Once he came out of the meditative state, he was still subject to the same desires (tanhā), and therefore suffering, to which he had been previously. Nibbana, rather than providing such temporary relief, must offer a permanent liberation. Following his enlightenment there was, however, much from this school that Buddha retained, though he made also significant changes.

Following this, still wishing to explore further meditative states arising out of yogic disciplines, Gotama fell in with another teacher, Udakka Ramaputta, a yogin who had explored a realm beyond even nothingness, which he identified as "neither perception nor non-perception." Again, Gotama proved to be a most adept student, soon achieving this level of yogic meditation. So skillful did he became, Udakka even offered to serve Gotama. But again, as before, when Gotama returned to his normal state following meditation, he felt himself still subject to those same desires which served to trap him in samsara and block his release to nibbana. His conclusion was that all these methods of yoga could only give a temporary respite from suffering, but not free one from it. Given his goal of nibbana, yoga of itself offered no solution, though it gave an effective means of movement toward that goal. It would remain central to Buddhist practice.

Abandoning this direction, Gotama now turned to tapas or asceticism, in the belief that this would enable him to burn up kamma, thereby bringing him moksa. He fell in with five other ascetics following an extreme lifestyle, often naked, even feeding on his own faeces and drinking his urine. Practicing breath control he was able to hold his breath for extreme lengths of time. Having reduced his diet to just a daily spoonful of bean soup, when he felt his stomach, he could press it almost through to his spine. So emaciated was he that his hair fell out and his skin withered. We are told he endured this practice for six years. This practice however again brought no solution because the body so starved only clamored more for attention, causing his lust and cravings to be even stronger than prior to his taking this path. Instead of freeing himself from human limitations, he had only succeeded in creating more tanhā, therefore dukkha, thus being more trapped in the cycle of samsara.

Finally, understanding the solution to lie not in asceticism, Gotama decided to abandon the extreme deprivation he had been practicing and pursue a path which came to be known as "the middle way," a path between indulgence and asceticism, for neither his luxurious palace life, nor its extreme ascetic opposite, had brought him any satisfaction. His five fellow ascetics were horrified to see their companion begin to take solid food, and left him in disgust believing he had forsaken the search for enlightenment.

A pivotal event during this time, which facilitated this decision, was an encounter with a milkmaid, Sujata, who upon seeing Gotama's severe appearance brought about by his extreme fasting, offered him milk, meant as an offering to the gods. This accidental encounter opened Gotama's eyes to the truth that it is compassion, not sacrifice, which lies at the heart of the spiritual journey. That the milk was meant for religious sacrifice is a sign that within Buddhism it is compassion (karuna) generated through correct insight (vidya), rather than religious sacrifice, which would become prime. The Brahmins, with their power associated with sacrifice within the Hindu tradition, are de-throned within Buddhism.

In Buddha's journey through asceticism, and rejection of such in favor of compassion, we find again a parallel with Jesus who, as he meditates on his mission before its commencement, nearly dies of hunger in the desert. Such was Jesus' hunger, temptation appeared to him in the form of stones made bread. Like Gotama, Jesus rejects this ascetic path, epitomized in John the Baptist, the one to whom he was initially drawn, who in fiery distain of the world, "lived in the desert feeding only on locusts and wild honey." As a result, Jesus would be charged with being a "glutton and a drunkard," though from reading the accounts of his life any charge of hedonism was clearly ill-based in that he, like Buddha lived a middle way, though for us in a consumerist age that middle way of each would seem to strongly lean to the ascetic side. As was Gotama prepared to receive Sujata's offering in-tended for the sacrifice, in like parallel to Buddha, Jesus is also prepared to set aside aspects of the religious tradition, especially those to do with sacrifice, when they stand in the way of the exercise of compassion. "So if you are offering your gift at the altar and there remember that someone has something against you, leave your gift there beside the altar and go, first be reconciled to them, and then come and offer your gift" (Matt 5:23-24). He also heals on the Sabbath and allows his disciples to pick ears of corn to assuage their hunger on that holy day.

Such occurrences allow a radically secular interpretation to be drawn of both figures, though that only one of several conclusions which can be drawn.

Disillusioned with the dhamma of other teachers Gautama now sought his own way to achieve his goal. While making rapid progress he remem-bered that event to which we have referred, from his youth, the ploughing ceremony, in which he felt something which all his striving had failed to give. In that ecstatic moment, which had come effortlessly and spontane-ously, he had experienced an intense compassion for all things. Was not nibbana then, to be found in that deep joy he had felt when his ego was completely latent? If so nibbana would be found not in the rejection of the world, but rather in the deep empathy he had felt for those living creatures harmed at that ceremony. Authentic rejection of the ego would be achieved not through asceticism, but rather through the compassionate embrace of the world. Nibbana would be found not in inhumane striving but rather in those things natural, normal, and indeed integral to the human condition. Rather than by assaulting himself Gotama would find enlightenment by cultivating deeply innate human tendencies. For six years Gotama had fought his humanity attempting to subjugate it, all without success, bringing instead only misery and suffering upon himself. What if there was another diametrically opposed way? Gotama became convinced that indeed the answers to these questions were in the affirmative. He had achieved that ecstatic state many years previously in solitude, so solitude he now sought.

While ahimsa, a philosophy of avoidance of harm to any creature, was strongly present in the Indian tradition, Gotama now learned such was insufficient, concluding instead that the attitude which stimulated such a position had to be extended to the positive, a loving compassion for all things. He had been successful in avoiding such akusala or unwholesome activities, harmful to kamma such as violence, stealing, lying, intoxication, and sex, but he now understood rather than mere avoidance, he must develop the kasula or wholesome state of mind, which would move him beyond egoism to that deep love for all things he had so momentarily experienced long before. Not lying was insufficient as one had to move beyond that to positive right speech, not stealing needed to be extended to the positive desire of acceptance of alms, and delighting in the bare minimum as a means of living. The cultivation of kasula, contrary to asceticism, represented a fulfillment of the deeply human, and was the means to enlightenment. The moral purity necessary for this, known as sila, Gotama soon achieved.

It is important to remember that these akasula things are wrong, not so much in that they break a moral or ethical code, but rather in that they tie us to tanha, that craving causing us to be caught in the cycle of samsara. Thus, sex for example was not something sinful and therefore wrong but rather more as something unhelpful, due to the lusts and desires (tanhā) it cultivated.

In further reflecting Gotama began to realize that desire, and the suffering to which it gave rise, was all pervasive. Even the search for Self was folly as it served only to create tanha.[2] He thus rejected the core idea of the newly composed Upanishads, of there being an eternal atman (soul), which was identified with Brahma. There was, Gotama asserted, nothing which had permanence. All was impermanent anicca, including oneself. Nothing remained permanent. Not even the bliss obtained in meditation lasted long.

2. By using uppercase Self I am referring to the type of deeper Self as identity as defined by Carl Jung. For Jung the Self signifies the unification of consciousness and unconsciousness in a person, representing the psyche as a whole, brought about by the integration of the various aspects of one's personality.

Further, desire also led to a breakdown socially of relationships between people, and indeed the cosmos itself, through greed. This last aspect
is well evidenced today by an increasing ecological crisis. In craving, desire
soon becomes coupled with jealousy and even hatred, directed often to
those who have those things we desire, or to those who stand in the way
of our desires. This causes division and hatred in the world. Such is doubly
foolish as these things, being impermanent, can never bring ongoing satisfaction, only serving instead to further ensnare us in samsara.

Given we can never have all the things we want, we are constantly
filled with frustration. Tanha extends to all areas of our life, not including
just physical things but also in areas such as seeking new stimuli, searching
for another to whom we may wish to converse, or even movement to a different meditation posture.

Having achieved sila (ethical behavior), it was not difficult for Gotama
to move to the next stage, single-mindedness or samadhi. This is also known
as samatha, the stilling of the mind. Gotama's method of reflection was not
cerebral, for he had tried that and been left unsatisfied. Rather it was carried
out by yoga in an altered state of consciousness, giving him a more direct
experience than mere rational theorizing could achieve. This style of meditation allowed Gotama to better appreciate those deep truths which finally
become the means to achieve enlightenment, to reside deeper within him,
so to become habitual.

Buddha's yogic practices were not however entirely self-directed.
Rather his goal was to engender compassion, which in this deep meditative yogic state could be extended to all four corners of the world. "Where
traditional yoga had built up in the yogin a state of impervious autonomy,
so that the yogin became increasingly heedless of the world, Gotama was
learning to transcend himself in an act of total compassion toward all other
beings, infusing the old disciplines with loving-kindness."[3]

From the perfection of samadhi Gotama was now able to move to attaining liberating truth, panna or bodhi.

The Buddhist scriptures condense the events concerning the enlightenment of Gotama, some claiming that after all his years of asceticism,
following just one meal, he was able to achieve enlightenment in a single
night. Others say he meditated forty-nine days (the square of the sacred
seven). Whether it was that night, a few, or many nights later, we are told
Gotama, desiring to achieve enlightenment (yathabhuta meaning "becoming true nature") sets himself down under a bodhi tree (ficus religiosus), a
tree long sacred in India, determined to remain seated in the asana posture

3. Armstrong, *Buddha*, 71.

in profound concentrated meditation (jhana), something he had practiced from his youth. The bodhi tree, situated west of the Naranjana River in the Kingdom of Magadha (modern day Bihar), now known as Bodhgaya, and is revered by Buddhists to this day. A bodhi tree still grows there, claimed to be an offshoot of that under which Buddha achieved enlightenment. To mark his enlightenment, the holiest Buddhist shrine, the Mahabodhi temple also stands in this place.

For Buddhists Bodhgaya is known as the navel of the earth, in like regard to Jerusalem for Jews, Christians, and Muslims. The bodhi tree acts as the axis mundi, the point common in many mythologies, where it is held that the divine breaks into the temporal, where humanity encounters the Absolute. Later, Mahayana would hold that this tree as axis mundi had also been the location for the enlightenment of vast eons for previous Buddhas. Of course, as found, in the biblical story the tree as axis mundi is also present, but as two trees, the tree of good and evil, along with that of knowledge, located in the primeval Garden of Eden. That same tree, it is claimed, later became the cross on which Jesus is crucified, the means through which salvation is procured. The place of the tree then is central to salvation in both Buddhism and Christianity. The distinction in the Buddha story is that there is no divinity entering the world to save it but rather a human being, highly advanced, but still nothing more than human, achieving enlightenment by himself without any divine assistance under the tree, while in Christianity the divine-human figure of Christ is crucified on the tree to bring salvation from outside as gift from the divine.

The earliest Pali texts tell us little concerning Buddha's enlightenment, only that he thought profoundly upon the transitory, conditional nature of life, along with reflecting upon his past lives. They center instead on the internal meditative process through which he passed, a profound meditation which led him to enter that same state he had spontaneously experienced as a child at the ploughing ceremony. Later in the Sutta-pitaka we are given more detail, being told that he, like a lion, had determined to remain seated under the bodhi tree until enlightenment was achieved, having a goal to achieve it that very night. We are told he first circles the tree, intending to sit where previous Buddhas had sat when they had achieved nibbana, but in each place the earth heaves, until he arrives at the eastern side, the side from which light first comes to the world, whereupon the earth stills itself as he sits. This posture of Gotama in a cross-legged asana position has become the archetypal images of the Buddha.

Gotama slipped into the first level of yogic trance (jhana) from where he moved successively through each of the four jhanas, until enlightenment was reached. On the first watch we are told, he acquired the power to recount all his previous existences, followed on the second, the ability to know the state of re-birth of all things in accord with the kamma they had accumulated. During the third watch Gotama attains the certain knowledge that all his defilements had been eliminated, so that no longer did he possess any craving (tanhā) nor therefore, kamma, and being free from ignorance, had perfect understanding. Gotama had "done what needed to be done" and thus had achieved nibbana, becoming now Buddha. Having achieved enlightenment, he had perfect moral purity (sila), perfect concentration (samadhi), and correct penetrating knowledge (panna). What was different with Buddha is that possessing such did not lead to a type of quietism, an exit from the world, but rather the practice of śīla, motivated by compassion (karuna). That compassion led him to choose to remain upon the earth to preach the way rather than immediately take his reward in nibbana. This choice not to exit to nibbana but rather to remain upon the earth becomes central to Mahayana. Nor did this mind-centeredness (samadhi) lead Buddha to rest in that, making of it an end in itself, as would be shown in exhibiting spectacular psychic and physical powers.

This inner meditative journey given in the earliest Pali texts is expanded upon in a clearly legendary manner, again in the Nidana Katha, There we find described details of the many forces pitted against Gotama, who is presented as one on the classic hero's journey, having to face off against a bevy of temptations, violent, lustful, and terrifying, sent by Mara, who appears, leading a mighty army, like a cakkavatti before him. Given that the goal within Buddhism is enlightenment, rather than vanquishing the demonic figure as does Jesus, the demonic there being equated to evil, Gotama seeks not to defeat but rather to enlighten Mara, understood not so much as evil but as deluded.

The temptations cast by Mara are detailed in the Sutta Pitaka, again in clearly legendary style. We find Mara first appearing with one thousand arms, each holding a deadly weapon, mounted on an elephant, 150 leagues high, casting a series of temptations at Gotama, who causes a metamorphosis in each as it approaches. Arrows and blazing rocks are turned to flowers, while temptingly beautiful maidens are changed to old women. The latter as temptation again is evidence for the negative view faiths in general have of women, often reduced to sexual temptresses. These temptations are all designed to appeal to the residual forces of tanha still present within Gotama.

Finally, addressing Gotama, Mara says, "show me one witness who can testify that you deserve to succeed where all others have failed." He even asks Gotama to move from his place under the bodhi tree, claiming it his to occupy, for he is the world ruler. Upon Gotama refusing to move, an argument ensues as to whom should sit there. Mara asks for validation from his armies who shout acclaim that such a position belongs to their leader. Gotama responds querying what Mara has done to deserve such privilege, before reaching down and touching the earth, which then heaving bears witness to his right. This posture of Gotama touching the earth is again one of the most common images in Buddhism.

The final temptation put by Mara is the most subtle, that of inviting Gotama to enter straight into nibbana. To succumb to that final temptation would preclude the saving doctrine being proclaimed, thereby keeping nibbana shut to any others. Realizing this, Gotama rejects the easy path, choosing instead to remain upon earth to commence his mission, preaching the truth he has found. In such Buddha is distinguished from the brahmins, whose interest was in keeping the sacred knowledge to themselves.

Finally, the earth responds with an enormous roar: "I bear you witness." In face of such an earthquake Mara and his army flee in terror.

In the desert, Jesus is likewise tempted by the demonic figure with temptations ever more subtle, concluding with that which offers the "good end" but through the wrong means. Again, accounts of Jesus' temptations become increasingly legendary. Initially, in the earliest Gospel, Mark, we are simply informed he was tempted, while in the succeeding Gospels we are informed of the spectacular nature of those temptations. In clearly legendary manner, Jesus is transported to the top of a mountain, and upon seeing all of the world's kingdoms is offered them on the premise that he will fall down and worship Satan. In such offering, as in the Buddha account, Satan is claiming they are his to give. Succumbing to these temptations would represent, like Mara's offer to Gotama of immediate entry to nibbana, the easy but wrong path to the goal, and as such is the most devious of temptations.

Having resisted all the temptations of Mara, Gotama is reborn as Buddha, the "awakened one," his enlightenment being accompanied by all sorts of cosmic signs.

> And when the sage entered Nirvana, the earth quivered like a ship struck by a squall, firebrands fell from the sky. The heavens were lit by a preternatural fire, which burned without fuel, without smoke, without being fanned by the wind. Fearsome thunder balls crashed down on the earth, and violent winds raged in the sky. The moon's light waned, and despite a cloudless sky an uncanny darkness spread everywhere. We are told that the blind received sight and the deaf have their hearing restored, the cripples walk, and the prisoner's chains are broken. The rivers, as if overcome with grief were filled with boiling water. Beautiful flowers grew out of season on the sal trees above the Buddha's

couch and the trees, including the bodhi tree, bend down over
him showering his golden body with their flowers.[4]

So great is the occasion that all the ten thousand worlds, heavens and
hells of the Buddhist cosmos, are shaken.

Much of the imagery above accompanying the Buddha's enlightenment will be familiar to Christians, for the cosmic signs accompanying Buddha's enlightenment, the event central to Buddhism, are matched by similar
archetypal cosmic events in that central to Christianity, Jesus' crucifixion
and resurrection.

On the night of his enlightenment, the now-become Buddha, we
are told, experiences full understanding all his past incarnations. Perfect
enlightenment having reached him, Gotama had now become the Manus-
ibuddha, the living Buddha (the enlightened one), Sambuddha, (the self-enlightened one), Shakyamuni (sage of the Shakyas), and Tathagata (the thus
gone). His followers will know him also as Bhagavat, meaning Lord. Here,
in such terms, clearly we have the later influence of Mahayana elaborating
and heightening the narrative.

The episode of Buddha's enlightenment is almost certainly compressed, but from such sudden enlightenment we are meant to learn that
our enlightenment can likewise be quickly achieved, if we are prepared to
be fully open to Buddha's message. Again, there is a parallel with some of
the disciples of both figures who make immediate decisions to follow them
in what are clearly compressed episodes. These accounts are not meant to
be taken literally, instead standing as a metaphor, for the radical call to commitment, for us not to delay, hesitate, or procrastinate, but rather to make a
decisive jump at the lifesaving message, given the urgency of the task.

Buddha remained in Bodhgaya for seven weeks pondering his future
ministry. Jesus, likewise, as have already seen, takes "time out," forty days in
the desert wilderness, to likewise prepare. For Buddha, the temptation which
he faced just prior to his enlightenment now returns. Would he become a
teacher or a recluse? Initially, he was deterred from taking the teaching path
by his knowledge of just how profound a state, at total odds with normal
human aspirations, is the dhamma, and therefore just how difficult it would
be to teach. Brahma, who had watched Buddha's enlightenment, intervenes,
knowing that if the Buddha fails to preach the path of his enlightenment, the
world, including Brahma himself, would be lost. He therefore kneels before
Buddha and begs him out of his compassion to undertake his preaching
mission. Buddha finally acquiesces and determines to preach. This clearly
mythological story reflects the inner turmoil Buddha experiences between a

4. Conze, *Buddhist Scriptures*, 63.

desire to retreat into solitude and that of preaching the path. It also is meant again to indicate that Brahma, the Hindu world creator, was actually dependent on Buddha, his superior for his creation. Just as Buddha is greater than Brahma, Buddhism, it is charged, moves beyond Hinduism.

Having determined to preach, something he did in the vernacular, rather than in Sanskrit, the sacred language of the Brahmins, Buddha seeks out his initial two teachers, Alara Kalama and Uddaka Ramaputta, but is told by the gods that they have died. Understanding that they could have achieved nibbana but were now condemned to another cycle of life, Buddha sharply perceives the urgency of his task. Given this he travels to Sarnath, a royal deer park near Varanasi, now a site especially sacred to Buddhism, to preach his first sermon. This sermon is preserved textually as the Dhammacakkappavattana-Sutta, literally the "setting of the wheel in motion," the wheel being a common symbol for the dhamma. The recipients are some of his former companions, including the five ascetics, who on the approach of Buddha immediately note the transformation he has undergone and rush to greet him as their master, washing his feet. Greeting him as a friend they are told not to identify him as such, as he is now the Tathagata, "the thus gone." He then begins to teach them, saying, "I have realized the undying state of nibbana. I will instruct you! I will teach you the dhamma." The ascetics, having heard his teaching and seen his transformation, determine to follow him, with one, Kondanna, immediately achieving enlightenment, so becoming the first enlightened by the Buddha's teaching, and as such the first Buddhist. Following his conversion, legendary tradition tells us the gods take up the cry "the Lord has set the wheel of dhamma in motion," and Buddha, delighted at his first convert, exclaims, "Kondanna knows."

The text is highly unlikely to have been Buddha's actual first sermon, representing instead a more developed exposition of his teaching, used as summary, projected back to being his first sermon. As with any good spiritual teacher, in reality Buddha's understanding and depth of teaching would have been in a process of continuing deepening development.

The five ascetics follow Buddha forming a begging group of arahants, practicing vinaya, a self-denial discipline, but not involving the extremity of mortification which they, and Buddha, had kept previously. Buddha teaches them in pairs while the others go to beg for sustenance, this indicating that probably the conversion of the ascetics took more time than in the classically known story. The other four ascetics, named here as Vappa (Sanskrit Vaspa), Bhaddiya (Bhadrajit), Mahanama (Mahanaman) and Assaji (Asvajit), soon follow Kondanna in being sotapannas—"stream enterers." Such a person, while not yet having been fully enlightened, has already entered the stream of enlightenment.

Following his delivering this initial sermon, and gathering his first disciples, Buddha establishes a monastic community, the sangha, to maintain and pass his teaching on. The sangha was to become central in Buddhism, one of its three central tenets. Born as a monastic faith Buddhism is still at its heart so to this day.

Three days after the ascetics had become sotapannas, Buddha preached a second sermon in the Deer Park during which he expounded an even more radical doctrine, anattā, the "no self." It was after hearing this sermon, we are informed, that the five ascetics or bhikkhus (Buddhist monks) all become arahants, "accomplished ones who have achieved nibbana." They never, however, become equal to Buddha, for he alone in this cosmic cycle has found for himself the way to nibbana. The term Buddha is reserved for those who discover the path to nibbana for themselves, rather than by hearing it preached.

Having now become enlightened, the new arahants, like Buddha, recognize just how urgent it is to preach the dhamma, an urgency arising from their understanding, as for Buddha, of the depth of dukkha, along with compassionate empathy for the suffering of others, and their need to escape samsara. Further, understanding the doctrine of anattā they recognize they must be selfless in preaching the saving dhamma.

The preaching of these few must have been highly effective because we are informed there was a great surge of those entering the sangha. The first of those entering was Yasa, the son of a rich merchant from Varanasi. He, like Buddha, had lived in the lap of luxury but had also become repelled by such existence. Awaking one night to servants surrounding his bed, and perceiving them as repulsive, he cries "terrifying, horrible!" immediately then deciding to leave to seek Buddha. Arriving at the Deer Park, Yasa meets Buddha who, allaying his dread, says to him, "it is not terrifying, it is not horrible . . . I will teach you the dhamma." On joining the sangha Yasa became the first arahant after the five ascetics, becoming also an intimate companion to Buddha.

Soon after Buddha is approached by Yasa's father, seeking his son. In turn the Buddha recites the dhamma to him and he, like his son, commits to it. He is acknowledged as the first to make what would become the essential Buddhist threefold commitment to Buddha, the sangha and the dhamma. Meanwhile, hidden from his father, whom Buddha is teaching, Yasa listening again to the dhamma, enters nibbana. Buddha then reveals Yasa to his father who begs him to return home, following which Buddha informs the father that such would be impossible for his son can no longer fulfill the mundane role of being a householder. Yasa's father then begs Buddha to visit his house for dinner, a request with which he complies. While there he preaches the dhamma to Yasa's wife and mother, whereupon they become Buddha's first female adherents. Following these conversions, the news spreads quickly through the nearby holy city of Varanasi, and many others come to follow the dhamma, so that we are told there are soon sixty arahants, along with the Buddha in the world. The wheel had begun to turn more fully!

Buddha, in an act which parallels the sending out of the seventy by Jesus, then instructs these first arahants to go into the marketplaces of the world and preach the saving dhamma. He also joins in this mission, and with such power and clarity was the message spoken the sangha began to grow rapidly, as did the numbers of the laity.

In his directing the sangha to carry on and broaden his ministry the Buddha is presented as a great organizer. As such he may be contrasted with Jesus, who while initially successful, at the point of his demise, would have been viewed as a failure. It was others, primarily Paul, with his distinct interpretation of Jesus' teachings, who would guarantee the long-term survival and growth of the movement which would become known as Christianity.

The accounts of the rapid expansion of the sangha, seemingly too incredible to be literally true, are intended to show the capacity of the dhamma to convict a person, doing so immediately and effortlessly. As such these accounts operate as hyperbole. We see the same in the great numbers who are said to have rapidly attached themselves to Jesus.

After these great events at the beginning of his ministry Buddha spends the next forty-five years teaching, though we are given little detail, with the last twenty years of his life initially left unrecorded. This absence was rectified in the later tradition in Sanskrit texts such as Agamasutras, the Buddhacarita, and to a lesser extent in the Lotus Sutra. This much later material is likely however to be almost exclusively framed by mythology and legend, rather than possessing historical veracity.

We do however have some details of a few episodes of the Buddha's mission. Early in his ministry we learn of one journey, where Buddha, while on his way to Uruvela, left to himself after sending the monks out to preach the dhamma, meets thirty young rowdy men pursuing a beautiful woman. Of them he inquires whether it is better to look for a woman, or to find yourself. Following his preaching the dhamma they are all convicted by his message, becoming stream enterers. On reaching Uruvela he does something even more dramatic, converting a whole sangha of forest dwellers under the leadership of the Kassapa brothers, some one thousand men, to the way of the dhamma. This story reflects how historically the new Buddhist way was able to make rapid inroads into the older Hindu tradition. Following their conversion, the vast assembly gather at Bodh Gaya to hear Buddha's third sermon, known as the Fire Sermon. By using the image of fire, sacred to the

Vedic tradition, but linking it negatively with the destructive passions which preclude enlightenment, Buddha is presented again as showing his way to be distinct, at odds with, and superior the Brahminic Vedas.

Buddha spent that winter in Uruvela, where it is recorded he carried out several miracles. Each of these have a deep symbolism, again often having to do with Buddhist triumph over the older Vedic tradition. Thus, he tames a cobra, housed in the sacred fire chamber, symbol of the divine in the Hindu tradition, entertains gods, who visit his lodge at night, splits logs used for the sacred fire ceremonies, ascends to the heavens before returning with a celestial flower, and reads the mind of one of the Kassapa brothers. These yogic powers, called iddhi, were associated with the learned power of the mind over the physical world. Though possessing such powers, Buddha, along with many yogins, warned against public demonstrations of them, as such could degenerate into magic directed toward a fascinated audience, easily seducing the one performing it into an ego entrapping celebration of their powers.

Buddha's reluctance to use miraculous displays of power matches that of Jesus, who while demonstrating miraculous feats, refuses to carry them out when challenged to do so as signs of his power.

Buddha next sets out for Rājagaha, accompanied now by some one thousand monks, where King Bimbisara, along with numerous Brahmins, greet him outside the city. They are amazed to find Kassapa, the leader of the local Vedic community is now a follower of Buddha. Buddha then preaches to the whole city, some 120,000 people, we are told, whereupon they all commit, an exaggeration surely, to become lay followers of the dhamma. Finally, even King Bimbisara falls before the Buddha and asking to become his disciple, invites him to dinner that evening. During the dinner Bimbisara donates to the sangha a pleasure park near to the city where the monks could live in seclusion, while also being close to the city in which they could preach. These places, known as aranas, were an ideal solution, allowing solitude for meditation, but also facilitating the preaching of the dhamma. Again, we find that while meditation is central to the Buddhist tradition, it is always linked to mission and preaching. One seeks nibbana so to assist others along the path. In contrast to Hindu monasticism the sangha always has a missionary goal, based, as we have seen, on Buddha's own choice when tempted at his enlightenment with passing into nibbana. Though he was beyond the world in panna (wisdom) Buddha chose to be for the world in karuna.

This gift created a precedent, and soon many other wealthy donors made similar gifts to the sangha, which soon acquired three large parks at Rajagatha, Kapilavatthu, and Savatthi as places where monks could retreat and meditate. They did not spend the year in these places, residence usually being restricted to the rainy season, with the rest of the time spent on the road preaching the dhamma.

Initially the monks, in preaching the dhamma, had travelled in the rainy season but gave up this practice due to it offending the idea of ahimsa, that of doing no harm to any living thing, a precept particularly difficult to uphold during the rainy season, when so many things were springing to life. Sensitive to this, Buddha introduced the monsoon retreat or vassa, making it obligatory for all sangha members. Traditionally monks in other orders had spent the vassa wherever they could, either alone or with others, who may have been following all manners of dhamma. Buddha made it obligatory for members of the Buddhist sangha to live together either in one of the aranas, or in an avasa, the latter being a rough residence the monks built from scratch for their habitation over the season. Living together they began to develop simple ceremonies which included times of communal meditation and teaching, the latter coming from Buddha himself, or a senior monk.

Buddhist monks, as well as holding to the five precepts of Pancasila, also needed to hold another five precepts concerning śila. They were to abstain from meals after lunch, shun all public entertainments, avoid garlands, ornaments, and perfumes, refrain from sitting or sleeping on comfortable furniture, and finally, to refuse to accept money. Though the full śila demanded by Buddha is a "middle way," it was still sufficiently demanding to make it only possible to achieve in a sangha, under the guidance of the Vinaya.

Buddha remained in the pleasure park at Rajagaha for two months, making it his arana, during which time two brahmins, who were to become his most important disciples, joined the sangha.

Sariputta and Moggallana had committed themselves to seeking nibbana and to that end had both joined the sangha of the skeptics led by Sanjaya. Neither had achieved enlightenment there, but they had made a pact that the first to achieve such would tell the other. One day Sariputta observed Assaji, one of the original Buddhist bhikkhus, begging for alms. He was immediately convinced that this monk had achieved the goal to which he and his companion were directed and inquired of him as to which sangha he belonged and to what dhamma he was following. In response Assaji taught him the dhamma, and though the lesson given by Assaji was brief it was sufficient to convince Sariputta to commit to the Buddhist dhamma, whereupon he immediately became a 'stream enterer.' As promised, he straightaway rushed to inform Moggallana of his discovery, who likewise soon became a sotapanna. Both men then headed to the Buddhist arana,

taking with them 250 of Sanjaya's followers. On their approach Buddha immediately perceived all that these two men would bring to the sangha, declaring they would become his chief disciples. These two men are claimed to
be the founders of the two main schools of Buddhism: Sariputta, Theravada,
and Moggallana, Mahayana. This clearly legendary story is meant to show
both the validity and necessary coexistence of the two schools, though that
has often not been the case.

Again we get a similar compression of such stories in the case of disciples of Jesus drawing others. A good example is Andrew converting his
brother Peter to the message of Jesus. (John 1:40-42). These compressions
are meant to show the urgency of response.

Buddha next made a visit to his father, Suddhodana, in Kapilavahhhu
with the now huge number of 20,000 Bhikkhus. Suddhodana made available to the Sangha Nigrodha park, just outside of the city, but he and the
townspeople refused to become followers. Buddha is forced to take recourse
to iddhi with the resultant spectacular displays of power causing the crowd
to commit to the dhamma. In one such famous miracle, that of fire and
water, he is said to have levitated with fire coming from his head and torso,
while water flowed from the lower part of his body. Such miraculous displays are, however, short lasting. Knowing this, the following day Buddha
sat with his father explaining the dhamma, who, this time upon hearing it,
immediately became a sotapanna. He then invited his son to his palace, and
following the meal all, bar one, Buddha's former wife Yaśodharā, still understandably bitter over his unannounced secret leaving, become followers
of the dhamma. It is said that Suddhodana then ordered that one male heir
from each branch of the Shakya nobility should enter the sangha.

Jesus likewise was found to be "a prophet without honor in his hometown," though the reception he finds his far more hostile. Jesus, unlike
Buddha, refuses to offer any miraculous signs to assuage the crowd's wrath
and only just manages to escape being killed. The differing violence in the
reactions may be due to the status each held. One was a former prince, the
other disparagingly met by cries: "is this not the carpenter?"

The distinct social status of each came may also be reflected in their
mission strategy. Buddha sought the support of those with status analogous
to him, kings and rulers, whereas Jesus' support is drawn from the outsiders
and those peripheral to the system. This status could also determine the
geography of their mission, Jesus mainly preaching in a rural environment,
while Buddha is largely committed to the urban environment.

Following this visit to Kapilavatthu many of Buddha's immediate
relatives commit, or by the orders of Suddhodana, are obliged to commit
to the dhamma. These include his now seven-year-old son, Rahula, cousin

Ananda, and half-brother Nanda, along with his brother-in-law Devadatta. They are accompanied by their barber, Upali, who initially joins them only to shave their heads as newly initiated bhikkhus, but who, on hearing the dhamma, becomes himself a bhikkhu, later becoming the leading expert in the monastic life.

Ananda, an enigmatic figure in the Buddhist tradition, becomes Buddha's personal attendant. Because of his proximity with Buddha, Ananda became a leading expert on the dhamma but fails to achieve nibbana during the lifetime of Buddha due to his not being proficient in meditation. Tradition has it that at the First Buddhist Council following Buddha's death, Ananda, having spent most time with Buddha, was the one able to recite from memory all his teachings. It was also Ananda who received advice from the dying Buddha that there was to be no successor as head of the sangha, Devadatta assumes in Buddhism a role analogous to that of Judas in the Christian story. That the family of Buddha enter the order parallels the case of Jesus, whose relatives become important, though only after Jesus' death, in early Christianity, his brother James holding perhaps the most prestigious position in the early Christian movement, the leader of the church in Jerusalem.

Outside the sangha very few achieved nibbana, one of those who did being Buddha's father Suddhodana, said to have attained nibbana in the fifth year of his son's mission. The very next day, we are told, he died.

Following Suddhōdana's death another important event occurs, one which would widen the impact of Buddhist teaching. Mahapajapati Gotami, the Buddha's aunt, who had brought him up following his mother's death, asked to be admitted to the sangha. Buddha rejects her request, even as she tearfully repeats it three times. There could be, he insisted, no place for women in the sangha. A few days later Buddha travels to Vesali on the banks of the sacred Ganges. One morning Ananda wakes to hear Mahapajapati, shaven and wearing monk's robes, having walked with her kinswomen all the way from Kapilavatthu, crying, and on inquiring the reason for their tears Ananda is told they were because Buddha would not have women in the sangha, Ananda tells her that he will speak with him. When Buddha refuses to reconsider, Ananda presses the point. The dhamma, he points out, was meant for all with no social class or caste of person excluded, including even animals. How could it be then that women would be excluded? Was rebirth as a man the best that they could hope? Still being met with refusal Ananda asks Buddha whether women are capable of being sotapannas and eventually arahants. On being told that they could, he replies to Buddha that nothing then stood in the way of ordaining Mahapajapati, especially given her kindness to him.

Buddha reluctantly concedes but sets eight strenuous conditions for her adherence. Those provisions made clear that the nuns or bhikkhunis would have an inferior status within Buddhism, this being in common with the other great historical faiths who place women in a secondary role. Thus, a nun—a bhikkuni—must always stand when in the presence of a bhikkhu, no matter how young the bhikkhu, and must receive teaching from a bhikkhu each fortnight. Bhikkhunis were not permitted to hold their own ceremonies and could not make their own retreat or "vassa" during the rainy season, being compelled instead to spend that time in the monk-led arama. Further, no bhikkhuni was permitted to teach or admonish a bhikkhu, while to be ordained, a woman had to receive permission from both the male and female sangha. Accepting these conditions Mahapajapati was ordained by a clearly reluctant Buddha, who makes the comment that with women included the sangha, which would have survived one thousand years, would now last but five hundred. If such statement is true, he was proved wrong.

Yet other sources, especially the Therigatha (Verses of the Elder Nuns), an early Pali text, inform us that Buddha praised the spiritual achievements of the bhikkhunis and prophesied that before his death there would be thousands of bhikkhus, bhikkhunīs, and laity, both male and female, to ensure the continued teaching of the dhamma.

In Mahapajapati, entering the sangha, there is a parallel with Jesus' mother, Mary, who becomes an important figure in the infant church, though that comes only after her son's death. Buddha's biological mother, Maya, also becomes an important figure in Buddhism after her son's death but from a locale beyond her mortal life.

Perhaps Buddha was actually more open in his acceptance of women. After all, it had been the milkmaid, Sujata, who had acted as a major stimulus to his own enlightenment. The conditions placed on Mahapajapati in this story probably reflect more a later patriarchal takeover of the sangha, rather than the intentions of Buddha. On the other hand, Buddha, as enlightened as he was, perhaps could not escape the social conditioning of the time, one which simply assumed women being inferior to men. Maybe he felt the lust and sensuality associated with women was a hindrance to liberation. Buddha's own story, after all, had seen him sneak away from his wife in the dead of night, regarding her as a hindrance to his goal. Near the end of his life, Buddha, asked by Ananda, "Lord, how are we to treat women?" responds, "Do not look upon them, Ananda." Ananda then asks, "If we do not see them, how should we treat them?" whereupon Buddha responds, "Do not speak to them, Ananda." And if we still have not got the point, the writer has Ananda follow up with a third question: "And if we have to speak to them?" "Mindfulness must be observed, Ananda," Buddha responds

(Digha Nikaya: 16). While most scholars hold this text to be a monkish interpolation, it makes clear the chauvinism of the tradition. Similar views occur early in the Christian tradition, including the Scriptures, curbing the more open manner in which it appears Jesus treated women. Male pursuit of spirituality across all faiths has been linked to the exclusion of women, seen as hindrances, primarily doing with sexual impulse.

In having women in their inner circles there is a parallel between Buddha and Jesus. Given the reactive antipathy to women which develops in both traditions, there seems to be little doubt women were actually part of the inner circles of both figures, their historical presence sufficiently strong so to make it impossible to later write them out. In the case of Jesus, Mary Magdalene, Mary, and Martha represent those women, while there are numerous others named in the Christian Scriptures as being leaders in the infant church. In both developed traditions of Buddhism and Christianity any radical equality would be lost to the patriarchal tradition, female orders becoming clearly subordinate to those of men.

We need to remind ourselves that it is only in the last half century that women have achieved, both in civil society and in religion, most steps taken toward equality. Prior to then women were viewed clearly as inferior, lacking many of the legal rights that men possessed. Religious traditions still until now lag behind social change.

The reticence of Buddha on this matter needs correction, as we have seen, by Ananda. In a similar very bald presentation, Jesus is presented as narrowly ethnocentric in his conversation with the Canaanite woman, who shows up his limited compassion in her response to his announcing that he had only been sent to the people of Israel (Matt 15:21-28).

The sangha, more reflective of the old oligarchic republics from which Buddha came than the hierarchical royal societies then evolving, was loosely knit, though each followed the same dhamma. However, once every six years the different sanghas came together for a large gathering where they recited the Pātimokkha, meaning bond, the basic code of monastic discipline, consisting of 227 rules for bhikkhus and 311 for bhikkhunīs. This creed-like statement of Buddhist belief and practice affirmed the centrality of nibbana, along with the right practices to progress toward it, meditation, and harmonious communal living. Buddha held the Patimokkha ceremony in high stead, with monks forbidden to miss it, as it served to keep the sangha bound in unity.

Following Buddha's death the sangha became increasingly hierarchical, with a more complex creed, recited on the uposatha (for the cleansing of the mind) days, replacing the earlier looser arrangement. Rather than reciting the dhamma, bhikkhus and bhikkhunis now recited the monastic rules and shared in the confession of sin, the latter indicating a growing structure and hierarchy. From these gatherings it is almost certain the Vinaya, the second of the three "baskets" of Buddhist scripture evolved. A similar development of institutional hierarchical structure is seen in the later writings within the Christian Scriptures, the so-called Pastoral Epistles (1 and 2 Tim, Titus).

The Vinaya served to order life in the sangha so to assist each monk or nun on their path to nibbana. The monastic life was to be marked by harmony and lack of concern for possessions to assist with meditation, for only in meditation was it possible to extinguish those fires of ignorance, hatred, lust, and greed which stoked dukkha. Possessions were minimal, with monks and nuns even being dependent on others for their daily food. Still today one of the strongest images associated with Buddhism is bhikkhus and bhikkhunis leaving the monastery early each morning to beg for food.

The final months of the Buddha's life are given in much more detail, particularly in an important Scripture, the Mahaparinibbana-sutta (Discourse of the Great Decease). The time of Buddha's death, despite his and the sangha's best efforts, was, we are told, a time fallen into depravity, in which greed, naked ambition, and violence abounded, with sense of the sacred lost. Even the sangha had been infected by the rampant egotism and violence of the age.

The Vinaya tells us how some in the sangha, rent by schism, even conspired to kill perhaps Buddha's most faithful disciple, King Bimbisara. The main culprit was Devadatta, Buddha's brother-in-law, who had been with Buddha from his childhood, with later texts telling us that enmity between the two relatives had existed from their youth. The earlier Pali texts know nothing however concerning this youthful conflict, informing us that Devadatta was a fine monk, especially an excellent orator. As Buddha grew older Devadatta became increasingly resentful, believing himself to be the natural successor to his brother-in-law. To that end Devadatta courted Ajatasuttu, son of King Bimbisara, impressing him with all manner of iddhi. Under Devadatta's influence Ajatasuttu set aside an area for a sangha under Devadatta's leadership at Vulture's Peak, just outside Rajagatha, while also making him a court monk. It is possible that, convinced that Buddha would appoint a successor, Devadatta and Ajatasuttu sought to ensure that control over the sangha would remain within the hands of the Shakya nobility. Buddha was aware of Devadatta's manoeuvrings but was unworried for he knew such machinations would only lead to a poor ending for Devadatta by serving to heap bad kamma upon him.

While one day when staying at the Bamboo Grove arama, outside of Rajagatha, Devadatta openly asked of Buddha that the sangha be handed to him saying, "The Blessed One is now old, aged, burdened with years . . . and has reached the last stage of his life . . . let him now rest." Buddha refused to accede to Devadatta's request, seeing no need for a successor, for he understood himself as never having led the sangha. Given that Buddha had not handed control even to his two most trusted bhikkhus, Sariputta and Moggallana, it was unlikely he would he pass his control to Devadatta. Angered, Devadatta stormed from the arana pondering his revenge. Meanwhile Buddha formally disassociated the sangha from Devadatta and instructed Sariputta to denounce him in Rajagatha.

Buddha believed there was no need for a leader of the sangha, for all which was needed for guidance was the dhamma, with each bhikkhu and bhikkhuni being responsible for themselves: "Each of you must make of themselves an island, make yourself, and no one else, your refuge." There being no need for hierarchical authority, the dhamma alone was to be their refuge. Indeed, dependence on another for its achievement was contradictory to Buddhism's essence The goal of nibbana was taken necessarily by an inner journey, though within the environment of the sangha guided by the Vinaya.

Buddha's desire that there be no future leader of the sangha were confirmed in the first gathering of the sangha after his death, where it was determined that they would rely on the teachings of Buddha, the discourses contained in the Sutta-pitaka, and the monastic discipline of the Vinaya-pitaka, in place of any living authority. Buddhism has passed through twenty-five centuries with no central figure other than Buddha himself. There has never been any central control, in the manner of the pope over much of Christianity. No one possesses authority to promulgate doctrine and creeds nor order the faith practice for the entire religion.

Just how far Devadatta had fallen from the way of the dhamma became clear next in his conspiring to have Prince Ajatasuttu kill his father King Bimbisara so as to ascend the throne, while he would deal likewise with Buddha. In carrying out his end of the bargain however Ajatasuttu was caught and confessed to all. Some sectors of Bimbisara's army wanted to not only execute Ajatasuttu but also his whole sangha, whom they judged to be implicated in the crime. Ajatasuttu, on being asked by his father as to why he wished to assassinate him, replied that he wanted the kingdom whereupon Bimbisara, so strongly influenced by his years of being a disciple of Buddha, handed it to him. His generosity was "rewarded" by his son then imprisoning and starving him to death.

Ajatasuttu and Devadatta, with part of Ajatasuttu's army, then conspired to execute the second part of the plan, the killing of Buddha, using bowmen trained as assassins. The first of these however, on approaching the Buddha, was overcome by terror and rooted to the spot. "Come friend, do not be afraid," Buddha persuaded, and then began to teach him. Soon the first, followed then by all the other bowmen, were converted to the way of the dhamma. Devadatta, left having to execute his plan himself set to do so. First, he pushed a great boulder off a cliff, under which Buddha was sitting, succeeding however in only grazing Buddha's foot. Unsuccessful in his initial plan, he next procured a fierce elephant Naligiri and set him loose on Buddha. Naligiri however, upon seeing his prey, overcome with the love emanating from him, stopped and lowered his trunk. Buddha, while stroking him, informed him that such violence would create bad kamma.

Such was the power of Buddha, even Ajatasuttu became a disciple, leaving Devadatta on his own. Refusing still to resile from his evil plan, Devadatta then sought support from younger members within the sangha at Vesali, arguing that the Buddha's middle way represented too much of a compromise with the world, and they should return to the harsher disciplines that Buddha had rejected when he left the ascetics. Devadatta proposed five new rules built around ascetic disciplines and asked that Buddha make them obligatory. Buddha refused, indicating that those in the sangha would be free to follow these dictates if they wished but would not be forced to do so. Devadatta was convinced he had won a victory, as Buddha would be perceived as being impious and lax. He gleefully announced to the assembled that he and any who wished to join him would leave to follow a way less corrupted by compromise with the world. Devadatta's appeal bore fruit with some five hundred monks following him to an arana established nearby at Gayasisa Hill. To win them back Buddha dispatched his two closest disciples Sariputta and Moggallana.

Enjoying his seeming triumph, Devadatta preached long into the night before retiring to sleep, following which Sariputta and Moggallana spoke, soon winning the bhikkhus back. Devadatta, distraught at his loss, according to some accounts suicided, or in others died before being reconciled with Buddha. Another, clearly legendary tradition has it that Devadatta, wishing to see Buddha before his demise, had himself carried on a litter to that end, but before he could reach Buddha the ground opened and swallowed him in a chasm leading to the underworld kingdom of Avici, the lowest of all the hells.

In the Devadatta cycle we find a strong parallel with the role Judas Iscariot plays in the Christian tradition, in that a close disciple conspires to have killed the one he had followed, successfully so in Judas' case. Judas, like Devadatta, becomes the classic evil one in the tradition. As dark figures, both are imaged in the respective faiths as sad foils to Buddha and Christ, unable to understand the heart of the message of the one they purport to follow. Twisted by their ambition, each carries out the most devious act of betrayal. Struck with perhaps remorse, or just pure anguish, each possibly suicides. The motives of both, however, are likely to be far more complex than that given in the respective scriptures, in which they are each classically portrayed, rather one-dimensionally, as archetypal shadows to the good.

Whatever the historicity of this Devadatta cycle, and at points it is clearly legendary, it indicates there was a risk to the unity of the sangha, and this must have concentrated the Buddha's mind during the final year of his life.

During that last year, Buddha was distressed to learn that his now follower King Ajatasutta was planning to launch a large attack against the smaller republics of Malla, Videha, Licchavi, Koliya, and Vajji. Thousands, he knew, would die in such violence, while the aggressive intent was contrary to his way. Ajatasutta's subsequent victory represented the triumph of hierarchical monarchy over the older style, loosely governed republics, whereas the rule of the sangha represented an adherence to an older model of government, now grown redundant in the world of commerce and politics.

Buddha then left Rajasatha and travelled north to Vesali for the vassa retreat, passing through Nalanda and then Paṭaligama, some two hundred years later the capital of the great Buddhist king Ashoka, who would demonstrate that monarchs could rule with the compassion of the dhamma. Finally, Buddha arrived at Vesali, dwelling in a mango grove belonging to one of the leading courtesans Ambapali, who after sitting at the Buddha's feet to hear the dhamma, invited him to dinner. Just after accepting her invitation, he received another dinner invitation from the Licchavi tribe, who had arrived in a splendid procession of carriages. So wonderful did they appear, Buddha informs them their splendor matches that of the gods, before preaching the dhamma to them. Having committed to the prior invitation however, Buddha dined at Ambapali's table who, following the meal, donated the mango grove to the sangha.

Following this, Buddha left Vesali to retreat further to the village of Beluvagamaka, whereupon he dismissed his monks, charging them to return to Vesali for the vassa. Only he and Ananda remained. Soon after the monks' leaving, Buddha became extremely ill to the point of dying, but refusing to complete the parinibbana (the final step into nibbana free from bodily constraint), which would complete the enlightenment, already won long before under the bodhi tree, he struggles on knowing he cannot die until he has bid farewell to the sangha.

In his weakened physical state Buddha is again assailed by Mara in a last temptation, repeating that faced immediately after his enlightenment.

Leave the earth now, tempts Mara, and enjoy your parinibbana. Again, though in his painfully physically diminished state it must have been tempting to want to leave his bodily existence, Buddha rejects this offer, informing Mara that he intends to live another three months yet.

When the time arrived for his death, Buddha calls the sangha together to bid his farewell. He informs them that they must each follow the dhamma for themselves, and that he has taught them nothing that they cannot themselves know directly through yogic meditation on the dhamma: "I have only taught you things I have experienced fully for myself." They are therefore, through meditation, to experience these things likewise directly, taking nothing on the trust of another. Enlightenment, again he emphasizes, is not a thing to be selfishly possessed, but rather is to be shared with others, compassion to be the hallmark of their lives. They are to live the dhamma "for the sake of the people, for the welfare and happiness of the multitude, out of compassion for the whole world, and for the good and well-being of gods and people" (Digha Nikaya: 16).

Now nearing death, Buddha left Vesali, heading north, accompanied by Ananda, to ever more remote villages, until arriving at Pava, where he stayed in a grove owned by Cunda Kammāraputta, the son of a goldsmith. By walking to ever more remote places, it is as though Buddha was walking out of the world. After listening to the dhamma, Kammāraputta invited Buddha to dinner. There is suspicion that the food Buddha ate was poisoned, whether deliberately or accidentally. After finishing his portion of the food offered, Buddha called for the rest to be buried, following which he became violently ill.

Despite being in a critical condition Buddha again set off to travel with Ananda, this time to Kusinara in the republic of Malla, again a further retreat from the world. This area was a place where previously his teachings had fallen on barren ground. While on the journey Buddha converts one of the Mallians, who upon taking the triple refuge, gave to both Buddha and Ananda a gold cloak. Buddha, upon putting this on, is told by Ananda that even the brilliant gold pales next to his skin. Buddha replies that this is because he will very soon achieve parinibbana.

Crossing the Hirannavati River, Buddha and Ananda, accompanied by numerous bhikkhus, reach Kusinara, whereupon they turn into a grove of trees where the mortally ill Buddha rests. While resting, one of his attendants began to fan him before being commanded to move aside as he is obscuring the view of the watching deities, said to fill the whole countryside. Buddha then commenced to give instructions for his funeral, which must be carried out in the style of a cakkavatti. His body was to be wrapped in a cloth and cremated with perfumed wood, the remains to be buried at the crossroads of a great city in a bell-shaped structure, to become known as a thupa (Sanskrit: stupa).

Just prior to his death Buddha is informed by a distressed Ananda that his two closest companions, Sariputta and Moggallana, had died. Buddha chided Ananda for his distress, telling him that the very essence of the dhamma was that nothing is permanent. The stress of Ananda is contrasted with the equanimity of Buddha who, rather than being saddened, is delighted to know that his companions had now achieved parinibbana. Ananda, with his inability to self-achieve nibbana, serves as a counterpart to the way of Buddha. Extremely close to Buddha, Ananda serves him diligently the whole time they are together and becomes the archetype of the one who through service of the Buddha enters nibbana through Buddha's grace. This way of puja, devotion, and worship becomes increasingly popular in the Buddhist tradition, particularly in Mahayana.

Finally, Buddha asks the monks present if there are any questions, they need ask. None are forthcoming, suggesting that he has fully taught the dhamma. All now being ready for his passing into parinibbana, Buddha pronounces his final words to the bhikkhus present: "All compounds grow old. Work out your own salvation with diligence," before charging, "Monks go . . . .preach this doctrine . . . for the good of the masses." In this final charge there is strong parallel with the resurrected Christ, in his parting words before his ascension, calling his disciples to take his message to the ends of the world (Matt 28:16-20). Buddha then passed through several levels of dhyana (meditation) before entering into parinibbana. Following his death Buddha's body was cremated, and in accord with his wishes, his ashes were interred in reliquary mounds called thupas/stupas. Each Buddhist temple, it is claimed, has ashes of the Buddha deposited in its stupa.

Buddha's death, like his enlightenment, was associated with cosmic events culminating in an audience with divinities. Similar cosmic events, as we have noted, take place accompanying both the death and resurrection of Christ.

Following his decease Buddha is transported in spirit to the second of the six Buddhist heavens, Trayastrimsa, the abode of the thirty-three main gods of Indian religion. During his three months there, among those he converted was his mother, Maya, who had died after giving birth to him.

Both the mothers of Buddha and Christ become disciples of their sons, though neither do through their earthly ministrations, but rather following each of their offspring's deaths, the Buddha story clearly having a much greater legendary component about it. One of Jesus' siblings, James, also becomes a prominent person in the church, while we are told that others of his siblings are also converted to the movement. The ambiguous, often negative relationship that both Buddha and Christ have with their families is viewed more positively following their deaths.

Buddha was even said to have returned to earth at Samskaya, located at one of the most western of the tributaries of the Ganges, on a gold, silver and precious stone staircase accompanied by Brahma and Indra. It is held by Christians that Christ will return to the earth at the eschaton. His return will be accompanied by similar precious stones.

By the time of his mortal end Buddha had many followers in a well-organized sangha. In this he could be contrasted with Jesus, who, as we noted, at the point of death was seemingly a dismal failure, with only his mother and perhaps closest disciple, John, present with him at the end. Having said that followers of Jesus were present right through the Roman empire at a comparable time, forty-five years after the commencement of his ministry, as were those of Buddha similarly widely spread.

THE LIVES: JESUS

We now turn to the one we call Jesus Christ. Again, we commence with the name. We have already examined how the term "Christ" is an honorific name depicting the high manner he is held by his followers, in similar style to the title Buddha, given by those following him. We shall limit ourselves then, to understanding the name "Jesus."

Again, we need again remember, names in the Ancient Near East were of great importance, a means of understanding, and defining those who bore them. The name Jesus, meaning "God saves," is a Hellenized form of the Hebrew "Joshua." This is no coincidence, for Jesus was seen by his earliest followers as a new Joshua, the one who had brought the people to freedom into the promised land, the culmination of a long journey, begun under Moses, from bondage and slavery in Egypt to liberation. In the Gospels Jesus is understood to be reenacting many of those things of that journey, strongly linked to both Moses and Joshua. Let us briefly examine these links, deliberately constructed as midrash.

In the birth narratives Jesus, or more accurately his family, must flee a king's vengeance just as his predecessor Moses had fled Pharaoh's wrath, only this time there is a sting in the tail, for the vengeful king is not foreign but rather the Jewish king Herod, and safety is found in of all places Egypt, a place often archetypically epitomized as evil. Again, it is not important as to the historicity of the event, something I wholly doubt, not believing that a ruler would feel in any way challenged by a peasant infant, but rather the presentation. Jesus is being presented as a new Moses, while the opposition which would develop between his followers and their parent faith is being extrapolated back even to the birth of the one they follow.

Before commencing his ministry Jesus, like both Moses and Joshua, spends time in the desert, in his case forty days rather than forty years, though the figure forty was meant to simply signify a long time. The temptations suffered in the desert both by Jesus and those long before, in the Moses-led exodus, are also paralleled. Though miraculously provided with manna in the desert, those of old want to hoard it lest it cease, whereas Jesus, faced with the temptation from the evil one, to turn stones into bread to satisfy his hunger, shows trust in God even though, unlike of old, nothing has been forthcoming to sustain that trust (Matt 4:3-4). Again, contrary to those of the past who, lacking faith, needed miracles to confirm divine presence (Num 20:1-11), Jesus rejects the tempting offer of a miracle (to fall from the temple with no injury and the miraculous offer of the kingdoms of the world) presented by "the evil one."

Following his return from the desert the parallels continue. In Jesus' baptism the waters are divided, again paralleling the miraculous division of the waters associated with both Moses and Joshua, at the Red Sea and Jordan River respectively. Following this, in Matthew's Gospel Jesus is presented next as one announcing a new law on a mountain. Again this draws clearly on the Moses narrative, in his reception of the law on Mount Sinai. Jesus however is presented as one superior, for while Moses merely presents the law, given him by God, Jesus himself announces the law. The superiority of the law he gives to the old is reinforced by his repetitious pronouncement, "You have heard it said (quoting the law) . . . .but I say to you" (Matt 5).

Why this concern by the followers of Jesus to use these Jewish forms? The answer is simple: the very earliest of Jesus' followers were all Jewish. This is something which cannot be emphasized enough. Jesus and his early followers are often imaged, as we have found, in Christian circles as rejecting their faith tradition, but that is not the case. Rather, they understood themselves as being part of the Jewish tradition, arguing from within that perspective their case for Jesus being the Messiah. By their use of midrash these followers of Jesus sought to show that their line of Judaism, with its proclamation that the Messiah had already come in Jesus, represented the true fulfillment of Jewish hope, while also showing their opponents to be wrong in their denying Jesus as Messiah.

Just how Jewish the earliest church was is seen in the struggle central to the Christian Scriptures: whether faith in Jesus should be retained within Judaism or, using a biblical analogy, this new wine could not be kept in the old wineskins and therefore must be shared beyond Judaism. This debate predominately frames the Christian Scriptures, and within them different understandings are present.

So intense is the struggle that at one stage, in an episode to which I have already referred, Jesus is said to say, responding to a Canaanite woman's plea for help, "I was sent only to the lost sheep of Israel . . . It is not right to take the children's bread and toss it to the dogs?" (Matt 15:24). The story is an interesting one in that the writer, Matthew, one of the more conservative writers in the Christian Scriptures, with his understanding of Jesus as not only remaining in the Jewish tradition but even tightening it, has Jesus present in towns, Tyre and Sidon, clearly outside of Israel. Why would he be in such a place if his ministry was as strictly delineated as Matthew claims? The woman in the story is shown as one of great faith in her response to Jesus: "Yes, it is Lord, but even the dogs eat the crumbs that fall from their master's table," a response leading Jesus to commend her for her "great faith" (Matt 15: 24-27). Matthew, in this story, is showing where he, the most "Jewish" of the Gospel writers, stands on the question of admission of non-Jews to the church. To do such he is prepared to go as far as placing the most unedifying words on Jesus' lips, before having him retract them, so to make his point. For Matthew those outside of Israel may become followers of Jesus, but from within a Jewish framework. Despite this his Jewish chauvinism is clearly present in his having the Canaanite woman self describe as a "dog."

It is possible, indeed probable, that Jesus historically actually did understand his message in a narrower manner of being directed to his fellow Jews, and only later did his followers understand its more universal relevance, hence the depiction in the above story of Jesus relenting, changing his mind. The changing of the mind, rather than being that of Jesus, is that of the church, as it moves from being entirely Jewish, to one admitting all. As such the account may be a construction. Jesus, after all, is never presented as being in the gentile centre of Sepphoris, just a few kilometers from his hometown, Nazareth. Buddha's entire ministry is likewise directed within his Hindu Indian context, only being spread beyond by his subsequent followers.

In his Gospel, Luke gives a distinctly different understanding of where he believes Jesus' sympathies lie. He has Jesus on visiting his hometown of Nazareth, being initially welcomed, a welcome which quickly sours when he speaks of God's gracious action being not directed at those in Israel, but rather to a foreign woman of Sidon and Syrian man (Luke 4:20–30). Luke is arguably the only non-Jewish writer in the Christian Scriptures.

Even with the admission of gentiles to the church won, the probable majority in the church asserted that faith in Jesus as the Messiah ought to be retained within the Jewish tradition, thereby requiring those non-Jews who became part of the church to hold to such Jewish rituals as circumcision and dietary laws. Only a minority, led by Paul, argued radically the contrary, that gentiles following Jesus did not need to submit to such Jewish ritual.

As these divisions deepened, the very survival of the parent-faith Judaism was threatened following the aforementioned revolt and subsequent Roman sack of Jerusalem in 66–70 CE. For those within Judaism, including most of the Jesus movement, this seemingly was the end of the world. Hence the mixture, in what are presented as Jesus' apocalyptic discourses, between the destruction of the Judaism, in particular the temple, and that pertaining to cosmic events to do with the earth's final destruction (Mark 13 and parallels).

In the face of such crisis a line more concerned with religio-cultural definition understandably began to win out in the mainline Jewish community, and the Jesus Jews (I believe this to be the most accurate term to use) were increasingly ostracized before finally being evicted from the synagogue. That accelerated the Jesus movement becoming a separate, later primarily a gentile faith. The total split between church and synagogue would however take a long time, and right up to the fourth century we know that Jewish Christians were attending synagogue, evidenced by fourth-century church councils legislating against Christian attendance at Jewish worship (cf. Council of Laodicea, canons 29, 37, 38; Apostolic Canons 70–71: see Apostolic Constitutions VIII.47.7–71).

The destruction of both Jerusalem and that central to it, the temple, meant that Judaism, as found, had to radically reorient itself, no longer able to be centered on the temple cult and ritual.

In understanding how Jesus is presented in the Gospels the date of this destruction is crucial, standing between the ministry of Jesus, which precedes it, and the Gospel writings which follow, meaning that between the time of Jesus and that of the writing of the Gospels everything within Judaism had changed. As we found, the Sadducees and Essenes were no more while the Zealots were greatly diminished.

Only the Pharisees bridge the period. The Pharisees, the term literally meaning "the separated ones," had represented the strongest challenge to the temple cult. They were primarily lay groups who believed that the holiness codes, pertaining originally to the priesthood, should be extended to all. They often met for table fellowship, and given Jesus' penchant for such fellowship it is clear he spent much time with them. Indeed, by many of his contemporaries Jesus, as seen, may have been regarded as a Pharisee. Certainly Jesus' manner of teaching is like that of the Pharisees, delivered to a group who chose to follow, having their goal elevation of piety. Contrary to the negative connotations which have become associated with the term, the Pharisees were generally held in high esteem by their peers. The negative understandings, part even of our common parlance, represents precisely the Christian propaganda, developed to denigrate the only surviving Jewish group.

Judaism after the revolt and subsequent defeat had become the religion of the book, with that book, the Hebrew Scriptures, being interpreted and taught by the Pharisees and Scribes, who established rabbinic Judaism. All Judaism from that time was to be rabbinic. A minority of Jews, however, believed in Jesus, and they, like the emerging rabbinic Judaism, also were a people of the book, though in this case a book developing new additions, later to become the Christian Scriptures. Given that the religious practice of each grouping was vastly different to that preexisting within Judaism prior to the destruction wrought by the Romans, both had to find means to assert that their understanding, though far different from the old, represented the faithful inheritance of the sacred tradition. Therefore, when arguing within this context great effort was made by the Jewish followers of Jesus to show that he fulfilled the Jewish expectation. Their accounts of Jesus are thus strongly shaped in terms of midrash, so to demonstrate that he stood firmly in, and was affirmed by, the tradition. Along with this creative construction of Jesus went also invective directed at the other side, who likewise, as just seen, were striving to show that it was their reformed Judaism which represented the tradition's true fulfillment.

The combination of the trauma of the temple destruction, along with already radical reform made within Judaism, meant most within that tradition came to increasingly reject the idea of Jesus as Messiah, hardening their attitude toward those within their community who followed him. This marginalization of the Jesus Jews became understandably stronger as this heterodox group increasingly accepted gentiles, the same people who had wrought the destruction of their temple and city, into their fellowship. Further, they increasingly were making no demand that these gentiles hold to Jewish religious practices. Such was viewed as being outrageous by nearly all within Judaism, especially when cultural survival was at stake. Even those within Judaism who had become followers of Jesus, as we have seen, found it difficult to accept these changes. How could so much of that which was at the core of the Jewish tradition and identity—circumcision, the cleanliness codes and the dietary laws—be done away with? How could it be possible that this still mainly Jewish group following Jesus were so readily accepting these gentiles into their fellowship who had so recently brought carnage upon Israel?

The rejection of Jesus as Messiah by the majority within Judaism was to be expected, given that he had fulfilled none of the Jewish expectations. The

Messiah had been expected to inaugurate a new era marked by the signs of the reign of God, the shalom, but Jesus, though he had preached this reign, had been summarily dispatched by the Romans in a manner which brought shame upon him, for did not their Scriptures clearly say, "cursed is the one who hangs upon a tree" (Deut 21:23)? The Roman presence following the failed revolt was even stronger, and nowhere was the reign of God to be brought by the Messiah seen. Clearly for most, Jesus as Messiah had failed.

The caustic nature of this split, as just seen, was responsible for much of the writing within the Christian Scriptures, including their construction of Jesus in his relationship to Judaism. A reading of these Scriptures will quickly show the invective hurled at "the Jews" and "the Pharisees." The Gospels' presentation of Jesus is strongly shaped by the increasing division between 'the Jews' and this new community, now both Jewish and gentile, following Jesus. Thus, in the Gospels Jesus is constantly presented as being in dispute with both his Jewish tradition and the Pharisees in particular. This is all indicative of the context of the Gospel writers' context, post 70 CE, rather than that existing during the time of Jesus. Jesus' actual dispute had not been with the rising group of genuinely popular religious teachers, the Pharisees, and Scribes, with whom he was identified as 'rabbi.' They, like him, rejecting the idea of religion being limited to cult and ritual, were often critical of the temple establishment. It would be accurate to say that both Jesus' and the Pharisees' dispute was with the religious establishment. The Gospels fail to, or are unable to hide that, as even a cursory reading of the passion narrative in any of them will show, for there it is clear with whom Jesus is in dispute. Given that it is generally accepted that the passion narrative is the most primitive part in the Gospels' construction we can suspect that it, rather than the rest of each Gospel, represents better the historical Jesus.

Having examined some of the issues concerning the Gospels' presentation of Jesus, let us turn to look at that life.

Unlike Gotama, Jesus came not from a privileged class but rather from perhaps the lowest of classes. We think anachronistically that Joseph being a carpenter signifies that Jesus was born into the middle-class family of a tradesman. A carpenter at that time, however, was not a skilled tradesman. Wealth was measured in holdings of land, and being part of the Roman Empire, progressively more land in Israel was being concentrated in ever fewer hands, a result primarily from increasingly onerous taxes. This left increasing numbers of landholders facing mounting debts, and as these debts mounted, they were often forced to sell their land, staying on as sharecroppers or tenants. While this offered short term relief, it could be no real solution, for after paying the landlord their due share there was even less than before to pay mounting debts, the result being finally they may have to sell themselves and their families into bonded labour or slavery. Looking at the stories Jesus tells, we can often see this context shaping many of them, the clearest example being the parable of the prodigal son where a son returns home seeking his father's mercy after having to sell himself into such labour. Elsewhere in a parable he speaks of a man and his family being sold into slavery (Matt 18:25).

Those, as was the case with Jesus' family, having no connection to land such as artisans, lay at the very bottom of society. Given this precarious existence right through his life it is little wonder that Jesus' best-known prayer pleads for "daily bread." To ask for security greater than that for the day was a stretch too far. That prayer was likewise meant for, and would resonate with, many others who found themselves in the same position under Roman occupation.

Jesus is also, we are told, related to John the Baptist, who given his father took turns at serving in the temple, is of the priestly class. We may not necessarily conclude however that being part of the priestly class implied one having wealth. Scholars also mostly hold that the supposed familial relationship between John and Jesus is most likely a literary or theological creation. The ages of the two mothers, supposedly cousins, are vastly different.

Jesus' birth is presented as being highly auspicious, virginal, associated with celestial events, wise figures from the east, and is located in a propitious place, and perceived by the local ruler as representing a threat. These are, as I have shown elsewhere, all almost certainly later accretions, informed by myth and midrash rather than history.

Jesus' actual birth, one where he is born out of wedlock to a young woman living on the periphery of the society, was most probably in a location, Nazareth, which distinct from Bethlehem the birthplace of kings, was unmentioned in the sacred tradition. The only likely visitors would have been the neighbors, while the celestial objects would have moved as they always did, with the chorus of angels being nothing more than a literary creation. Jesus' birth, far from worrying Herod, would not have even registered as a blip on the historical record. Though it is likely the birth of Gotama was mythically inflated in importance, that of Jesus is massively inflated.

As we have seen in our examination of the Gotama nativity story, we have parental dreams associated with both he and Jesus, these dreams having to do with the special status of the respective children. While in the Gotama cycle it is the mother who is the recipient of dreams, with Jesus it is the "father," Joseph, who has multiple divinely inspired dreams.

We cannot know where Jesus got his undoubted wisdom, though there are hints that even as an adolescent it was present. In one account, the only given of "the lost years," between his nativity and his ministry, we learn of Jesus being in discussion, even debating, the priests in the temple, while his parents think he is lost. The factual basis for this story is, however, highly doubtful.

Along with the overwhelming majority of his social class, it is likely that Jesus would have been illiterate. He would have had however, a good understanding of the scriptural tradition, held in oral form, and as we have already found in our discussion concerning the Buddhist sangha, memory in oral tradition in antiquity could be prodigious. Such memory and familiarity with the Scriptures was expected within Judaism.

Before he commences his own ministry, Jesus appears to have been a disciple of John the Baptist. The baptist was an important person, believed by many people to be the Messiah, and there are those, the Mandaeans, who follow him to this day. We know of this close connection between John and Jesus because in three of the Gospels Jesus submits to being baptized by John, the embarrassment of that being tempered by the unlikely reasons given in each Gospel for that baptism. In the other Gospel, that of John, though Jesus is not baptized by the baptist, the connection between the two is still clearly drawn. Though clearly different to the baptist, Jesus continues to hold some of his views right through his ministry, and finally, each being seen as a dangerous subversive, they share a common gruesome fate at the hands of the authorities.

Jesus commences his ministry in Galilee, aged thirty, the same age as Buddha, and soon gathers a reputation as a miracle worker and healer, drawing large crowds. He also teaches, that teaching centered on the "kingdom of God," fitting firmly within the Jewish tradition, though Jesus seems to understand himself as having some pivotal role in the kingdom's coming. This kingdom, or reign of God, preached by Jesus is the Jewish "shalom," the right and just relationship between things, both people and creation, all existing in harmony under God's benevolent rule. Jesus' miracles and healings, bringing wholeness, are meant to be anticipatory signs of this coming reign, being understood by their recipients and onlookers as such.

The Roman occupation was understood by most Jews at the time as representing the major hindrance to God's reign. That is understandable given the Jewish tradition had at its core the Exodus story, the account of the nation's escape from bondage in Egypt. God was understood to be the God of liberation and now that Israel was again under the heel of an oppressive superpower, it was widely expected that the divine would act to bring that same freedom from the oppressor as had been wrought long ago. This expectation had led to the formation of the nationalist movements, the Pharisees, the Zealots, and the Essenes, and messianic figures, all having as common goal the overthrow of the Roman invaders. Jesus was strongly associated with these anti-imperialist nationalist movements, as of course was his mentor John the Baptist. The location of John in the desert on the Jordan was an obvious reference to the Exodus, for the crossing of the Jordan was the final step of those of old to enter their freedom in the promised land. Across that river the people had been led by Joshua, of which, as we have seen, the name Jesus represents a Hellenized form. Jesus likewise identifies himself by his going out to John in that place for baptism, where he, like those before, passes through the water, in his case symbolically in baptism, to freedom. All would have understood the symbolism, including the Roman authorities.

The connection between John the Baptist and Jesus is particularly strong, drawn from familial connections in their births to their common fate, gruesome execution for sedition.

Jesus, like Buddha, then retreats into solitude, spending time we would suppose reflecting on his mission and ministry. Like Buddha he is faced, as seen, with temptation, emanating from "the evil one" to take a different route in ministry.

Rejecting such temptation from that point Jesus lives a life of radical freedom, preaching a message of liberation.

Initially in his ministry Jesus is presented as drawing great crowds. His preaching is classically Jewish, built around the coming of the Messiah and the inauguration of the kingdom of God (the shalom), a time when cosmic harmony will dwell. His parables are directed to the kingdom: "The kingdom of God is like . . ." He appears as a teacher of wisdom and worker of miracles, these prefiguring God's reign in the wholeness they bring. He acts out the role of the expected Jewish Messiah and seemingly is identified by many as being such, the crowds following him increasing.

But then in the accounts we have he seemingly radically reorients his ministry in such manner that most of those following fall away. Jesus is increasingly presented as one never comfortable with a style of popular ministry, particularly in Mark, the earliest of the Gospels, where a device known as the "messianic secret" is employed. Thus on each occasion Jesus carries out some miraculous event; these being interpreted as messianic signs, he adjures those around to keep secret what they have witnessed. Of course, this clearly can only be a literary device for it is beyond reason to expect witnesses who have seen such incredible feats to remain silent. It is as though we are being prepared to find that Jesus is more than a spectacular charismatic figure identified with the popularly expected Messiah. As the story advances Jesus no longer is pictured as the miracle worker and healer operating with a charismatic power, attractive to the crowds, instead becoming one who increasingly speaks of his imminent suffering, understood in some manner as being redemptive. He also calls his followers to imitate what he will do, to "pick up their crosses and follow." In the Roman world being called to pick up one's cross was far more than a metaphor. This understanding of redemptive suffering is not entirely new in the Jewish tradition, having roots in some passages, known as the suffering servant passages, particularly in the Deutero-Isaiah tradition (Isa 42:1–4; 49:1–6; 50:4–9; and 52:13–53:12).[5] Clearly the Gospels have another such passage, Ps 22, in mind in their narrative of Jesus' crucifixion, that account being another example of midrash.

Suffering is redemptive in the Judeo-Christian story, something diametrically at odds with the attitude found in Buddhism, where the path to salvation, better understood as enlightenment, is one whereby suffering must be transcended, left behind. In Buddhism suffering is understood to be a direct result of our still being bound to samsara and as such hinders liberation, rather than facilitating it, as it does in the Christian story.

It is difficult to know the historicity of this radical change in Jesus' understanding and ministry, or whether, more likely, it serves as a theological construct. As such it is almost certainly an attempt by the Gospel writers to make understandable what appears to be the failure of Jesus' mission in that the hoped-for kingdom did not come. There was no demise of the oppressive Roman empire and a beginning of a new age of peace and justice. Instead that empire had decisively dealt with whatever threat Jesus presented by having him summarily executed.

Given that failure, the Christian writers creatively drew on their Jewish scriptural tradition reorienting Jesus, moving him from one proclaiming the reign of God to one increasingly understood as the means of redemption, particularly through his death and resurrection. That redemption no longer lay in a new transformed earth but rather in a heavenly sphere, separate from the earth, as an individual after-death experience. That change is most strongly found in John's Gospel, where Jesus preaches himself exclusively, rather than the kingdom. Jesus himself, particularly in his crucifixion/resurrection cycle, increasingly becomes the redemptive reality, rather than the kingdom of God. This happens very quickly, shaping the earliest layer of the Christian scriptural tradition, the letters of Paul. Indeed, Paul is perhaps most responsible for it. That transformation of Jesus' message is

5. The book of Isaiah was written by different authors over a period of some two hundred years from the eighth century BCE to the sixth century BCE, responding to different contexts. Scholars usually divide the text into three parts: Proto-Isaiah (chapters 1–39), Deutero-Isaiah (40–55), and Trito-Isaiah (56–66). Deutero-Isaiah comes from the sixth century BCE.

so successful that for most today the entire Christian message is popularly summed up in the preaching of the redemptive nature of Jesus' death and resurrection, while his vision of the reign of God is little known and rarely mentioned.

Though the Gospels are written later than Paul, they are unable to hide the real emphasis of Jesus' teaching. Apart from John's Gospel, he is seen in them to be time and time again proclaiming the kingdom of God. The passion narrative particularly gives the truth away as to the actual message of Jesus who until his death was clearly understood as a seditious figure. There is no attempt, not even in John's passion narrative, to hide this reality. Indeed, in John's Gospel the seditious nature of Jesus' challenge to the kingdoms of this world is drawn sharply in that the kingdom, represented by Pilate, is contrasted with that having Jesus as its representative. The contrast in kingdoms and their power takes, however, a more metaphysical turn.

The culmination of Jesus' life comes as he enters the city at the heart of the faith tradition and religious order, Jerusalem, at Pesach or Passover, the great Jewish nationalist celebration, commemorating release from slavery in Egypt. This was the greatest of all Jewish festivals. Tens of thousands of pilgrims made their way to the temple in Jerusalem, swelling the population of the city perhaps tenfold. Later in the divine story the Jewish people believed that God again had acted to free them from captivity to another superpower, Babylon. The expectation was that, now captive to Rome, this same supernatural power would surely soon free Israel. All, whether Roman or Jewish, understood just what this celebration meant in this context. For Rome the occasion clearly represented a danger. The procurator or prefect was compelled to leave his preferred seaside residence at Caesarea Maritima, to be present in Jerusalem, all leave was cancelled, and the military, overlooking the temple from the Antonia Fortress, was placed on high alert.

Obviously in such a context any actions taken by Jesus would be greatly amplified. Yet every action he takes is deliberately provocative, designed to radically challenge. The provocative seditious nature of Jesus' ministry is found in

- the popular entrance into Jerusalem on Palm Sunday
- his overturning of the money changers' tables in the temple
- the threat he makes to call down an army of angels at his arrest
- the charges brought against him: "he said he was the king of the Jews"
- the nature of his death, crucifixion being a highly public execution, mostly used for subversives as a warning to others

- in the sign placed above Jesus while on the cross, mocking him as "King of the Jews," crucifixion being the punishment summarily meted out to such claimants.

Let us look at some of these events more closely.

First, this Galilean Jesus, Galilee being viewed as a place of discontent, comes cheered by the masses, riding on a donkey into the city, a style of entrance understood as messianic, despite its humble sound (Zech 9:9–10). The king/Messiah, it had been prophesied, would so enter Jerusalem, hence the cry of the crowd identifying him as the son of David, Israel's greatest king, by whose line it was expected that the Messiah would come. That the Messiah would bring deliverance makes this entry extremely incendiary.

In case the challenge was not sufficiently clear, after retiring to the city surrounds, Jesus returns the next day proceeding to the temple, where creating a great disturbance, he overturns the tables of the money changers, whose role was to change the commonly carried pagan Roman currency into the ritually clean coinage needed to purchase sacrificial offerings. Roman coinage carried a graven image, such being forbidden in the temple, made worse by the claim that the one imaged, Caesar, was asserted, as inscribed on those coins, to be the "divine son of God." By having the coins tossed to the floor he is figuratively overturning that contention.

We cannot know if the exchange rates were extortionate or not. In any case Jesus makes no investigation as to whether some money changers were fairer than others but rather indiscriminately commences to overturn the tables. All of this under the noses not only of the temple establishment but also the Roman forces resident in the overlooking Antonia Fortress.

Jesus' actions may be understood as cleansing the temple or more radically as figuratively destroying it. In support of the more radical position elsewhere, including his trial, we find Jesus speaking of himself as replacing the temple. Equating the temple to his body, he asserts that it may be destroyed but that he is able to raise it in three days (John 2:19; Mark 14:58). From very early in the Christian tradition Jesus' death as sacrifice is understood as replacing the temple sacrifices. In his trial before Pilate, Jesus' opposition to the temple, including the threat to destroy it, is the main charge laid against him. By his action Jesus is attacking the whole temple complex, built around the assumption that the prime purpose of religion was cult and ritual. For Jesus, it is by actions, directed toward the divine reign, rather than the temple cult, which allow a person to enter communion with God. As we have seen, Buddha likewise, as found, sees cult and ritual as being an insufficient religious response.

Cultic-ritual worship centered on a temple and represented no threat to the Romans; indeed it was quite welcomed. Rome, full of the temples of its conquered peoples, was happy to co-opt all sorts of religions and cults in service of the empire. A faith, however, that moved past such into the socio-political realm was understood to be unacceptable.

Not content with his provocative entry into the city and his temple actions, Jesus next engages in dispute with the religious leaders, going as far as calling them "snakes and vipers" and "whitewashed tombs . . . full of hypocrisy and iniquity" before charging that tax collectors and prostitutes will enter the kingdom before them (Matt 23). We can assume that Jesus' barbs were not restricted to just the religious hierarchy. Some of his opprobrium must have been reserved for those representing the source of oppression, the Romans. That this barbed criticism occurs at the liberation feast of Passover while Israel was under Roman oppression supports this conjecture. In any case, some of the iniquity of the religious leaders would be due their collaboration with the Romans.

Of course, such opposition to the order of things cannot go unpunished and within a few days, on the very eve of Passover, a time when his actions would be most incendiary, Jesus is arrested by the Jewish leaders. Their motivation may well have been a concern to keep the peace for fear of Roman aggression at such a sensitive time, that being mingled with their opposition to his teaching and practice. After all that "peace" allowed them to carry out what they considered central, the temple cult. In a rebellion, or even commotion, that liberty would be at risk. The Romans held the necessary temple vestments and could well refuse to hand them over.

When Jesus is finally arrested there is again an underlying sense of subversiveness about the entire scene. Jesus makes a threat that he could call down legions of angels, while Peter, whom we are told is carrying a sword, cuts off one of the arresting party's ear. Why are members of the party surrounding Jesus armed? Were they hoping that resistance to the arrest would spark a widespread revolt? Were the legions of angels metaphorical representations of the legions of the populace who would rise? Whatever the case the whole episode is filled with resistance to the order.

Even Jesus' betrayal by Judas may be linked to the idea of sedition. Judas may have had the idea that by his betrayal he would force Jesus to act, calling down those "legions of angels" (the raising of a popular movement?) to lead a rebellion against Rome. Or conversely his actions may have been anger directed toward Jesus' refusal to act in the seditious manner, using the divine power by which he was still widely expected to act. Judas' disappointment, or even anger, could perhaps explain the crowd with Jesus on Palm Sunday, expectant of rebellion, being largely disappointed, gone by the following Friday. That Jesus refuses to act in the expected seditious manner does not signify that he is any the less seditious figure. His whole response and demeanor perhaps mocks the Roman claims more radically than that which was expected would.

Sedition again enters in the charges brought against Jesus. We are told there were many charges (Matt 27:13), and we have noted those concerning the temple. That probably truest to the mark is stated thus: "We found this man perverting our nation, and forbidding us to pay tribute to Caesar, and saying that he himself is the Messiah, a king" (Luke 23:2). There is truth to their charge, for Jesus saying, on examining the Roman coin, "Pay to Caesar what is due to Caesar, and to God, what is due to God," given his, and his interlocutor's theological understanding, could only mean that what was due to God would leave nothing left over for Caesar (Mark 12:17). It is interesting that this charge is found in Luke's Gospel as Luke spends much of his time as an apologist for the faith, attempting to present Christians as a respectable group within the empire, with whom the Romans ought hold no fear. That strengthens the case for its legitimacy.

In each of the Gospels Jesus is charged with being a king, and in none of them does he deny being such. As we have seen, king was synonymous with Messiah, the expected one who would cleanse the land of oppressors. Under the current situation, however, the only king permitted in Israel would be the one appointed by Caesar, serving as vassal to him.

Jesus is brought, we are told, before both Herod Antipas, tetrarch or governor of Galilee, and the Roman prefect, Pontius Pilate. In the Gospels we find him dealt with rather summarily, though probably not as summarily as the probable reality. The Gospels tend to inflate the trial in its importance, but their inflation tells us much as to how they viewed Jesus. We read how the crowd is given a choice of having Jesus or the rebel Barabbas released to them. Though no such custom is known, we may well ask, why in the biblical account is Jesus being linked with a political subversive rebel such as Barabbas? Following his trial, he will again be connected to such subversive figures in those who hang on the cross beside him. Not common thieves, as is often thought, but political bandits or rebels.

In John's Gospel account of the trial we find a classic theatrical reversal of roles, where seemingly it is Pilate who is being tried by Jesus. The Johannine account of the trial is an engagement between two alternate kings, their sources of power being drawn from different spheres, all built around the question of where true power lies. Is it with the temporal Rome or with Jesus, symbolizing divine power? That two diametrically opposed conceptions of power are clearly in play make this scene even more subversive.

Tried by the occupying power Jesus dies the death of a political rebel on a cross, a means of execution reserved by Rome for such figures. This method of execution was slow and incredibly painful. Every detail was attended to, so as to ensure a prolonged agonizing death. Thus, the spikes were driven into the heel of the foot, the most painful place, while also ensuring that the one hung did not bleed out. The victim was thus left to slowly asphyxiate. To prevent such, those crucified would initially push themselves up despite their pierced feet, until that became too much and then dropping forward, they would slowly and painfully suffocate. If Roman patience ran short, soldiers would break the victim's legs so to hasten the death. The Romans weren't the only ones to use such cruel means of death, Israel having used it in 88 BCE when the Judean king and High Priest Jannaeus employed the method to dispatch eight hundred of his opponents.

The manner of Jesus' style of death is evidence of the nature of the charge against him, as Rome showed just how seriously it viewed sedition by reserving this, its most barbaric form of torture, for it. Other than that of Jesus, the most famous Roman use was in the execution of thousands involved in the slave revolt led by Spartacus a century prior. On the way to their place of execution a victim was made to carry a wooden board on which was written their crime. This was then affixed to the cross above their head. We are told that the wording in Jesus' case, written in three languages no less—Aramaic, Greek and Latin—was that he was "Jesus of Nazareth, king of the Jews." Thus written, the message that Jesus was regarded as a subversive political rebel could not be clearer. Nor, given that such execution was public, on the busy thoroughfare just outside the city gate, could the lesson be more blunt. Rome knew only one "king," Caesar, with all others, such as Herod Antipas, serving as vassals, needing to offer their allegiance to him. Those coins, which he had not long before overturned, made clear after all the unique divine status of Caesar. To proclaim that there was another kingdom, led by one other than Caesar, to which a person owed ultimate loyalty, was sedition, for which the punishment was this gruesome death.

Christianity, like the other western faiths, Judaism and Islam, is essentially sociopolitical. The manner of Jesus' death is further evidence for believing that at the core of his teaching was his proclamation and enacting the reign of God.

Jesus must have known just how incendiary his actions were and what was to be the likely response of the establishment, both Jewish and Roman. It is almost as if he baits them. Not being able to get into the mind of Jesus we can never know why he so acted. Did he really expect some sort of divine intervention on his behalf, legions of angels to descend from heaven? Could he have believed the people would rise with him and reclaim the land from the occupier? Was it that he saw his suffering in some mysterious way as being redemptive in and of itself? This last understanding was, as we have seen, present in the Hebrew Scriptures. Whatever the case, it would have been obvious to an objective outsider that the outcome of his actions was not likely to be good for Jesus.

It is almost as though Jesus commits himself to such a torturous path. We have seen how Jesus is presented, ahistorically I believe, as one who reoriented his ministry from one centered on miraculous healings, wisdom parables, and teachings concerning the reign of God, to becoming one centered on the necessity of his own suffering, understood to be redemptive. Thus he seemingly gives himself in sacrifice. While the idea of the efficacy of sacrifice had deep roots in the Jewish tradition, it would become core to Christianity.

Within Judaism this idea of sacrifice as redemptive informed animal sacrifice, an essential part of the temple worship, more so at Passover, when thousands of animals were sacrificed, many of them lambs. These sacrificial offerings were made in the belief that one through them could draw nearer to God, bridging a separation caused by human wrongdoing. Only partly was this about turning the divine righteous wrath from them, for contrary to what many Christians believe, the Jewish concept of God is not one of the divine as being wrathful, demanding propitiation. God is understood rather as graceful, the heart of Jewish faith being built around God's gracious choice of them as a people. Though propitiation for sin did play a part in the practice, sacrifice was primarily concerned with the positive, communion with God.

This sacrifice is the reason for John's Gospel having a different setting for Jesus' death. According to John he dies on the sixth hour of the day of the "preparation for Passover" (rather than Passover itself as in the synoptic Gospels), the day, indeed the very hour, on which the lambs are being slaughtered (John 19:14), meaning Jesus' death is linked with those lambs being sacrificed. The image of Jesus as the "lamb of God" is central to John's Gospel, in turn becoming something coming to lie at the heart of the Christian tradition. John's Gospel in particular, so full of theological reflection, shows this increasing tendency in the Christian tradition to make of Jesus' death a redemptive sacrifice.

Both the preaching of Paul and the writing of John are built around this idea. This sacrificial idea develops further in theories of atonement to the point, that the divine, conceived as perfect, unable to stand imperfection, demands the death of the perfect divine son, so to enable others, made clean by the sacrifice, to dwell in the divine presence, following their death in an otherworldly domain. These theories we will later examine.

Ironically the faith of Jesus, so strongly critical of cult and ritual is turned into a religion built on cult, ritual (sacrifice), and temple (church). Again there are similarities with the development of the Buddha cult, particularly in Mahayana.

The Christian story then moves to the resurrection, wherein it is claimed that on the third day Jesus is resurrected to life. There are five varying accounts, that variance showing us that there was no objective experience of this event. That stands in stark contrast to the passion where the accounts, more historical, share much in common. Beyond the supposed proofs of an empty tomb, the nature of how the grave clothes are left, and the various visions, the strongest actual evidence for the resurrection actually lies in the profound change exercised upon Jesus' disciples. Resurrection becomes central to Christian preaching, for given the failure of Jesus to bring the reign of God the success of his mission becomes increasingly linked to this event.

The resurrection cannot be simplistically dismissed. It appears there must have been some event, sufficiently strong, which turned Jesus' followers from the disillusionment, despair, or even anger they may have felt toward Jesus following his demise, to become fearless champions of his cause. It seems something dramatic happened, causing their view of him to be totally transformed. From fear and timidity, they emerge to fearlessly proclaim him, placing themselves in great danger by such proclamation of one so recently executed by the Roman authorities for sedition. They even begin to change their day of worship from the Sabbath to the day of resurrection (Sunday), and most incredibly as strict Jewish monotheists, begin to elevate Jesus to heights which will eventually see him pronounced divine. Thus, Saul, who had been the strictest kind of Jew, can as Paul, some twenty years of Jesus' death, announce, "Christ Jesus: who, being in the form of God, counted it not a prize to be on an equality with God, but emptied himself, taking the form of a servant, being made in human likeness; and being found in such fashion, he humbled himself, becoming obedient even unto death, even death on the cross. Wherefore also God highly exalted him and gave unto him the name which is above every name; that in the name of Jesus every knee should bow, of things in heaven and things on earth and things under the earth" (Phil 2:5-11).

Paul is clearly placing upon Jesus ontological form distinct from that which others possess. The literary style of this passage indicates that it may go back even further, for it reads like an exclamatory style of hymn or credal statement of faith. He is perhaps even quoting older material which already has Jesus holding a unique ontological status.

Paul, remember, was Jewish, the very epitome of being so. In the very same letter he informs us that as Saul he had been "circumcised on the eighth day of the people of Israel, of the tribe of Benjamin, a Hebrew of Hebrews; as to the law, a Pharisee" (Phil 3:5). That such a strict monotheistic Jew as Paul, writing so soon after the time of Jesus, could make such claims of Jesus is amazing.

To simplistically dismiss the resurrection as announced in the Gospel accounts does not exhaust its possibilities to profoundly represent something beyond the literal narrative objective. What that is I understand as being beyond our cognition, lying instead in the deeply experiential domain. Certainly, the earliest followers of Jesus experienced it profoundly. It would be objectified in different ways, in each of the Gospels. Again, I have examined the nature of the resurrection in detail elsewhere.[6]

Given the reputation and the esteem in which both figures were held, it is understandable that fsiths soon developed bearing their names. How representative these faiths were of their founders is of course a question for great debate. Indeed, we can ask if it is even appropriate to speak of founders, for as we have seen, it is extremely unlikely that either Buddha or Christ set out to establish new faiths.

Along with Muhammad, they represent the three most influential faith figures of the contemporary world. As we have noted, the meaning of the titles Buddha and Christ make clear the extent of esteem in which both were held by their followers. In Jesus' case that title of Christ/Messiah still did not however satisfy his followers, for from within the Jewish tradition the Messiah was nowhere expected to be divine but rather human, an agent only of God. Unsatisfied with this, Christians made of Jesus someone increasingly ontologically different, until finally in Christian orthodoxy he becomes the divine "Son of God," the second part of the Trinitarian Godhead.

Likewise Buddha continues to be increasingly elevated by Buddhists. Within Mahayana he becomes divinized, indeed moves beyond the gods. Finally, as we have seen, he comes held to exist in "trinitarian" form as Tri-yaya; Nirmanakaya (the physical body of the historical Buddha), the Sambhogakaya (the bliss body of the enlightened Buddha), and the Dharmakaya (the absolute unity body of all things, beings and phenomena, beyond existence or conception).

Though new religions were founded and named after them, both Buddha and Christ themselves were profoundly shaped by the traditions into which they were born and upon dying would have still been regarded as part of their traditions, though understood as radical or even unorthodox.

6. Queripel, *On the Third Day.*

Hinduism, as we have found, was a fluid, developing tradition at the time of the Buddha, flowing in new directions as evidenced in the Upanishads but also into new faiths emerging from it, not only Buddhism but also Jainism. As seen, each of these movements represented a change from the old externalized ritual cult centered around the Brahmin priesthood to a far more internalized pursuit by individual adherents. The Upanishads charged that each person need individually be responsible for making the identification of their inner essence, the atman, with that which is the essence of all, the Brahman. Jainism taught that we are born with a soul which has the capability for divine consciousness, bringing with it infinite knowledge (siddha) but is caught in kamma from which we must free ourselves by right thoughts, actions, and speech. Those that achieve siddha are called jinas (conquerors). Jainism, as such, represents a similar though stricter response than Buddhism which likewise has at its core the escaping samsara for nibbana, using similar though less extreme means.

In similar manner, the Judaism of Jesus' time was in a state of transition. As in India, the old priestly order represented by the Sadducees, was being challenged by the Pharisees, the Essenes, and Zealots, along with popular charismatic figures, John the Baptist and Jesus, among them.

Jesus, while influenced by his tradition, pushes it in new directions. Like Buddha he understands faith as being more deeply personal than just observance of the cult. It calls for a radical inner transformation. For Jesus even the Torah, which lay at the heart of Judaism was not sacrosanct, able to be abrogated in the face of human need. The centrality of love, or agape, for Jesus is similar to the role Buddha gives to karuna.

Both Buddha and Christ embraced this fluidity in their traditions to such extent that their early followers determined that neither could be contained within those traditions and so developed new faiths bearing their name.

This primarily was due to both Buddha and Jesus rejecting that which lay at the heart of the faiths they inherited, the cultic apparatus, with its assumed automatic efficacious effect, built around the priesthood and its ornate rituals, claimed to have sacral backing. Such priesthood built on the power of sacrifice would find no formal place in the faiths named after our two figures, though it later returns in Christianity.

India at the time of Buddha was marked by an increasingly rigid system whereby status in life was set by the caste into which one was born. The four Indian castes had originally been occupational with a fluidity about them, but by the time of Buddha they were firmly set, justified, and sanctified by sacred tradition. Even today, with that same support, contrary to the Indian legal code, they still exist.

At the top of the order was the sacred priesthood, the Brahmins, their power lying in their sacrifices, as prescribed in the sacred Vedas, said to recreate the original primal sacrifice which brought all into existence. This power extended to that of life and death, with even the gods being subject to the correct rendition of the sacrifice the brahmins offered. In the divinely ordained order below the brahmins lay the ksatriya (those involved in government and defense), followed by the vaisya (farmers and breeders of stock, those, who in an agrarian age, essentially sustained the economy), and finally the sudras (slaves and others peripheral to the society). Others were believed to reside outside the caste system or varnas altogether, the avarnas, Dalits, or outcastes. The sacred nature of this was held to be static, ever unchanging.

Buddhism represented a protest against this sacred hierarchy. Buddha, born into the second of these classes, the kshatriya, held all those within the sangha to be equals, though with the caveat, as we have seen, that women were either excluded from or placed in a secondary position within that institution. The sangha to this day knows no caste.

Sacerdotal duties carried out by the Brahmin priesthood, which by correct performance necessarily brought atonement with the various gods, represented the core of Vedic religion. Holding the power of sacrifice, the Brahmins were, and still are, believed to be the highest of the Indian castes. Both Buddhism and Jainism, along with movements within Hinduism itself such as those of the Upanishads, represented a movement away from the automatic, transactional, to something which involved a far deeper commitment and effort on the part of the devotee. Rejecting caste linked to cultic sacrifice, Buddha asserted, "The person who is tolerant to the intolerant, peaceful to the violent, who is free from greed, who speaks words that are calm, helpful, and true and that offend no one—them I call a brahmin."

In like manner Israel had developed its own sacred order, built around the temple with its concentric series of ascending courtyards. This layout of the temple was an overt expression of Israel's stratification, having in ascending order a court of the gentiles, a court for women, then of men, followed by that of the priesthood and at the heart, the Holy of Holies, reserved for the high priest's entry only annually.

Jesus rejected this hierarchy into which he had been born. He was not the first nor the only one in his tradition rejecting the old cult, similar rejection having long established roots in the prophets, while contemporary to Jesus found also in the Pharisees, along with other popular charismatic figures such as John the Baptist.

Jesus' rejection was to be expected as he himself was an outsider. From Nazareth, born he was born into the poorest of classes, with aspersions cast as to his mother's moral turpitude and the legitimacy of his birth. At one stage, as he is disputing the Pharisees, they caustically say, "we know God spoke to Moses, but as for this man, we don't know where he comes from" (John 9:29). The aspersion being cast to the legitimacy of Jesus' birth are hardly subtle.

Right through his ministry Jesus rejected social and religious hierarchies, most clearly seen in his choice of meal companions. Table fellowship was critical to social status at the time, being framed by such things as who would invite you to their table, at which tables you would choose to sit, how high up at those tables you would be seated, and who you could successfully invite to your table. This had to be done carefully lest one would lose face and be shamed, shame being something to this day strenuously avoided in the Middle East. With a wry sense of humor, on one occasion in a story, Jesus mocks such attempts to secure prestige by careful calculations (Luke 14:7-11). Seeking honor at table one diner pushes himself too high, only to find himself shamefully demoted to the only seat left, that at the foot of the table, when someone of higher social rank enters.

The followers of Jesus continued to reject a hierarchy of salvation. Understanding the significance of Jesus' rejection of such, Paul, despite his evident chauvinism, was able to write in one of his earliest letters, "There is no longer Jew or Greek, there is no longer slave or free, there is no longer male and female; for all of you are one in Christ Jesus" (Gal 3:28). There would be no exclusive or privileged access to salvation for a chosen people. We have seen how the issue at the heart of the Christian Scriptures was whether a chosen people, the Jews, had a advantaged access to divine grace or whether such was available to all equally, both Jew and gentile. The conclusion finally reached was that all could enter God's reign with no restrictions of Jewish practice being placed on gentiles converting to the way of Jesus. Again, as with Buddhism, the "blind spot" concerned women, clearly placed in a subservient position from very early in the Christian tradition, though seemingly not at its most primitive level.

Buddhists rejecting the Hindu caste system, centered on the temple and priesthood, declared all to be equal within the sangha, while Jesus rejected the hierarchical structures, often built around holiness codes, which marked Judaism. His new community were first known as "people of the way," a distinct way to the world.

This rejection of old religious forms and hierarchies, by both Buddha and Jesus, and their followers, would have profound social ramifications.

Despite shortcomings in their practice, neither Buddhism nor Christianity in theory institute formal social hierarchies. In India today, where caste is still a powerful force, conversion to either Buddhism and Christianity offer a means of escape from its strictures.

6

THE TEACHINGS

In the teachings of both Buddha and Christ there are great profundities, though we never can be absolutely sure whether those teachings are from their mouths or are later attributed to them. Given the extremely long oral tradition, this is particularly a problem with the teachings of Buddha.

There are commonalities in the teachings, and similar sayings and general teachings may be laid out alongside each other, that being an easy enough task. Simple conflation, however, is a mistake. Buddha and Christ come from different directions and arrive at distinct conclusions regarding the human condition and its resolution.

The core of their teachings is quite distinct. Buddha turns inward, away from the world, while Jesus turns outward to the world.

For Buddha, that lying at the heart of the human condition, a condition in essence marked by suffering, is misconception, a belief in, and concern for, the ego or self. This concern for self is misplaced, as nothing, including most radically the "self," has ongoing or indeed any existence. One need overcome the ego and its desires to escape the ever recurring existence represented by samsara. Externalized ethics are of course present in Buddhism; indeed the Buddha is known as "the compassionate one," but they do not represent its essential core. That core is all about correct perception. From that perception, ethics, particularly compassion, will flow.

Jesus, on the other hand, understands the genesis of human suffering as being sin, understood as ethical wrongdoing. Such actions were contrary to the shalom of the reign of God. Later within Christianity this breaking of the corporate concern was held to have metaphysical effects in that it also meant one was not only alienated from those to whom they had done wrong but also from God. The self, rather than being viewed negatively as in Buddhism, has in Christianity nothing essentially wrong concerning it. Rather, created as necessarily good by a good God, it is called to ethical living, toward the reign of God, and metaphysically to eternity. The wrong in human living is not found in its essence but rather in its failure (as seen mythologically in the primal garden of Eden story) to live ethically. Only later does the idea that essentially there is something wrong with our human essence enter into Christianity, being found in the idea of "original sin." Let us more closely examine the teachings of each.

BUDDHA

Turning to the teachings of each figure, we again will commence with the one chronologically prior.

The teachings of the Buddha are known as the dhamma (Pali) or dharma (Sanskrit). The word comes from the Sanskrit root "dhr"—"to support" or "to remain," so best means something like "the moral and spiritual law of righteousness, the eternal true law of the universe." To follow the dhamma means one chooses to live harmoniously in accord with how things essentially are, that being understood as beneficial, the best way to live. In this it is comparable with the Greek concept of the eternal law, both physical and metaphysical, known as the "logos" (word), believed to hold all in place, and by which one in accord ought to live. This logos concept becomes central to Christianity, where Jesus come to be understood as the Word, or logos, the one in whom even the cosmos finds its accord (John 1:1-18).

In Buddhism the teachings of the Buddha are core, for they represent the signposts for the adherent to follow if they are to successfully achieve liberation to nibbana. Jesus likewise centered his ministry on teaching, though in Christianity it is not Jesus' teachings which become central, as seen, but rather the Easter events around his death and resurrection, with those serving as the means of liberation. In Buddhism there is like elevation of the Buddha himself as the means of effecting salvation, but that does not come until much later, with Mahayana. Contrary to Christianity, however, that understanding is never universal in Buddhism.

The goal of the Buddhist is that of nibbana, literally meaning "going out" or "extinguishment," thereby being freed from samsara, the endless turning of existence. It is kamma, understood as a fire linked with desire (dukkha), which keeps a person in that cycle. With the fire of desire doused, a person is liberated to nibbana, such extinction being not annihilation but rather understood as a fullness of boundless existence beyond the constraining ego.

At the heart of Buddhist practice is the taking of refuge in what are called the three jewels of the faith, the triratna: refuge in the Buddha, the sangha, and in the dhamma. Later Tibetan Buddhism would add a fourth, the finding of a teacher or lama to show the way. One becomes a Buddhist by making a commitment as follows: "I take refuge in the Buddha, I take refuge in the dhamma/dharma, I take refuge in the sangha," this being repeated three times.

In his teaching the Buddha strongly rejects metaphysics, having no interest in speculations on the divine, the ontological status of humanity, cosmological arguments of how the world and the universe came into being, nor whether the arahant (the worthy one seeking) exists after death. Even though the universality of dukkha or suffering is central to his experience, Buddha does not entertain speculative thought as to when or how dukkha commenced, or whether it has been eternally present, nor its root cause. All these speculations Buddha regarded as being non-edifying and unhelpful, drawing us from that which is central, our pursuit of nibbana. There is a certain empirical nature about Buddha's teachings in that he held all his answers came out of human experience and as such are intended to be pragmatic. While not sharing the philosophical objection to metaphysics of Buddha, Jesus likewise rejects pointless metaphysical speculation. On one occasion being asked as to what had caused a man's illness, his own sin or that of his parents, Jesus replies by not answering but rather deflecting the question before healing the man (John 9:1-6).

Buddha refused even to describe nibbana, believing it to be essentially beyond words, "incomprehensible, indescribable, inconceivable, unutterable." He compared it to the wind, something which cannot be seen, but which has clear effect. Jesus similarly spoke of the divine Spirit as wind: "We know not from whence it comes, nor where it goes" (John 3:8).

When speaking of nibbana Buddha's preference was to use negatives to say what it is not: a state 'where there is neither earth nor water, light nor air; neither infinity nor space; it is not infinity of reason but nor is it an absolute void . . . it is neither this world or another world; it is both sun and moon (Udana 8:1).[1]

For those unenlightened the state is indescribable and mistakenly can be thought of as nothing. For those who successfully extinguish the ego and thereby reach such a state it is perceived clearly as not being a void. On the rare occasions Buddha attached positive attributes to it, he noted nibbana

---

1. Armstrong, *Buddha*, 166

was "the truth, the subtle, the other shore, the everlasting, peace, the superior goal, safety, purity, freedom, independence, the island, the shelter,
the harbor, the refuge, the beyond" Later Buddhists, especially those in the
Mahayana, would equate Buddha himself with nibbana.

Again rejecting speculation, Buddha charged, enquiring as to the
whereabouts of one in Parinibbana is like asking where a flame goes when
it is extinguished.

To one monk who kept pestering him concerning his philosophical
position on different matters, Buddha replied that the questioner was like
one who, shot by an arrow, was more concerned about who shot him and
from which village they came than in getting the treatment that would save
him (Majjhima Nikaya i.4.26).

Buddhist teachings gather around what is held to be objectively prov-
able: the Four Noble Truths, the three marks of existence (anicca, anatta,
dukkha), and developing such spiritual qualities as equanimity, patience,
generosity, loving-kindness, compassion, and insight.

There is nothing metaphysical or otherworldly in the search for
nibbana.

Rather, Buddha believed the search to be entirely natural, in deep accord with both our deep human essence and that of the cosmos, written like
a type of DNA into the essence of each of us and all things, as natural as the
law of gravity. Thus, rather than being a denial of our human essence, the
path to nibbana utterly fulfills us, with our deepest realization being found
in this search. It is the path most congenial to our human condition and as
such will bring us our greatest happiness and fulfillment. When we fail to
follow the dhamma we choose the way of lesser satisfaction, create kamma,
thereby bringing "hell on ourselves" without need of reference to an external judge. Resisting that which is most beneficial we become like, in images
used in Buddhism, a misaligned wheel or bone out of joint.

Given such, in a deep sense there is a self-interest in it.

States which caused dukkha, such as greed, anger and envy, are not
sinful in the sense that Christians see them but more so not beneficial, in
that they hold the one possessing them to dukkha and therefore to the endless cycle of samsara and unhappiness.

By following the prescription Buddha had discovered, any living being—human, god, or animal—could find their enlightenment by working in
accord with their essential being. In this understanding of working with the
natural order there is a similarity to the type of truths discovered, roughly
contemporary with Buddha, in China by Lao Tzu, the founder of Taoism,
and also in the Greek concept of the logos.

Buddha believed all the answers he gave were latent within each human, who was therefore able to discover these things for themselves without
recourse to divinity. Believing that such wisdom lay not only within him but
also with all, Buddha often used a Socratic style of teaching, a question and
answer method drawing from a person the knowledge they already possessed but had not realized. A famous instance of him doing this with the
Kalamans is given in the Kalama sutta. Buddha commenced by telling them
one of the reasons for their confusion was that they were too expectant of
other people providing answers for them. "Do not be satisfied with hearsay
or taking truth on trust," he adjured them, "but rather search your hearts
for what you already know." Buddha himself of course had passed through
such rigorous self-examination. He asks the Kalamans, concerning greed,
whether it was good or bad. Did not this attribute cause the one holding
it to be despised and shunned by others so that they became unhappy? Do
not likewise the attributes of hate and clinging to clear delusions bring unhappiness to the one possessing them? Did not the "fires" of greed, hatred,
and ignorance cause unhappiness? On their confirmation that indeed they
did cause unhappiness, the Buddha tells them, "Not to rely on any teacher.
When you know in yourselves the things that are helpful, "kasula," and the
things that are unhelpful, "akasula," then you should practice this ethic and
stick to it, whatever anybody tells you" (Kālāma Sutta, Anguttara Nikaya
3:66). In like manner he also convinced the Kalamans that they would find
happiness in the practice of such virtues as benevolence, generosity, and
compassion. In doing so they would find a deep contentment born of equanimity, a goal held very highly within Buddhism.

The advantage his listeners had was that they had an interlocutor, who
having found the path, could present them the right questions.

Everything, Buddha insisted, must be tested against human experience. To the Kalamas he adjures, "Don't go by reports, by legends, by traditions, by scripture, by logical conjecture, by inference, by analogies, by
agreement through pondering views, by probability, or by the thought"
(Kalama Sutta, Anguttara Nikaya 3:66).

He illustrated this in a well-known story, to which we have already
referred, in which he claims his teachings are analogous to a raft used to
cross a river. Once the river is crossed the one using the raft does not pointlessly carry it on. Rather, having served its purpose, the raft is left behind.
As such it will be of use to another, whereas to pointlessly carry it on would
serve only as an encumbrance. "In just the same way, bhikkhus, my teachings are like a raft, to be used to cross the river and not to be held on to. If
you understand their raft-like nature correctly, you will even give up good
dhamma, not to mention bad dhamma . . . Would he be a clever man if,

having reached the other shore he was to cling to the raft, take it upon his back and walk about with the weight of it?" (Alagaddupama Sutta of the Sutta-pitaka Majjhima Nikaya 22). Such attitude appeals to many in an age of postmodern skepticism and scientific investigation.

Later highly speculative metaphysics enter Buddhism in the greatly detailed elaborations of the Mahayana tradition. Those things so firmly rejected by the earliest Buddhist tradition—ritual, metaphysics, grace and the supernatural—all make a return. The same holds for Christianity. One could speculate that these things seemingly have an essential place in any religious tradition and when excluded will find a way back in. The radical departure has a strong propensity to return to the norm.

Buddhism's teachings are not externalities, calling for an assent to doctrinal orthodoxies, though there are certain things which must be taken as givens: dukkha, anicca, anatta, and "the Fourfold Path." Acceptance of Buddha's diagnosis of these realities sets one on the right path for the journey. Having committed to that journey truth is found in following it rather than in external signposts.

In this there is a distinct difference with Christianity where an externalized orthodoxy in terms of doctrine became central, though in its earliest manifestations, as we have seen, Christian belief was far broader than what it was to become. Whereas Christianity is understood as calling for a formal ascent to a certain body of doctrine, often expressed in creed or catechism, in Buddhism one does not hold formally to a set of beliefs so much but rather meditates upon the core premises. There is then in Buddhism a greater experiential component than in Christianity. While Buddhism certainly has beliefs, the truth of one's faith is determined not by an assent to orthodoxy, as found in a Christian catechism, but rather by the effective outcome of commitment to a way, the path laid out by Buddha. Orthodoxy became the core of Christianity, whereas Buddhism is best understood as orthopraxis.

For Buddha, though, truth lay within, rather than in some external authority; the finding of that truth is not easy, however, despite it being in accord with our deep inner essence. Further, one does not merely give intellectual ascent to it, but rather it is a thing of such profundity that a person on finding it has not only their deepest understanding transformed but also their whole being. The discovery of this is only possible by use of the most rigorous methodology, for only such would enable a person to perceive a true reality at complete odds with that commonly perceived. Only a long and sustained cultivation of the mind through yogic meditation (citta bhavana) made it possible for a person to master the mind, rather than the mind mastering them. Both understanding and meditation are essential in reaching nibbana, the Samyutta Nikaya claiming "those having both meditation and understanding are close to nibbana." This understanding then is not merely an intellectual affair but is found through profound meditation and manifests itself in compassion.

We fail to see this essential truth because we are caught up in ignorance or avidyā. "I see no other single hindrance such as this hindrance of ignorance, causing us . . . to run round and round in circles" (Itivutaka: 14). Wrong perception is the Buddhist "sin," giving rise to all other problems.

The mind colors all reality. Every experience of suffering and dissatisfaction has its source in ignorance, avidya, based in the mind. "Phenomena are preceded by mind, led by mind, formed by mind. If one speaks or acts with a polluted mind, suffering follows, as a wheel follows the foot of a draught-ox. Phenomena are preceded by mind, led by mind, formed by mind. If one speaks or acts with a pure mind, happiness follows, as an ever-present shadow" (Dhammapada: 1–2).

Right perception of reality, vidya, lies at the heart of Buddhism, built around understanding both anicca and anatta. All things, including the self, are illusionary. When unable to perceive such, wishing to grasp things, including a concept of "self," we fall into suffering. Buddhism calls for "right perceiving" with the Buddhist "sin" being avidya, understood as absence of vision or ignorance. The Dhammapada opens with the lines "all we are is a result of what we have thought." In Buddhism one needs correct understanding of existence to make any progress, something as discovered by Buddha, clearly laid out in the faith.

This is quite distinct from the Judeo-Christian tradition wherein sin is understood much more in terms of ethics, sin literally meaning "missing the target," the target being one of correct behavior.

In Buddhism, lack of true insight or understanding (avidya) sets one on a course of twelve conditioned and conditioning links, which led one ever deeper into dukkha, therefore samsara. These are imaged on the Buddhist "wheel of life," the Dharmachakra.

- Ignorance or avidya, imaged as someone blind stumbling, causes formation
- Formation, seen as a potter at their wheel, is the source of consciousness
- Consciousness, pictured as a monkey, is the root of name and form
- Name and form, imaged as two people in a boat, gives rise to sense organs
- Six sense organs, viewed as an empty house, lead to contact

- Contact leads to sensation, imaged as a person with an arrow in their eye
- Sensation seeds desire, viewed as a person consuming alcohol
- Desire, imaged as a monkey snatching fruit, causes attachment
- Attachment in turn causes existence, viewed a pregnant woman
- From existence comes birth, pictured as a woman giving birth
- Birth brings dukkha, which causes
- Sorrow, despair, misery, grief, anguish, aging and death, imaged by a person carrying a corpse

Gotama found the most vulnerable points in these twelve links to be ignorance, craving, and grasping. He thus determined that at these weak points he would break free of samsara. He began to train himself with the goal of doing so. The means to this would be ethical discipline, a concentrated mind, and wisdom or penetrating insight.

In his effort to achieve this he discovered there are three phenomenological or soteriological stages culminating in nibbana. The first, showing one to be free of avidya, is dhatu-kusalata, the possession of the ability to see samsaric existence as composed only of phenomena. The second stage, manasikara-kusalata, is the capacity to reflect upon phenomena as being anatta, anicca, and dukkha. The possession of these things then leads to the third stage, the elimination of all desires and liberation to nibbana.

Much of this complex Buddhist phenomenology is found in the third of the three baskets of Buddhist Scriptures, the Abhidhamma Pitaka. Though this understanding with its theoretical complexity may seen obtuse, it was not something meant to remain in the realm of the theoretical but to have practical, far changing effects on how a person lived. As we have seen, Buddha's teachings are always intended to move beyond the speculative or theoretical to the practical and experiential.

The first step to enlightenment was to cleanse the mind of the illusion, avidya, of the permanency of things, with its attendant desire to possess them. That achieved, the person searching would be ready to move on. The journey, having commenced through a process of via-negativa (a giving up), then moves to a via-positiva (a taking up), the expansion of the wisdom heart and the attaining of the Bodhicitta (enlightened mind).

Ignorance could, with right meditative insight, be progressively left behind as one ascended higher as first a stream enterer, a once returner, a non-returner, and finally an arahant. In this journey, avidya progressively becomes vidya, or penetrating insight.

The veracity of Buddha's method was not proven as metaphysical truth, given by the gods, nor in its scientific accuracy, as proven by intellectual reasoning, but rather by the practical utility of whether it worked. Buddha himself, no longer subject to desire, and therefore suffering, was convinced by his profound equanimity that this indeed was the case. "The recluse Gotama does not have any superhuman status, any distinction in knowledge and vision worthy of the noble ones. The recluse Gotama teaches a dhamma merely hammered out by reasoning, following his own line of inquiry as it occurs to him, and when he teaches the dhamma to anyone, it leads him when he practices it to the complete destruction of suffering" (Majjhima Nikaya 12).

On another occasion upon meeting a mendicant, Buddha said, "No teacher have I. None need I venerate, and none must I despise. Nibbana have I now obtained, and I am not the same as others. Quite by myself, you see I, the dhamma won. Completely have I understood what must be understood, though others failed to understand it. That is the reason I am Buddha. The hostile forces of defilement have I vanquished . . . .and, having calmed myself, I am on my way to Varanasi, to work the weal of fellow-beings still oppressed by many ills . . . . Having myself crossed the ocean of suffering, I must help others cross it. Freed myself, I must set others free."[2]

Jesus likewise has a suspicion both of teachers and the tradition, being instead prepared to subject their words to his own thinking and experience. Concerning the received tradition he asserted, "while you have heard it said . . . I say to you," and of the tradition, "it is not possible to put, 'the new wine . . . into old wineskins." We are told that unlike others, "the teachers of the law" who regurgitated old teachings, Jesus was seen to be one who taught "with authority" (Matt 7:29).

The Thomas tradition within Christianity knows something similar, regarding both self-experience and reliance when it has Jesus proclaim, "I am not your teacher. For you have drunk, you have become intoxicated at the bubbling spring that I have measured out" (Gos. Thom. 13:5). "If you bring it into being within you, (then) that which you have will save you" (Gos. Thom. 70:1). "Whoever will drink from my mouth will become like me. I, myself will become them, and what is hidden will be revealed to them" (Gos. Thom. 108).

While there is a strong rationality about Buddha's teachings, there also exists the dimension of deep compassion. In like manner Jesus spoke of the need to be "wise as serpents and gentle as doves" (Matt 10:16). Compassion is probably that attribute most associated with Christ, best exhibited in his

2. Conze, *Buddhist Scriptures*, 53-54

words, which come to apply to his life, "greater love has no one than to lay down their life for another" (John 15:13).

The compassion of Buddha is most clearly seen in his not hoarding the wisdom he discovered which could have brought him to Parrinibbana but instead choosing to remain upon the earth to share it, so delaying his own liberation. Later, Buddha in one of his previous emanations, as seen, would be pictured as one sacrificing himself, on one occasion by self-emulation, for others.

At the core of Buddha's teaching lies the universality of suffering, dukkha, arising from desire or craving, tanha, that causing an accumulation of kamma, in turn trapping us in samsara, the every recurring cycle of life. The escape from this suffering, and therefore samsara, Buddha understood to be his goal.

The method he discovered was one of seeing reality correctly (to possess vidya), this built on the impermanence, indeed the unreality, of all things, including oneself. Things themselves exist but always in flux, possessing no abiding substance, being instead shunyata (emptiness). Once that was realized one would cease to crave for them. Then a person, no longer accumulating kamma, would be liberated from samsara. To escape samsara one needed not so much to change one's life as to change one's mind, for it is the deluded mind which keeps one trapped in recurrent dependent arising (pratitya-samutpada).

Craving is not necessarily material or evil. It may be a desire for the spiritual or the good. Whatever the case it causes suffering, so tying us to the cycle of samsara, a chain of ever dependent origination or causation, which leads us to ever coming into being, so precluding our entry to nibbana. Cleansing ourselves of avidya, we are able to develop our true being, the Bodhicitta, the one overflowing with compassion for all things, as distinct from the ego. Buddha claimed to not only have overcome this ultimate existential issue but to also have provided a methodology for the happiness of all living things in the journey to nibbana. This happiness had a reciprocal relationship with four social emotions: friendliness, compassion, sympathetic joy, and impartiality, all of which we are called to practice.

The veracity of these truths is found in examining them. Life, we are deeply aware, is full of uncertainties and vicissitudes, and even with the best of fortune we are unable to escape suffering. The greatest certainty in life, that we will die, is a cause of suffering, perhaps its major source, as it strips from us the illusion of that permanency we so desire. Mortality represents the greatest threat to our self-identity and, as we have seen, the desire to preserve our ego is the root course of our suffering. To seek preservation of the ego, yet knowing it will ultimately be utterly extinguished, can only cause us immense grief and anguish at the deepest existential level.

Gotama tried, or had imposed upon him, two paths to avoid suffering. The first, foisted upon him by his father, was based on satiation with the luxuries of the world. The second, which he chose, clearly in reaction to his previous excess, was the path of extreme asceticism. He remained on this latter path for several years, finally understanding that rather than assisting him achieve his goal of release from the world, this method instead only tied him even more strongly to it. Perhaps the words of a much later Indian, Mahatma Gandhi, are most appropriate: "to the hungry person God can only appear as a loaf of bread." Deprivation only serves to attach one closer to the things of the world by intensifying desire. As such it can never lead us beyond them.

Buddhism has, as we have found, been charged with being a negative religion due to its depreciatory view of life being essentially marked by misconception resulting in suffering. It ought not however be thus viewed, the Buddhist retort being that this view is neither negative nor positive but rather one simply honest and that the Buddha's goal is clearly positive, to put an end to this suffering: "Both in the past and now, I set forth only this: suffering and the end of suffering."[3]

Great drama, music, and poetry are often built around suffering because ultimately suffering is a profound reality in human life. Regards the existential reality of our mortality suffering may be said to encompass all of life. Each faith acknowledging the reality of suffering, seeks its root cause. To that they give alternative answers. Buddhism asserts it to be the result of ignorance or misperception, avidya, while Christianity claims it to be a result of sin, understood as ethical wrongdoing. Both present a solution, for Buddhism the path of true visioning, for Christianity, an openness to accept divine love and so to be one of love to others.

Buddhism, moreover, does not just remain in the negative with suffering but asserts positively that there is a way out so that rather than being resigned to suffering as fate, we are able to transcend it. Given the profundity and universality of suffering this makes the message of Buddha one which, rather than being negative, is deeply positive, while also being highly cognizant of reality. The Buddha was determined to preach this positive message, even when greatly tempted to leave it a secret by entering straight into nibbana.

Such negative casting of Buddhism is particularly unfair when we could charge that in like manner it could be possible to call Christianity a

3. Keown, *Short Introduction*, 48.

negative religion, especially in terms of how much of Christian spirituality develops with its emphasis on the via negativa, the rejection of anything in the world, especially human desires, as possessing anything divine about them. It asserts there is no way out of suffering except for divine intervention, present in another as Christ, we ourselves being unable to move past its all encompassing presence. In such understanding God is known not as being analogous to the world but rather as its negation. Given this, salvation can come only from outside the world with nothing within us being able to achieve such. That, it could be charged, is to take a pretty bleak view about human nature.

As with Buddhism, Christianity has at its core the realization that human life is deeply marked by suffering. Suffering enters from the very beginning in the Adam and Eve story, a story informing us, as we have seen, that the idea of remaining in some primeval innocence untouched by suffering is an impossibility. To do so would not be to live as an adult human. This, rather than some transactional change in divine-human relationship caused by human sin, as Christians would later come to hold, is the point of the Genesis story. We find likewise in the Buddha account that Gotama is unable to remain in primal innocence, despite his father's best efforts.

Suffering is integral to life. The concern for suffering, and attempts to understand it, extend right through the Judeo-Christian story, most vividly being present in Christ himself. The core symbol of Christianity, the cross or crucifix, testifies to the integral link between Christianity and suffering.

Rather than being a negative faith, Buddhism understands itself as bringing equanimity and deep inner joy and contentment. Thus, in the Anguttara Nikaya we read of the joys and happiness available to both the recluse and the householder.

Given neither of the path of indulgence, as planned by his father, nor that of asceticism had led him to his goal, Gotama chose what became central to Buddhism, "the middle way." It is interesting to note how asceticism as a means of escape from the world informed a movement associated with early Christianity, Gnosticism. Gnostics, whether Christian or otherwise, likewise believed that ties to the world could be starved into submission. Thus, the extreme acts of many early Christian ascetics, often known as the desert fathers, were influenced by Gnosticism. Like Buddha, Jesus rejected this way, strongly associated with John the Baptist, leading him to be charged with being a "drunkard and a glutton" (Matt 11:19).

Gotama did not resign himself to suffering but instead searched for a way out. Of his teaching he would later claim, "I show you on one hand suffering, and on the other hand, the way out of suffering" (Majjhima Nikaya 22, Samyutta Nikaya 22:86). He concluded that while of those things around us we can have no control, be it success or failure, gain or loss, of the mind we can. Through rigorous discipline Gotama would seek to still the mind, center it, and thus find right perception.

Of Buddhist teaching, the comparison with a surgeon is often made, for like a surgeon, Buddha first diagnoses in detail the disease, gives its cause, determines a cure, and finally sets out the needed treatment. Let us then explore his diagnosis and cure.

Buddhism is built around four factors of faith or truths (Ariya-sac-ca-Pali, Aryasatya-Sanskrit) representing confidence in the truth of the Buddhist path, śraddhā. These are three tilakkhana, representing the fundamental facts of existence, and the Four Noble Truths. The tilikkhana are

a. anicca, which, forming the basis for the other two, asserts all things are in a state of flux with nothing permanent.

b. anatta: Not only do things, but we also have no permanent physical form, something which, as we all painfully know, changes, breaks down and finally decays. We also have no permanent personality or identity as "Self." The "I" is just a convenient label for a series of interconnected events There is no "I" which needs to grasp and own, and even if there were, those things the I would wish to grasp also have no intrinsic existence.

c. dukkha or suffering, something arising not so much from impermanence itself, but rather from the illusion of permanence. It is this illusion which causes suffering.

From the core ontological realities given by the tilakkhana come the Four Noble Truths, the "cattari ariyasaccani."

It is claimed that in delivering those truths Buddha needed few words, just twelve sentences, even using this economy of words to explain these truths in three different ways. These are laid out in the Dharma-cakra-pravartana sūtra.

Such paucity of words was sufficient for the five ascetics to become arahants, while of the pantheon of gods who had been listening, it is said, they became bodhisattvas.

The first of the Buddhist Four Noble Truths is that life is full of affliction or suffering. The term dukkha, as we have seen, is used either of wheels whose axles are off-center, or of bones slipped from their sockets. As neither of these things are meant to be, nor is life necessarily meant to be lived in dukkha. Buddha held suffering to be self-evident, with all life marked by it, sometimes as physical, other times psychological, even existential suffering or angst to do with our mortality. "What, O monks, is the Noble Truth of suffering? Birth is suffering. Sickness is suffering. Old age is suffering. Death is suffering. Pain, grief, sorrow, lamentation, and despair are suffering. Association with what is unpleasant is suffering, disassociation from what is pleasant is suffering. Not to get what one wants is suffering. In short, the five factors of individuality are suffering."[4] Even when life seems good, Buddha held that it still has within it unsatisfactoriness. Dukkha extended through all the six realms of existence, from the lowest hell to the highest of the heavens and was experienced by all living beings, even the gods. Only in nibbana, beyond these realms, is dukkha absent. The Judeo-Christian story also strongly recognizes the reality and universality of suffering. Suffering and brokenness must be acknowledged as poignant realities.

Suffering or dukkha arises because all sentiment beings are empty of atman, while all phenomena or dhammas are without sabhāva (intrinsic nature). This includes things, experiences, beliefs, and systems of thinking, and most of all our own self-identity. All these are anicca, lacking permanence. Nothing was permanent, everything at any time being just a combination of constituents. Our belief that things had a permanency was illusionary, leading us to want to possess them, resulting in craving or tanha, that causing our enmeshment in samsara. On realizing they have no essential reality we are cast into a state of angst. To believe things remain in a set state for anything more than a fleeting second is to be caught in a state of avidya. All is ever changing in a dance of the cosmos, something confirmed in modern physics.[5]

Around the second of the tilikkhana, the no self or annata, Buddhism developed a whole complex ontology. While the idea of anicca, the first of the tilikkhana was already part of the tradition, the idea of the no self arose from Buddha's insight.

Both the I and any idea of a higher form of the Self had no existence but rather also were illusionary. Rejecting the idea of the eternal soul, Buddha conceived the idea of anatta, charging that not only was there no eternal soul, there was not even at any point a transitory self. As seen, the idea of the permanent Self or atman had been growing increasingly important in contemporary Hinduism, especially in the Upanishads, which spoke of rebirth as the transmigration of an eternal soul, the atman, from one body to another. In the Upanishads, the atman had even come to identified with the divine principle, the Brahman. Buddha, seeing no evidence for this, rejected it as speculative metaphysics.

4. Keown, *Short Introduction*, 50.

5. Some texts do, however, allow for an eternal essence, which they call tathagatagarbha, that being the potential tathagata or Buddha nature within, which by rigorous effort, like that made by Gotma, can be brought to realization.

In Buddhism the absolute contrary is taught. Instead of an understanding that there is an eternal identity which forever passes on, Buddhism teaches that not only is there no eternal identity, there is never even
a momentary identity. All constituents of being represent only sequences of
transitory events. Successive reincarnations are not animations of an eternal
atman but are rather like an ocean wave. The nature of the wave is dependent on what it has been, in the sense of a small wave does not suddenly
become large. However, in the wave it is not molecules being passed on
which are the cause of the wave's size and shape but rather the energy passing successively through different parts of water. Thus, Buddhism teaches,
there is nothing in the next incarnation which will be identical with what is
now in me, yet what is within me will profoundly shape the next incarnation in the manner of a wave. There is a causal connection, shaped by the
kamma accumulated, in the manner of a wave's size and shape being a result
of energy in a wave being passed on.

Buddhism asserts there is no constant in a person, the first-person
pronoun being just a convention we use. Having no self a "person" instead
consists of "khandhas" (sometimes spelled skandhas), an ever-changing
bundle of five constituents or aggregates. These khandhas are body (rupa),
feelings (vedana), perceptions (sanna/samjna), volitions (sankhara/samska-
ra), both conscious and unconscious, and consciousness (vinnana/vijnana).
At any point we are a specific configuration, this always being due to the
causal consequences of earlier combinations. Modern biology confirms
this physically at least, informing us that 98 percent of all our bodily atoms
are replaced annually. Absolute contingency lies at the heart of Buddhism,
hence the continual need for mindfulness. It is the reading of these khandhas as permanent, and our wishing to hold on to them as some kind of self,
which is the core ignorance, and therefore source of suffering in Buddhism.

Buddha's conclusion arose from his own exploration. Prior to his enlightenment Buddha had sought to uncover this real Self which lay beyond
the transitory ego. But far from finding this he found no sense of even the
self. It was not his essential personality which Buddha discovered was extinguished but rather all those things which created kamma: greed, hatred, and
most of all illusion. Buddha instead found peace in "selflessness," determining that nothing, including "Self," as defined by the atman, was eternal, and
that it was our conception that things were, which caused our suffering. To
hold on to either, things or a Self, caused dukkha. All things were impermanent "maya" (illusion), lacking real existence. "Impermanence, unsatisfactoriness, and non-self are the three characteristics to be found in all that

exists. Unless we identify them within ourselves, we will never know what the Buddha taught."[6]

Buddha taught that until we deal honestly with this reality of annata, rather than trying to ignore it, there can be no hope for a cure. While we continue to think and act in the traditional manner, caught in avidya, our lives will be marked by suffering, "When we realize we are nothing but energy particles coming together and falling apart, nothing but the five elements, then what is the 'me' we are so zealously protecting?"[7] Given this, meaning and therefore happiness, could not be found in one's own person, for such did not exist.

Jesus had a similar view of the ego or self, though such does not arise from a deep ontological framework as in Buddhism but more so out of the damage the pursuit of egotistical interests can cause in our relationship with others. Again, external ethics are core to Christianity. The Christian tradition nowhere contains an understanding of the "no-self" but rather calls for a transformation of the self so that it moves from selfish ego to being self for others. Egotism is always viewed harshly in Christianity. We are called to live corporately, love being the highest attribute. The rejection of egotism is most clearly evidenced in that even one's spiritual capabilities have no value unless subject to the command to love. Egotistical boasting of such is met by Paul's admonition that pursuit of holiness without love is worthless. "If I speak in the tongues of men and of angels, but have not love, I am a noisy gong or a clanging cymbal" (1 Cor 13:1). That Jesus rejects such spiritual egotism is found in his refusal to demonstrate great feats and miracles, which would testify to his holiness. In Christianity, the self always exists for the service of others, deeply motivated by love. One is called to "pick up their cross," this representing a radical dying to the self. The core of Christianity sees Jesus' giving of himself to a torturous death for others. Paul can later say, "it is no longer I that lives, but Christ who lives in me" (Gal 2:20). Selfish ego is to be transcended in Christianity.

Buddhists took this teaching on impermanence sufficiently to heart for us to not to find any image of the Buddha until five hundred years after his death. For possessing no permanent form, especially following his passing into Parinibbana, how could Buddha be imaged?

Though people often speak of a person being re-born in Buddhism this is not really the case. There is no straightforward rebirth of an individual for there is no "I" to be reborn, just a combination of khandhas. For ease of communication, I will speak of a person's rebirth but the truth, that

---

6. Khema, Being Nobody, 18.

7. Khema, *Being Nobody*, 18.

it is rather bundles of khandhas reborn in accord with accumulated kamma, must be kept in mind.

In meditation the khandhas are contemplated each in turn, with the changes in them demonstrating how each being subject to dukkha could not therefore be the true Self.

In another sermon, often known as the Fire Sermon, Buddha declares, "All is aflame. What all is aflame? The eye is aflame. Forms are aflame" (Adittapariyaya Sutta). The body, mind, and emotions, as represented by the five khandhas, fed by greed, hatred, and delusion, are on fire with lust for those things in the world. These three fires, understood negatively, deliberately represent a critical counter to the three sacred fires of the Vedic tradition. One must smother the flames by being dispassionate through the pursuit of mindfulness. Detached from the fire of the khandhas the truth of the dhamma would be recognized and the path to nibbana begun.

Along with the five khandhas there are twelve ayatanas: the six cognitive faculties (the five sense organs and the mind) and the six corresponding categories of objects. This classification of the elements of the world is based on human experience and is used by Buddhist philosophers to explain how everything in the temporal world is transient and non-substantial. Essentially there is no reality beyond our experience, and recognition of this opens the path to nibbana. As such Buddhism is a form of philosophical Idealism.

In Vajrayana, a link is made between the five Dhyanibuddhas (meditation Buddhas) we previously examined and the five khandhas.

In turn they are:

a. The bodily form "rupa," linked with Vairocana, imaged in yellow, identified with the sun at the zenith and like the sun, representing the creative power of the universe.

b. Sensation or feelings, "vedana," represented by Ratnasambhava, understood as born of the jewel, who heads a grouping of deities, the Ratnakula, all of whom wear a jewel. He, dwelling in the southern quarter of the universe, is again associated with yellow, and has a consort or shakti, Mamaki.

c. The third of the Dhyanibuddhas is Amitabha "of unlimited splendour," representing perception, "samjna," living in a western paradise known as Sakhavati, the place of the setting sun, and so colored red.

d. In the eastern heaven of Abhirati, colored blue, dwells Aksobhya, "imperturbable," the one of unlimited splendor. He is linked with the khandha of consciousness, "vijnana."

e. The last of the dhyanibuddhas is Amoghasiddhi "unquenchable power," symbolizing volitions and interdependent conformity, "samskara." Colored green, Amoghasiddhi is associated with the north.

This family of five Buddhas became standard, often placed in a circle within a mandala. The historical Buddha, Sakyamuni, is usually placed in the center with the four other Buddhas, from other eons placed around him, representing the four cardinal points of the compass.

Each of these Dhyanibuddhas may appear as emanations, known as a Dyhanibodhisattvas. These include Samantabhadra, Ratnapani, Avalokitesvara or Padmapani, Vayrapani, and Visvapani. Avalokitesvara, the Bodhisattva of compassion, is the best known of these, understood to be the guardian deity of Tibet, as well as being a popular figure of devotion in Mahayana. His shakti or consort, Pandara, is the Buddhist equivalent of the Hindu god Vishnu, the most auspicious of the creator deities. Avalokitesvara becomes known as Kuan Yin in China and Kannon in Japan. Although male in India, he becomes a female mother figure, cradling an infant in her arms in China, Korea, and Japan.

Buddhist meditation may be divided into two types: analytical, a state in which you analyze the Buddhist teachings, and intuitive, a state in which one stops analyzing and comes to appreciate reality directly.

The schools of Buddhism have varying goals for meditation. While in Theravada the goal of meditation is the development of vidya, so freeing oneself from samsara, the aim in Mahayana is to develop compassion in order to free all beings, while in Vajrayana the objective is to understand the vast, open, and luminous quality of the world. In Zen one aims to breakthrough to their own true Buddha nature.

While for most Buddhists meditation has the goal of bettering one's kamma, within the sangha meditative practice has a deeper goal: the elimination of all those impurities binding us to samsara and the attaining of nibbana. Those in the monastery seek to free themselves from the binds of desire (kamadhatu), form (rupadhatu), and no form (arupadhatu). Having advanced this far they will have developed many spiritual supernatural powers (iddhi), including psychic power (mahabhijna), but more importantly meditation and controlled breathing exercises known as dhyana. This practice of dhyana leads to a joy and peace which subjugates anger and angst, giving rise to a supreme concentration which then moves past investigation and reasoning. Meditating upon all these things, a monastic seeks to note the changing nature of their thoughts and sensations, increasingly becoming mindful of all things continually arising but then falling away, while strengthening the desire to be free of the chain of causation. The realization that all is anicca and anatta becomes progressively ever clearer. Finally the feeling of joy in achieving such subsides, to be replaced by equanimity, a perfect evenness of mind and temper. At this point one was ready to enter nibbana.

Within Buddhism there are two major types of meditation, having very distinct goals: samatha and vipassana. Often, particularly in Theravada and Vajrayana, the former is understood as preparation for the latter, while in Mahayana they are practiced together. Samatha has as its aim, calmness, sharing that goal with meditative practices found in many traditions. Unlike samatha the goal of vipassana, a meditative style peculiar to Buddhism, is not peace but rather insight, which may serve to break peace. Vipassana has as goal the development of a critical, penetrating insight, focused around thoroughly knowing the anicca, anatta, and dukkha teachings of the Buddha. The violent, sudden insight to reality in Zen, "satori," serves as a stark example. Some practitioners of vipassana go as far to say that samatha, by the calmness it brings, may serve to hinder the real insights to be achieved in vipassana, as the practitioner may wish not to move past the intoxicating calm offered by that style of meditation.

Buddha cautioned his followers that no matter how expanded the mind was, it was still conditioned (samkhata), created by previous states of mind. Attachment to such high state is still attachment and is therefore not truth.

In like manner Buddha cautioned against using the supernormal powers which can come from long meditation. Once upon meeting a yogi by a river, who boasted that after twenty years practice he could now walk on water, Buddha responded, "but tell me why have you spent twenty years cultivating this ability when there is a ferry just over there?"

The capacity to have vidya as opposed to "commonsensical" misunderstandings necessitates profound skills of meditation core to the Buddhist tradition, in which there are extensive details given as to techniques.

Meditation is directed to four abodes known as the brahmaviharas (literally 'abodes of Brahma'), these being loving-kindness (metta), compassion (karuna), empathetic joy (mudita), and equanimity (upekkha). These are also known as the appamanna (the four ascending meditative practices, divided into two sections: the rupa jhana, four meditations on form, followed by the arupa jhana, four meditations on formlessness. In the former the seeker moves through progressive stages:

- to detach the sensory desires.

- to cease deliberation and discursive thoughts, be they good or bad.

- to losing feelings and emotions, thereby moving to equanimity.

- and finally, to a point where, moving beyond all effects, one no longer feels neither sadness nor happiness.

One then moves to the four realms of arupa jhana wherein the adept successively

- arrives at an infinite place beyond color or shape.

- moves to a perception of infinity.

- transcends the subject-object distinction.

- Before finally arriving at a place, dwelling in the nothing, wherein they experience a total cessation of all feelings and ideas, being free from kamma.

In this intricate detailing of meditative techniques, Buddhism differs from the initial layer of the Christian tradition. While we are told several times of Jesus spending time in deep prayer and meditation, even a whole night, we only see him doing so as observers. We do not enter the method of his meditative prayer. The extensive methodology of meditation in Buddhism is entirely absent from the initial layer of Christianity. We do know however that Jesus' prayer could be sufficiently intense so to manifest physiological effects, with him sweating blood in the garden while contemplating his imminent trial, torture, and execution. It is only later in the Christian tradition, first with the "desert fathers," followed by the Neoplatonists, and later again in the monastic tradition, that we find developed all manner of techniques for prayer and meditation. While not widely known, even in the West, methodologies for meditation and contemplation given in the Christian tradition can approach the detail and complexity of Buddhist techniques. A clear example is that developed rigorously by the Jesuits in a thirty-day retreat.

Within both Christianity and Buddhism these intricate methodologies of prayer and meditation are largely observed only by those who have committed their lives to their respective faiths through entry into the monastic life. This is even more the case in Christianity where there is often little discussion or teaching of methods for contemplative prayer.

Within Buddhism however, the monastic life has a deeper link with the wider faith, the role of the laity in Buddhism often understood as being one in service to the sangha, primarily by the provision of their physical needs. Most Christians have little contact with the Christian monastic tradition, monasteries being less numerous and not core to contemporary Christianity, centered rather around the church. Further, many Buddhists are expected to "take monastic robes," even for just a short period, this find-ing no parallel in Christianity. It can fairly be said that Buddhism is a faith centered on the sangha, especially in its Theravada and Vajrayana forms, whereas Christianity is not. The core of Christianity is the gathering of the laity at church, while in Buddhism such gathering of laity is rare, only found at large festivals. This gives the average Buddhist a stronger link with the fountains of meditation than a Christian has with meditative prayer. That such hunger exists in Christianity can be seen in growing links with the monastic tradition in many places, most clearly seen in the tens of thou-sands visiting the contemporary Taize Community in France, with the Iona Community in Scotland standing as another significant place of retreat.

Despite the closer link with the sangha the devotional life of the Bud-dhist laity may however be intermittent and fleeting. Often it will consist of a quick offering and prayer at a temple.

Within Buddhism, by disciplined meditation it is possible to affect re-birth or even to pass into nibbana, such being determined by kamma. Bud-dha derived his idea of kamma (literally action) from his Hindu tradition, where it likewise was understood as being something accumulated from thoughts, actions, and desires, causing one's place of rebirth.

Kamma is the result of a chain of causation whose twelve links, com-mencing with ignorance, form a wheel controlled by the demonic anti-Buddha, Mara. It is not one's actions which cause kamma but rather the intentions which lie behind the actions. All things arise, dependent either on something else or on a combination of numerous things. Nothing exists independently in or of itself, the only exception being nibbana. All dhamma (phenomena) are dependent on and arise from previous dhamma. Every-thing ought to be understood as a dynamic network of interrelated causes and effects rather than as a collection of separated static objects, nothing having any essence apart from the constituent parts it contains in any mo-ment. All happenings, including that happening which we view as "self," are conditioned, and in turn condition, future happenings. With its idea of dependent origination or arising, Buddhism stands between eternalism (a permanent soul) and annihilation. The former holds that there is a true self, an atman, which endures forever, while the latter believes that all is impermanent with no connection between events, all being chance. Again, Buddhism chooses the middle way.

Behavior is directed by differently rooted systems. Bad behavior, akusala, arises from greed, hatred, and delusion, while that which is good, kusala, grows out of non-attachment, benevolence, and right understanding or insight. Even good behavior, though, enmeshes us in samsara by accu-mulating kamma.

Good kamma, called punna, guaranteeing a better rebirth, is the prime aim for a layperson, for only a bhikkhu or bhikkhuni can realistically hope to extinguish kamma. In most schools the best a layperson can hope is, by the accumulation of good kamma, to have a more propitious birth; until finally born as a bhikkhu or bhikkhuni, they will have the chance to reach the goal of nibbana. As seen, one of the best methods for a layperson to win good kamma is by assisting the monastery. Mostly that occurs by their giving food to the monastics as they make their daily rounds. Other means of service include the offering of robes to monks and nuns, partaking in the services conducted by the bhikkhus, and the donation of funds for the upkeep of the monasteries.

Having an impersonal origination and causation, kamma is something written into the cosmos as natural law (paṭiccasamuppāda) rather than a thing understood either as the result of moral reward or punishment meted out by a god.

Kamma determines where the khandhas find rebirth, governing such things as the family, social class or caste, physical appearance, and most importantly character. While kamma has a powerful effect, it is not appropriate for a Buddhist to just go along with it in a manner of resignation. Instead they are called to resist their kammic impulses, so to develop a better character, exhibiting new patterns of behavior. Such will result in better kamma, leading to a better rebirth. Kamma correctly understood is not about avoiding responsibility nor an excuse for fatalistic acceptance, but rather an incentive to use what one has been dealt in the most creative and propitious manner.

In some traditions within Mahayana, kamma/karma can be passed to another in the style of supererogation associated with Christianity. A person could call upon a Bodhisattva for extra good karma, as would a Christian call upon a saint, or Mary, who having an excess of goodness, can share that with others. Of course in Christianity, the one with unlimited excess of good is Christ, whose name can always be called upon for divine forgiveness and grace. Within Buddhism though, with the exception of Pure Land forms, such grace could assist a person in their rebirth, but karma still being present, it could never bring them to nirvana. Such magnanimous sharing does not lead to a depletion of karma for the one giving it but rather to an increase, due to the generosity of their giving.

Some schools of Buddhism have rebirth as being instantaneous while others, like Vajrayana in Tibet, detailed in the Bardo Thodo, believe there is a forty-nine-day buffer period between lives, during which time the spirit of the deceased remains with them before being reborn. Dying is viewed as a propitious opportunity for a properly trained practitioner to pass directly to nirvana. In the Bardo the steps in dying are well laid out, and one, if having rehearsed them, can use them to escape from samsara.

Given that there is no self as ego, never mind Self, understood in the deeper Jungian sense, which passes from one life to another, nor an eternal soul, what was it that determined a person's birth status? Views on what is reborn vary. While some hold there is an inexpressible self or avacya which migrates from one life to the next, the majority hold to the radical no self-view. It is generally held that a person's consciousness (vijnana), though evolving, exists in continuum, and it is this which undergoes rebirth, that consciousness, often being represented in the last idea or impulse before death, with that having been conditioned by the kamma of their now lived out life. This determines the life form in which the khandhas will find their place, seeding the unconscious receptacle or alaya, the storehouse of consciousness, which in turn becomes the decisive factor of a new name and form of a child in the womb of another. When that child takes bodily form, it links with that consciousness, and a new life cycle begins, the conditioned and conditioning links continuing to play out. There being no permanent self or soul, our life is like a fire, never static, but a thing in constant flux. Likewise, the kamma accumulated in one life is passed to another as one flame lights another. That new flame lit, while being dependent on the other, is not however the same flame.

That suffering is a result of our craving or tanha is the second of the Four Noble Truths in Buddhism. This arising of craving is known as samudaya. It is of course, utterly foolish, for given the impermanence of things they can never really be possessed, meaning we can never find fulfillment in them. That we seek to do so is illustrative of our utter ignorance or avidya. "This, O Monks, is the truth of the arising of suffering. It is this thirst or craving (taṇha) which gives rise to rebirth, which is bound up with passionate delight and which seeks fresh pleasure now here and now in the form of (1) 'kama taṇha,' the thirst for sensual pleasure, (2) 'bhava taṇha,' thirst for existence in samsara, and (3) 'vibhava taṇha,' thirst for non-existence or annihilation as means of escape from samsara" (Dhammacakkappavattana Sutta).[8] Again, in the last, we are reminded of the danger of ego in pursuing even the good goal.

Having its root meaning as being "attached to a place," taṇha has its genesis in greed, delusion, and hate, these imaged in Buddhist iconography respectively as a cock, snake, and pig, their tails in each other's mouths as they race around the inner spokes of the Dharmachakra or "wheel of life." We, like they, in our accumulation of kamma, are trapped in the

8. Keown, Short Introduction, 53.

ever-revolving wheel of samsara. Surrounding the hub of the wheel are two semi-circles, one light and one dark, representing the two types of dhamma one can create, positive and negative. These realms are those of the gods, semi-gods, and humans on one side, and animals, hungry ghosts, and hell on the other. Even the highest of these however is not the Buddhist goal, given that each is still trapped in samsara.

The third truth is that the accumulation of kamma may be countered by practicing proper disciplines, nirodha, literally meaning cessation or removal. Given that illusion and ignorance resides in the mind, it must be disciplined to perceive correctly, so it ceases craving for that which can never satisfy. When we give up this craving our suffering ceases, for we are then rid of those things such as anger and lust which tie us to the cycle of samsara. We replace them instead with attributes such as wisdom, love, understanding, and compassion, this assisting our movement toward nibbana. Such involves great discipline, achievable only through the rigorous practice of yoga. "This, O monks, is the truth of the cessation of suffering. It is the utter cessation of that craving (tanha), the withdrawal from it, the renouncing of it, the rejection of it, liberation from it, non-attachment to it" (Dhammacakkappavattana Sutta).[9] Such leads to "extinguishment" or "going out." This is not the self or ego going out, for such does not exist in the Buddhist conception, but rather the extinguishment of those three things which cause kamma: greed, hatred, and delusion, which manifest themselves in such things as dependence on material possessions, greed, jealousy, anger, covetousness, and sexual lust. The true mark of those, who in this lifetime are living in nibbana, is a total absence of these, they being replaced by peace, deep spiritual joy, equanimity, compassion, deep wisdom, and insight. This achievement may seem to be beyond us, but the good news is that Buddha has shown us the way for this journey. That brings us to the last of the Four Noble Truths. Having diagnosed the situation Buddha now offers a cure by detailing a path out.

The final noble truth is that there is a path (Pali magga, Sanskrit marga) out of this tanha, a proven method of Nirodha, which leads to nibbana.

> And this, monks, is the truth of the Path which leads to the cessation of suffering. It is this Noble Eightfold Path, which consists of—right view, right resolve, right speech, right action, right livelihood, right effort, right mindfulness, right meditation.[10]

9. Keown, *Short Introduction*, 56.
10. Keown, *Short Introduction*, 58.

This is known as the "eightfold path," a path, as the middle way, avoiding the extremes of both opulence and asceticism. The process is extremely difficult for the mind must be trained to include emotions, thoughts, and understandings entirely foreign to the narrow limits of our natural being.

The path Buddha presented was a practical program rather than one of metaphysical truths, its proof being in how it works. It may be summarized as follows:

- Right view or knowledge. The acceptance of Buddhist teachings, thereby acknowledging that a pathway exists.

- Right resolve or aspiration, making a serious attempt to develop right attitudes, so to make a single-minded commitment to the path.

- Right speech entailing speaking the truth, along with speaking in a sensitive manner, e.g. avoiding gossip and slander.

- Right action, avoiding such things as killing, stealing, taking intoxicants or drugs, and not thoughtlessly satisfying sensual, including sexual pleasures.

- Right livelihood, pursuance of an occupation which causes no harm. Professions to avoid include being a slave trader, prostitute, butcher, brewer, arms trader, or tax collector.

- Right effort, making a strenuous moral exertion to control one's thoughts, so to develop a positive state of mind.

- Right mindfulness, the cultivation of constant awareness, a mind centeredness, entailing a rigorous self-examination of thoughts, and the development of clarity regarding non-permanence.

- Right meditation or absorption, the development of very deep levels of calm and equanimity using various techniques, especially yoga, leading to a true focus, which gives direct perception moving beyond maya, the false perception of self and reality.

These eight may be categorized otherwise as morality (sila), meditation or correct centeredness (samadhi), and wisdom or panna (Pali)/prajna (Sanskrit). The first of these, concerning morality and ethics, informs communal living, while the latter two, centered around meditation and insight, have to do with internal processes. They ought not be considered as sequential stages but rather as interrelated parts of an integrated whole, each reinforcing the others.

The first five of these steps in the Eightfold Path, known as the Five Precepts or Pancasila, are recommended to everybody, and commitment to them is a major part of the ceremony performed when one becomes a Buddhist.

There was nothing terribly original about the Buddha's description of our problems, for nearly all his contemporary yogins would have agreed with his analysis of the human condition given in the first three truths. The originality of Buddha was his claim that he had found a way out of the human dilemma through his Fourth Noble Truth, the Eightfold Path. Yet, later in Mahayana even concerning this, Buddha did not claim originality, saying only that he had rediscovered an ancient truth which had been taught by previous Buddhas, but which had been forgotten in the periods between each Buddha.

As we found, Mahayana brought massive changes within Buddhism, with even the ontological understanding of the Buddha changing radically. From being a self-enlightened human, who discovers the path to enlightenment, before teaching it to others, who likewise must make their own self-propelled journey, in Mahayana Buddha becomes one, who, having status beyond even divine, is able to offer salvation to those who seek it, through the grace he offers. While in Theravada all things were understood to be contingent and impermanent, in Mahayana, Buddha becomes eternal and transcendent, therefore distinct from all else, which remains conditional and impermanent. Mahayana claims that Buddha having called nirvana indescribable, indicates the existence of the unconditioned Buddha and other beings in a transcendent realm. This change also effected both the style and goal of meditation.

In Mahayana the Eightfold Path became refined into five stages, understood as: accumulation of those things necessary (sambharamarga), preparatory conduct or training (prayogamarga), vision (darsanamarga), meditation or contemplation (bhavanamarga) and finally no further training (vimuktimarga). The first two stages, expected of all Buddhists, lay, or ordained, are understood to be preparatory levels, from which the initiate launches on the path proper from within the sangha.

Having achieved prayogamagga and taken the robes, the monk begins the journey on the path of darsanamarga. On this part of the path there are sixteen key points or moments of comprehension, which upon completing the initiate enters the next stage bhavanamarga, where through disciplined mind control they achieve a series of revelations which enable profound understanding of the true meaning and reality of the Four Noble Truths, particularly in how they extinguish dukkha. Following this, using enhanced meditative methods, the bhikkhu/bhikunni achieves the seven "constituents of enlightenment," the study of dharma, energy, mindfulness, concentration, joyful zeal, aptitude, and equanimity, enabling them to fully understand the second (tanha) and third (nirodha) truths. The arahant/ arhat (Sanskrit) will then clearly understand the origination of suffering, which being now extinguished, causes moksha, or liberation. Then follows the final stage, vimuktimarga, a passive part of the journey wherein the individual is carried forward, driven by the momentum of the previous stages, toward nirvana. This process most likely will take place over several lifetimes, with the initiate living as a deeply committed ordained monk or nun within the sangha.

In some traditions this brings the arhat to the point where they enter "the stream," thereby being destined to no more than seven future incarnations (in other traditions seven years) on the wheel of life before entering nirvana.

The Bodhisattva practice in Mahayana revolves around the Six Perfections or Paramitas. By practicing these perfections, the Bodhisattva passes through ten stages of bhumi (lands), stages of awakening, on the way to nirvana. Once the seventh bhumi is reached it is impossible for the one practicing to fall back from their goal, nirvana being assured.

These were impossible to traverse in one lifetime, the realistic goal being to cover them in several lifetimes. Mahayana scholars outlined an elaborate pathway to best achieve this. A major part of this path was the fulfillment of paramitas, with numerous meditative techniques and theories built around these paramitas. These successively were:

- dana paramita, the perfection of giving to monks and nuns.
- sila paramita, the perfection of morality.
- ksanti paramita, the perfection of patience or preparedness for endurance.
- virya paramita, the perfection of vigor.
- samadhi paramita, the perfection of meditation.
- dhyana or prajna pramita, the perfection of wisdom

These are best pursued within the sangha, given that following this highly disciplined path was extremely difficult within the normal human sphere of activity. Only in the monastery, free from those distractions necessary in worldly interactions and living, could a person, through the strict practice of yoga, devote themselves sufficiently to the path. Without the insights gained through yoga, such things that ran so contrary to human experience, such as the knowledge of anatta, could never make sense. Many merchants became followers of Buddha, but given they were bound by their economic interests they could rarely be free of dukkha. The best they could realistically hope for was to live a life befitting of the kamma they had created, while hoping to find a more auspicious locale after their death, perhaps as a monk which could set them on the path to nibbana. Enlightenment from the lay state, while possible, is very rare, mainly found in Mahayana, particularly in the Pure Land schools.

Two distinct styles of message were thus tailored for ordained and lay followers. While the former were recipients of the full teaching associated with the dhamma, the laity received teaching that emphasized the need to live a compassionate and ethical life, so that the kamma they necessarily produced would be of a better kind. Laypeople were encouraged to take the five precepts to do with śīla: not to take life, steal, lie, partake of intoxicants, and to avoid sexual promiscuity. On the uposatha days, long established in the Vedic tradition, the laity carried out extra practices such as abstaining from sex, dressing soberly, not indulging in entertainments, and not eating until midday. These were practices associated with monastic novices, so could perhaps serve to give a taste of monastic life, thereby possibly encouraging it at a future stage. Any monk, before they embarked on the practice of meditation found in the sangha, needed to have practiced the five sila precepts.

Within the scriptures there are sermons directed to the laity. In the Sigalovada Sutta, often known as the "code of discipline for the householder," the recipient, Sigala, was instructed in śīla to avoid alcohol, late nights, laziness, and bad company. There is also a lay version of the Fire Sermon in which the lay follower is instructed to tend the three good fires, taking care of his dependents, caring for his wife, children, and servants, and to support the bhikkhus and bhikunnis in the sangha. The idea of ahimsa (respect for all living things and avoidance of violence) was also understood to be central to lay devotion.

The ultimate goal of Buddhist practice, nibbana, could be entered in embodied form, as it was for Buddha. In such manner it was known as sa-upadi-sesa. Such did not eliminate suffering, Buddha himself still experiencing such, right through his life, up to his violent illness and subsequent death. In this embodied state it represents a transcendence of suffering, a means to pass through it, rather than being governed by it. Having achieved this egoless state of sa-upadi-sesa, Buddha was convinced there was no fuel left to spark any tanha, and given the absence of desire, no kamma produced. He knew himself therefore as being free from the endless round of samsara.

An arahant in sa-upadi-sesa has extinguished the fuel comprised of craving, hatred, and ignorance and therefore dukkha, but still being in this bodily state, the five khandhas continue, meaning that from this burning remained the residue "sesa" of the fuel "upadi." This continued while one was in the body with its senses, mind, and emotions. As such there was always the potential for further conflagrations leading to another existence rather than nibbana. When, however, one in such state left the body there could be no more igniting, and with no chance of being caught up in samsara, entry into nibbana was guaranteed.

While nibbana means "extinguishment," it does not signify that the person having achieved such becomes nothing. That certainly was not the case with Buddha, who after all developed a whole movement through the sangha, teaching and traveling to many places, during the forty-five years subsequent to his enlightenment. Rather it signifies nothing in the sense that a person in nibbana lies beyond that which can be defined. Even after physical death it is wrong to say that the enlightened person, having entered parinibbana, does not exist as though extinct. It is equally wrong to speak of annihilation as it is to speak of an ongoing existence for a soul or self. Again, Buddhism chooses the middle way.

Buddhism has ethical implications particularly in regard to anatta and anicca Following Buddha, one is called to a life reflecting the absence of the ego. It is the illusion of ego identification which leads us to unethical actions such as, among others, greed, competitiveness, pride, and violence, so free of the illusion of the ego a person no longer seeks to fill it at the expense of others. This makes for better community, both in the sangha and the wider world. It is good again to be reminded that communal, not individual, living in the sangha represents one of the three jewels of Buddhism.

As we have noted the West has sometimes regarded Buddhism as having a self-centered nihilism in that it neglects the realm of social ethics. This, using a concept at the heart of Buddhism, is to radically misconceive.

As seen, ethics represent the first part of the Eightfold Path, expressed in the Five Precepts or Pancasila, which all Buddhists are called to observe. The core of Buddhist ethics lies in the inviolability of life, something which Buddhism, along with its contemporary faith, Jainism, brought to the forefront. Both strongly rejected animal sacrifice, which had been at the heart of Indian religious practice. This in turn influenced the wider Indian tradition so that even in the Brahminic tradition animal sacrifice increasingly became rejected in favor of symbolic offering such as fruit, vegetables, and milk. Within both Buddhism and Jainism the principle of ahimsa led to such practices as the straining of water and refusal to travel during the monsoon because of the chance in either case of killing small insects. In certain Buddhist cultures some even frown upon agriculture given the ploughing of fields leads to the death of many soil organisms. Buddha himself as a young boy, as we found, was upset for this reason when he saw a ploughing ceremony. Such ecological concern speaks poignantly to our modern context.

Within the sangha, beyond the initial "Pancasila," there are four other levels of ethical codes. The first of these is the Eight Precepts (atthangasila), followed by the Ten Precepts (dasasila), these both supplementing the Pancasila by detailing such things as the times when meals may be taken, the prohibition of frivolous activity, perfumes, and adornments, high beds, and the accepting gold or silver (now understood as money). Then follow the "Ten good paths of action" (dasakusalakammapatha), governing the actions of the body, speech and mind. These include things found in the Pancasila but go further, calling for abstention from speech, which is slanderous, harsh or idle, not to succumb to greed nor hatred, and to have right views. Finally, there is the strictly monastic disciplinary code (patimokkha), canonized in the Vinaya. The number of rules varies between the schools, but there are some two hundred which in great detail regulate communal life in the sangha. These are normally recited aloud in a fortnightly gathering, and monks wishing to confess to breaching them do so, expressing their regret, resolving not to repeat their mistake, while declaring their reliance on the three jewels of Buddhism to assist them. Some things led to a monk being automatically expelled from the sangha: sexual intercourse, stealing, killing a human, and lying about one's spiritual attainments.

The rule offers great detail on such things as the height of a monk's bed, how monastic construction is to take place, and the type of robe to be worn.

These are comparable with the Christian monastic rules developed by Saint Benedict in the sixth century. The Buddhist version is however significantly longer than that of Benedict and also details the context from which the ruling arose.

Buddhist ethics arise from three cardinal virtues: non-attachment (araga), benevolence (adosa), and understanding (amoha). The development of these virtues is crucial for the Buddhist as it enables them to fulfill the incumbent moral precepts, as only by developing correct disposition and inclination is it possible to act ethically. Thus, to keep the first precept of the Pancasila, the prohibition of killing, it is necessary not just to feel restrained by rule, but rather to develop a compassionate regard for all living things. Abstention of itself is not sufficient.

Ethics can be very tightly held in Buddhism, sometimes to an extreme. With the prohibition on killing, within the commentary on the Dhammapada we learn how on one occasion when the Sakyas, the kin of the Buddha, were under attack, they preferred to be slaughtered rather than break the precept forbidding the taking of life. Within that text we find words which illustrate the folly of violence, understood not only as destructive but also unproductive for the one aspiring to it. "He abused me, he struck me, he overpowered me, he robbed me. Those that harbor such thoughts do not still hatred . . . Hatred is never appeased by hatred. By non-hatred alone is hatred appeased. This is an eternal truth" (Dhammapada 3-5). We find a something similar in the Jews refusing to fight on the Sabbath in the second century BCE Maccabean revolt (1 Macc 2:32–38), though this had to do more with the day rather than an adherence to non-violence.

In the Jakatas we read of kings and princes who, rather than defend their kingdoms, were prepared to renounce their thrones. Of such renunciation of throne, we have already noted the case of Bimbisara. Of Buddhist rulers, Ashoka is held to be the example par excellence as one transformed by Buddhist ethics. In expanding his empire he had used violent means, a war with Kalinga resulting in 100,000 deaths. On becoming a Buddhist, so horrified was he by this huge loss of life, he renounced violence as a means of conquest, and committed himself to conquer only by the dhamma in future.

Nonetheless within Buddhism a type of "just war" theory developed. In an early second century Mahayana source, the Satyakaparivarta, we find the argument that war may be pursued as a last resort when all other means have failed. The text uses concepts of compassion to justify even torture, retributive violence, and harsh punishment, as means of spreading Buddhism. A text from the medieval period, the Kalachakra Tantra, speaks of a "holy war" between Buddhists and "barbarians," predicting the coming of a Cakravartin, who will lead the Buddhist forces to victory over evil. Here we are close to many of the Jewish messianic expectations, strongly present around the time of Jesus, regarding the Messiah, one who would come in divine power and strength to overwhelm the forces of evil. Influenced by such messianism, the Dead Sea Scrolls, roughly contemporary with Jesus, speak of the "Teacher of Righteousness," in whose name "the sons of light" shall battle the "kittim" under the "Prince of Darkness," understood to be the Romans. So pervasive was this idea, Jesus was often tempted by it, challenged to "call down fire and lightning." Like Buddha, Jesus decisively rejected such understandings. As with Buddhism, we find in Christianity the development of just war theories, most identified with Augustine, permitting a Christian to go to war if certain conditions have been met, with pacifism, a widespread movement in the early church, becoming progressively marginalized.

As we examined, in recent times both Buddhism and Christianity have been widely used to justify violence.

While for most Buddhists sila has great importance, there are some who hold it in little regard, asserting that any actions, even those good, arising from desire, tie one to this world by creating kamma. One must transcend even ethics. This however is a minority view and is problematic in that the Buddhist texts continually call us to good actions, particularly compassion, while Buddha, known as the compassionate one, and others, after their enlightenment, continued to live good lives, holding high concern for ethics.

Particularly within the Mahayana tradition a growing flexibility developed concerning ethical precepts, with context becoming increasingly important in how they were understood, that flowing from the belief that Buddha taught guided by context. His teachings, therefore, could be regarded as provisional rather than as eternally binding. Thus, it was argued, with compassion central, this allowed the bending or even breaking of precepts when they stood in the way of that compassion being exercised. This discretion could especially be exercised by Bodhisattvas. It has even been argued that a precept so central as the not taking of life could be laid aside in order to stop someone from committing an action so heinous that it would condemn them to severe karmic consequences. There is something very similar in the Christian tradition which goes right back to Jesus, who was prepared not only to break the oral law of the tradition, but even that law itself found in the Torah, regarded in his tradition as being absolute. Thus, he heals on the Sabbath and satisfies his disciples' hunger on that holy day of rest. From such Christians have developed the concept of situational ethics.

It is best to see ethics within Buddhism as not being a goal in and of itself. The ultimate value of ethics is found in that they make possible the achievement of enlightenment. An unethically lived life would make such a goal unobtainable. Indeed true panna (insight) necessarily leads to love and compassion to arise naturally. In Christianity, likewise, the ethical life is lived out of a radical internal conversion or metanoia, meaning a total turning around.

It is generally held that not every desire in Buddhism is necessarily wrong, the desire to do good, to bring compassion to the world, being viewed positively. There are two words used in Buddhism picked up in the English word "desire." The first is negative, tanha, but Buddhists also use another word, "chanda," as representing a much more positive form of desire. Having positive desires for oneself and others, such as advancing toward nibbana, or wishing to extend compassion to the world, is understood as chanda. Such extension of compassion to others lies at the core of Mahayana. It is best to recognize only the inadequacy of a life lived to high ethics alone. As well as having sila, one needs to also possess panna, a profound understanding of wisdom, achieved through samadhi (meditative consciousness), particularly regarding the human condition. Sila and panna are best understood as belonging together, neither sufficient unto itself. This is seen in that generally, Buddhists understand that there are two ladders to enlightenment: kamma yoga (right action) and bhakti yoga (right devotion and love to the Buddha). Both wisdom and compassion are dependent on each other. Panna falls short entrapped in egotism without karuna, the compassion which stimulates sila, while sila can be easily misdirected without the eyes of panna.

As in Christianity, Buddhist ethics often came to be shaped by relationship to political power. This especially is the case in Theravada, where the sangha, the monarchy, and the laity all stand in reciprocal relationship to each other. Modern Thailand is a clear example. The laity serve the sangha in such things as providing land for the monastery and the service of meals, such allowing them to advance in their journeying toward nibbana; the king commits to defending the faith, while those in the sangha bring blessing to both the king and those resident in the kingdom. This is not greatly different to the relationship between these different orders evident in medieval Christendom until the Enlightenment. King Ashoka in Buddhism and the Emperor Constantinople in Christianity play very similar roles in their taking each faith from being countercultural protest to becoming mainstream. That change sees a necessary compromise in each faith's ethics, which increasingly come to serve the state and justify state actions.

Clearly ethics stand close to the heart of the ministry of Jesus. The core of his teaching is the kingdom of God, the bringing of the shalom, understood as universal harmony. The ethics Jesus announces, however, are so rigorous they can only be held by a person radically transformed. Rather than a code, requiring just external adherence, the ethics of Jesus can only be kept by a transformed person who has deeply internalized them. As in Buddhism it is not enough to just not transgress by avoiding doing the wrong. Instead, a person needs to affirm the right. It is not sufficient to not kill, steal, or lust. Rather there is a need for an inner transformation making these things unappealing. Jesus often takes the negative prohibition and turns it to its positive.

As we have found, Jesus himself was not one to hold dogmatically to the ethical codes of his time as contained in the Torah, sometimes abrogating while on other occasions heightening them. Thus, despite announcing in the Sermon on the Mount that he has come not to do away with even an iota (the Greek i, therefore smallest letter) of the Law/Torah, he pronounces, While you have heard (in the Torah) that you shall not murder, I tell you that you must not even be angry with another, and while in the Torah adultery is forbidden, Jesus announces, the one who looks at another with lust has committed such (Matt 5:21–48). Jesus is clearly calling his followers beyond mere keeping ethics as rules observation. When he disregards the Torah he does so in the name of something greater: love and compassion. Thus, as we have seen, he heals numerous people on the Sabbath and rejects criticism of his disciples taking grain to eat on that day. In his either heightening or abrogating the strictures of the Torah, Jesus is showing that mere keeping to an ethical code by itself is not sufficient. One must go deeper to an inner transformation of the heart.

We may conclude that ethics, though important for both Buddha and Jesus, are not the starting point. Neither are teachers of morality. Rather, for each ethics arise out of something more profound. Ethics represent not external codes with which an adept must struggle but rather are the fruits of a deeply transformed person. Holding to a right ethic should be a natural outcome from the transformation already experienced.

Both Buddha and Jesus teach a subversive wisdom, centered on a "way," offering a sharp critique of the accepted, and apparently sensible, conventional wisdom of their surrounding culture. Each offer a radically alternative way of perception and living. Buddha established his way in the eightfold path and sangha, while Jesus' way was so distinct, as seen, his earliest followers were first known as "people of the way," before later being called Christians. Jesus often speaks of "seeing," "light," and "sight" as signifying true insight of reality, while his aphorisms and parables turn conventional wisdom on its head. Everything for Jesus needed to be understood in the subversive terms of the kingdom of God with its radical contrary understanding. For Buddha "enlightenment" likewise meant an absolute new way of perception, something in sharp contradistinction to normal perception, understood by him as illusion. Both Buddha and Jesus call us to a radical shift in perception and from that in our living.

Central to that new living for both Buddha and Jesus is the call for a turning away from egotism. For Buddha egotism as illusion represented the root cause of our suffering, and if we were to ever to be free of such suffering, we must see the absolute folly of living to such, as ontologically there is no self. Egotism is ultimate foolishness for it represents absolute misconception. While Jesus lacks a systematic ontological framework from which he critiques ego, he speaks of how those who empty themselves will be exalted, adjures us to become children, understood as an egoless state, while also calling his followers to take up our cross and follow, the last image being the strongest annihilation of the ego. Thus Paul could exclaim, "I have been crucified with Christ. It is no longer I that lives, but Christ who lives in me"

(Gal 2:20). The Buddhist "letting go" and the Christian "dying to oneself" have similar roots.

With Buddhism rejecting caste, it had a special appeal to those who stood outside or at the base of the old caste system. Buddha charged, "one does not become a Brahmin by long hair, or by family, or by birth. The one in whom there is truth and holiness is the Brahmin" (Dhammapada 393). With the old ordering of society breaking down, the new faith became attractive to the growing numbers of merchants, viewed as being well down the caste system. The Buddhist ethical precepts of sobriety and harmonious existence were also beneficial to their commercial interests and practices. A comparison may be made as to how within Christianity, Protestantism, by its emphasis on the similar values, appealed to the same class of people.[11]

It would be fair to say that the subversive wisdom of Jesus extends more overtly into the sociopolitical realm than does that of Buddha. The two figures were born into very different social strata, and this may be key to explaining this difference. Further, Buddha used his connections with the privileged to propagate his faith, whereas Jesus, whose main connections were with the Galilean peasantry, lacked such means. In addition to being a wisdom teacher, something he shared with Buddha, Jesus was also a social prophet calling for a radical reordering of society. The differences between the two come not only out of the different social classes into which they were born but also out of the religious background from which they come. While both Hinduism and Judaism developed strong hierarchies in terms of social classes and formulated theologies to justify such, particularly to do with the priesthood, Judaism contained within it something largely missing in Hinduism: a prophetic movement, offering a sharp social and faith critique of both the social and religious order. Jesus was influenced by and drew much from this prophetic movement. Over Jerusalem, remembering the martyred prophets, he exclaims, "O Jerusalem, Jerusalem, who kills the prophets and stones those sent to her" (Matt 23:37; Luke 13:34).

The difference in their stance toward the order into which they were born can be seen in the deaths of each. Buddha grows old in deepening wisdom, while Jesus is brutally executed by the authorities as a young man.

This does not mean that the teaching of the Buddha lacks political ramifications, for we have seen it clearly does. His teaching undermines the caste system, while creating a new social order in the sangha and among Buddhist laity. Again the concepts of anicca and anatta have strong social

---

11. This type of connection was extensively explored by Weber, *Protestantische Ethik*.

ramifications. Political movements, as we have seen, both for good and bad, have a base in Buddhism.

The distinction is more that Christianity, as with all the classical Western faiths, are at their heart political; faiths having their genesis in India, including Buddhism, are not. Solutions built around politics they hold to be illusionary, part of the deception of maya. The core image of each faith makes that clear.

While there are commonalities in the faiths there are also some very clear differences. The sharpest of these has to do with their cosmologies. Here there is a massive contrast. The cosmologies of Christianity and Buddhism, as well as being entirely different in terms of time and size, are also opposites in orientation.

Each is framed by the cultural milieu from which they arise, Buddhist conceptions arising out of a wider Indian cyclic understanding, while the Christian linear understanding comes directly out of Judaism, that in turn being framed by the wider lineal understandings of the Ancient Near East. Thus, within Christianity there is but one genesis of the universe, followed by a linear movement of history in which a unique drama of fall, redemption and culmination (eschaton) is played out, with the process being teleological in that it is oriented to an end. Within this movement the divine breaks in from time to time, that presence mainly confirmed in history, human affairs very much the focus. The most important intervention for the Christian is of course the incarnation of the divine into history in the person of Christ, claimed to be God himself, present in history upon earth.

We will be familiar with the controversies to do with such figures as Galileo, with the challenge he presented to the cosmology held by the church, due to its understanding of both the extent and geocentric understanding of the universe. Temporally, as calculated by biblical genealogies, the universe was held in the West to be but a few thousand years old. Spatially it was understood to be a geocentric three-story universe of very limited size consisting of earth, hell, and heaven, the latter being located spatially "above, out there," with hell understood to be below, with we, in our mortal existence, being in the middle. The Western belief as to the extent of the universe, both in size and age, in light of modern knowledge is almost quaint.

For the Buddhist, on the other hand, time moves in great cycles of tremendous length with historical events repeated in each succeeding eon. The scale of this Buddhist cosmology is truly immense, measured in kappa or kalpas, each being billions of years in length. The duration of each of these is likened to the time taken to wear away a great mountain by a person wiping a cloth upon it once every hundred years. In Mahayana the historical Buddha is understood as being only the latest of a vast array of Buddhas, gone before him over an immense time span. Gautama, it was claimed, had been preparing himself for his task since the time of his predecessor Dīpankara many aeons before. It is therefore, asserted that on the night of his enlightenment Gautama came to know all his predecessor Buddhas; their names, castes, and professions back to 91 eons, each eon being roughly equal to the span of the solar system (Majjhima Nikāya i. 483).

Given the enormity of the Buddhist cosmology the number of times kamma can be passed from one life form to another is stupendous with samsara, meaning "endless wandering," being seen for what it is.

The cyclical rise and fall of each cycle is linked in a cause and effect manner to the lives of humans present within each. We find this in a Buddhist creation myth, found in the Aggañña Sutta, which tells of how the inhabitants of a destroyed world cycle are born into a new one. Cycles come into being, rise, endure, and slowly disintegrate, before finally being destroyed in great cataclysmic events. They then emerge again as another eon commences. Those who populate these eons rise and diminish with the eon. Indeed, the cycle is driven by human action. In times of gathering greed and ignorance the cycle is in a downturn, while in the upturns in the cycle inhabitants possess a growing higher ethical nature, manifested in the size of their physical being.

Initially in the cycle upturn there is no sun or moon and therefore no time, with people being self-luminous, formless, and sexually undifferentiated. As the world system evolves these beings grow less ethereal and more physical, becoming ever more attached to the world as they begin to consume it. The "fall" in each cycle commences with the entry of tanha (desire) marked by rice eating, resulting in humans losing their ethereal self-luminosity. They develop instead solid bodies with sex-differentiation, along with sexual desire. The loss of human luminosity makes necessary the appearance of the sun and moon, and with these celestial objects comes time. With human beings, having become entirely physical, there is an increase in the need to consume, leading to ever heightening conflict. As people begin to acquire property, greed leads to stealing, this all driven by tanha. This division and argumentation leads to the need for a leader to keep the peace, with a king being elected to rule. Initially that rule is just and fair, but government, like all else in decline, becomes increasingly corrupt, with growing inequalities ever more prevalent within society. Finally, such leads to revolt, with resultant chaos and plunder. Piety is lost and irreligiosity spreads. Eventually, humans fall to a beastly state, living extremely short lives, until the descent cannot go deeper and the cycle turns. Goodness begins to increase, eventually leading to the birth of a sankka, a universal king who brings a reign of righteousness. This king, forgiving and compassionate, understands that punishing evil is ineffective and so chooses a better path wherein he facilitates capital to traders, provides land to farmers, proper wages to workers, and tax exemptions to the poor. The upturn finally results in the birth of a Buddha. That having happened the cycle then again begins to go into a long downturn as over time the memory and power of the teaching of the Buddha fades. The manner of human living then has cosmological effects. Some accounts inform us that the era of this Buddha's teachings is half over and that knowledge of the dhamma will diminish over the next 2,500 years.

The details of this enormous cosmology are mainly contained in stories concerning the first mythical king of the current eon, Mahasammata (the Great Elect).

This endless cycles of massive eons makes possible all to be saved.

The Buddha of the next cycle will be Maitreya. Now residing in Tusita (the fourth of the six Buddhist heavens), it is expected that he will make his appearance in some thirty thousand years. (Given that possibly the name is derived from mitra, meaning friend, there may be a connection to Mithraism). In Central Asia (Tibet and Mongolia) the inscription "come Maitreya, come" is often found. Such eschatological thinking is not something greatly stressed in Southeast Asia, however. While marginal in the East, eschatology is central to the faiths of the West: Judaism, Christianity, and Islam. In Christianity it is not another figure who will come but rather the now glorified Christ who will descend this time not in humility but as the triumphant one of power.

The massive Buddhist cosmology also shapes the realms of rebirth. There are five of these, though later a sixth, that of the giants, is later added. They are known as the bhavacakra, pictured on the dharmachakra and are often depicted in Buddhist art. The three upper realms are considered places of auspicious rebirth, while the three lower are understood to represent inauspicious abodes. The heavenly realm (Deva), that of the demigods (Asura), and the human realm (Manussa), represent favorable realms of rebirth, while an inauspicious rebirth leads one to be reborn into either the realms of the animals (Tira-acchana), the hungry ghosts (Preta), or into hell (Niraya). Each of these abodes have numerous realms within them.

The best one can achieve, short of entering nibbana, is to be reborn as a god in the heavenly realm. This highest realm, from the fifth century CE, was further divided into twenty-six levels, known as mansions, so that in all there are thirty-one realms for rebirth. Within these upper realms exist the gods from the Hindu tradition, most notably Indra and Brahma, each of whom play an important part in Buddhist literature. There is also "the heaven of the thirty-three," an abode ruled by King Sakka. These gods dwell on Mount Meru in a style resembling the gods of that other divine mountain,

Olympus in Greece. This mythical image of the divine mountain is a direct borrowing from the older Hindu faith. The greatest physical depiction of this mythical mountain with its surrounding waters is found in both Angkor Wat in Cambodia and Borobudur in Indonesia. These gods, though living in bliss, are still caught in the wheel of samsara so are clearly inferior to Buddha, indeed to any who have achieved nibbana. Often caught up in their bliss the gods neglect to practice the dhamma, thereby exhausting the good kamma which had led to their being reborn in such realm, leading them to be reborn in a lower realm. They then appear frequently on the earth, especially intent on listening to the Buddha, so to find nibbana. Also important are the "tusita" devas, those, including future Buddhas, awaiting their final rebirth on earth. Included in these is Maitreya.

The highest gods being so sublime and remote have little or no involvement in human affairs. The top five heavens, the Pure Abodes, being so distant from the earth, are reserved for those never returning to this realm. In the lower mansions are found the lesser gods or devas, often just reborn from the human state. Due to the good deeds and developed understanding they possess, these humans have been reborn as gods, enjoying blissful divine existence. Rising through the levels of the heavenly abodes the lifespan of the gods increases until it reaches billions of years. This, however, is marked by relativity so that for even the lower gods a human lifetime seems but a day.

Below the heavenly realms lies the abode of the demigods or Asuras. Their existence is almost as blissful as that of the gods but is marked by conflict both among themselves and also in fruitless warfare waged against the gods. Again we have a similarity to the gods of Olympus, forever in conflict.

The next level is the realm of humanity. Rebirth as a human being is not easy but is highly desirable, for though lower than the realms of the gods, it is from this level that one is most likely to achieve nibbana, given that life in the highest levels is so blissful, those resident there perceive little need to strive for it, while those in the realms below the human are too preoccupied with suffering to consider nibbana. Those at the human level suffer the vagaries of life, like those seen by Buddha, while with the charioteer. Witnessing such, they, like he, can be stimulated to seek nibbana as a solution to life's problems. Again, the middle way, between the opulent easy life of the gods and the suffering of those in the lower realms, is understood to be advantageous.

Below the human level is the level of the Titans: demonic, warlike beings, subject to violent impulses in their never satisfying grasping for power, that insatiable thirst making them the very opposite of the Buddhist ideal.

The realm below this is inhabited by ghosts, former human beings, who, having developed such strong attachments are bound to the earth. Their desires can never be satisfied, so they live continually frustrated. Often depicted as wraith-like creatures, they have enormous stomachs but tiny mouths, unable to take in the "food" to satisfy their greed. With the extreme tanha they accumulate they again stand as the antithesis of the Buddhist way.

Beneath this is the second lowest of the realms, that of the animals. Birth in this domain is particularly undesirable for here, being subject to base animal instinct, and with limited intelligence, one is unable to see the need or the means of escape from this state. Animals are also subject to enslavement and often death at the hands of human beings but also by other animals and so need live in constant fear. In such fear is no equanimity, so central to Buddhism.

At the lowest level are the hells, of which there are eighteen, Buddhist depictions of hell ranking alongside those of Christianity in their graphic depictions of torturous suffering. Thus, in popular Buddhist art we find figures boiled in oil or being dismembered limb by limb. Unlike the Christian hell however, the Buddhist hells are not places of finality. Release will occur when accumulated evil kamma has been burnt up. As such these hells align more with purgatory in some Christian understandings rather than the eternity and finality of the Christian hell. Within Buddhist cosmology there are also cold hells where punishment is by freezing rather than roasting.

Migration between the world systems is due to kamma with each system being replete with its own worlds, heavens, and hells.

The notion of the six realms with their thirty-one levels is accompanied by another view in which the Buddhist universe is divided into three spheres. The lowest of these spheres, that of the senses (kamavacara), includes all the spheres up to the sixth level of the heavens. Above is the sphere of pure form, rupavacara, a rarified spiritual state in which the gods communicate by telepathy. This extends up to the twenty-seventh level, beyond which is the highest level, the sphere of formlessness, arupavacara, a sublime state, in which beings exist as pure mental energy. In these upper four levels the gods perceive phenomena in increasingly subtle ways, from infinite space, infinite consciousness, nothingness, and finally to neither perception or non-perception, the last being the highest level into which anyone can be born. Buddha in his meditative practice prior to his enlightenment achieved both of these highest spheres. As amazing, however, as these states are, they are all still caught up with the creation of kamma, being bound therefore by samsara. Like Buddha, one must aim to move past even these to nibbana.

No such intricate description is given of heaven in the Christian tradition, though we get some passing references to different levels of heaven into which one may be birthed. The Gospel writer John writes, "in my Father's house are many mansions" (John 14:2), while Paul speaks on one, probably himself, caught up to the "third heaven" (2 Cor 12:2). In the second century CE Bishop Irenaeus of Lyon differentiated levels of heaven: "Those who are deemed worthy of an abode in heaven shall go there, others shall enjoy the delights of paradise, and others shall possess the splendor of the city; for everywhere the Savior shall be seen according as they who see Him shall be worthy" (Book 5, 36:1). Roman Catholics also have a realm of purgatory as a place for those dying still needing to purged of sin before entering heaven, while there was also limbo, as a place for unbaptized infants, only recently abolished. Given that in Christianity one does not go through multiple rebirths or incarnations, this aspect finds lesser emphasis than in Buddhism.

The interaction between the state of the universe and the actions of its inhabitants has implications for Buddhist ecological thinking. Given that the well-being of the universe is linked to the ethics of those living within, in that part of the cycle where ethical living dominates, the universe exists in a harmonious state, with the opposite applying in the downward part of the cycle. Likewise, Christianity has a strong ecological framework, found particularly in the bookends of its Scriptures. In them we find a cosmic harmony both in the beginning, in the opening chapters of Genesis, and likewise in the final chapters of the last book in the Christian Scriptures, Revelation. That harmony is even said to be founded in the person of the Christ, "the one in whom all creation is held together" (Col 1:16-17). As with Buddhism, in Christianity cosmic harmony is linked with ethical living, existing before sin enters the world, and again when evil is overthrown at the eschaton.

Both Buddhism and Christianity share in understanding that lying at the heart of them to be indefinable. The Buddhist nibanna and the Judeo-Christian God are beyond definition, each needing to be experienced rather than defined and controlled.

There is again a parallel in Jesus and Buddha both having divine status imputed to them, indeed in the case of Buddha, a status beyond divine. We can be almost certainly sure that neither claimed that status for themselves. Concerning Buddha, there is no credible suggestion that such status was claimed by himself or applied to him by his contemporaries, only being bestowed on him much later in Mahayana. Buddha himself had no desire for divine status, as such would not help him in achieving his goal, for gods, like humans, were caught in samsara. Divine status given to Buddha is still rejected by Theravada. Jesus' claiming of such would place him at such odds to his Jewish tradition, to be non-understandable.

The timing of this elevation for each is different. In the case of Jesus it was given him not long after his lifetime. Though Jesus is presented in John's Gospel as claiming divinity, biblical scholars are almost universal in seeing this as being John's understanding, rather than the actual preaching of Jesus. The Gospel of John is probably written around eighty years after Jesus' life, so in terms of such elevation it is very early. It stands at odds with how Jesus is presented in the other Gospels, where, as we have noted, Jesus' teaching is built not around himself but what he calls "the kingdom of God," placing him firmly in the Jewish tradition. The idea that someone from within the strict Jewish monotheist tradition could speak of themselves in the way Jesus is presented as doing in John's Gospel, while expecting a receptive hearing, is simply inconceivable. Elsewhere, as we have explored, elevation began with Paul, or even earlier, with Jesus being held to have a distinct ontological status, beyond the human. That elevation would be completed some three hundred years later in the Council of Nicaea.

While Buddha was given an elevated position in Theravada, he remained human. Not until the coming of Mahayana was he elevated to a distinct ontological status.

Even when given divine status by their traditions, both Buddha and the Christ fully retain their human status. Indeed, in Christianity the understanding of Christ as being fully human is held as a test of orthodoxy. The humanity of Buddha is most powerfully affirmed in Theravada, which makes no other claim of him than that he having established the path as an enlightened being has passed into nibbana. Even in Mahayana Buddha, though he acquires further status, still fully retains his human status as nirmanakaya.

The paths by which both Buddha and Christ were ascribed divinity share many commonalities. The esteemed status in which both became to be held is initially found retrospectively in the birth stories, each creatively constructed using myth and legend to make such status clear. Again, certain mythic motifs linked to that serving as core event for each, the enlightenment of Buddha and the death and resurrection of Christ, are clearly archetypal, indicating that these are later legendary appendages to each story, rather than having historical basis. In each instance we find incredible cosmic events present to show just how earth- (indeed cosmos-) shattering was each event.

In reality it is likely that both figures were first understood as great wisdom teachers, imparting wisdom beyond that of others, while also being viewed as workers of great miracles. From there elevation begins, much

quicker for Christ understood as the "son of man," an enigmatic figure having a variety of meanings but often linked to the apocalyptic judgment, then
becoming in turn Messiah (still understood as human) before elevation to
distinct ontological status, divine as "son of God." The ascension of Buddha, as we have seen, is slower and more disputed, for while the much later
Mahayana tradition views him, as we have seen, to be beyond even divinity,
Theravada, while ascribing special status to him, rejects the idea of divinity.

It is highly likely that neither Gotama nor Jesus would recognize themselves in this divine guise, for we know that in their historical forms both
strongly rejected such appellation. Buddha made it clear that the goal of
nibbana meant that one must aspire to go beyond the gods, while adjuring
people not to follow him but rather to find their own way to nibbana using
the teachings he gave. That Jesus would proclaim of himself that he was
divine is inconceivable in the strict monotheist Jewish context in which he
lived. Even if he understood himself as playing the role of Messiah, this was
still a human role, though divinely blessed.

As charged, that the elevation comes after each, attributed to them by
their followers, rather than being self-proclaimed, is I believe far preferable.
Self-attributed claims to divinity would make each into egotistical braggarts
of even dubious psychological state. On the other hand, such status being
attributed to them by others shows just how highly regarded both were
perceived.

BUDDHA'S TEACHING: AN ALTERNATE VIEW

As we have seen, with its depreciation of both the self and the world in
such concepts as anatta and anicca, along with its goal of eliminating desire, Buddhism has been often perceived as a negative faith, denying our
essential humanity, which it seemingly calls us to extinguish in its goal of
nibbana. Further, by such demands as the elimination of the self along with
any desire, it is charged it presents us with an impossible task. Tackling these
issues, Buddhist scholar David Brazier has presented another way of understanding Buddhism. He does so in his work *The Feeling Buddha*.[12] In the following I am essentially presenting a summary of his work, which deserves
to be read in full. Where I refer to connections with Jesus and Christianity
however, those are my own conclusions.

Brazier, radically reinterpreting Buddhism through the eyes of his own
faith experience, seeks to make it a far more positive faith, more amenable

12. Brazier, *Feeling Buddha*.

and understandable to our human condition. Of his work he notes, "the conclusions I have come to are far from orthodox."[13]

He commences by charging that the traditional view that the Buddha seeks to escape suffering is inadequate. "Generally, Buddhism is presented as a way to overcome suffering. It is formulated as a remedy to all the pain of life. This book does not present that way . . . affliction and trouble are essential as the grit is to the pearl."[14] Instead he claims Buddha's call is to embrace suffering, as it is precisely the grit which creates the beautiful pearl. A core image he uses is one common in the Indian tradition, the lotus, something of beauty, which grows out of often dirty swamps.

The traditional understanding of Buddhism he charges arises because of the long time between the life of Buddha and the time when the accounts were written. "There must have been a great deal of scope for distortion to enter the teaching over such a period."[15] The Buddha's life, rather than being one of absence from suffering, was deeply marked by acute suffering from the very beginning, with his mother dying while giving birth to him. As a child he again knew suffering, first when his cousin Devadatta killed a swan and again later in his experience of the ploughing ceremony while grieving the death of so many organisms in the turning of the earth. Later, just prior to his leaving the palace to seek enlightenment, he again experienced suffering in his journeys with the charioteer Channa. Following his leaving of the palace it was Buddha's deep entry into suffering from great hunger, during his time with the ascetics, which enabled him to experience the simple act, which was transformative for him, his receiving from the milkmaid Sujata milk meant for a sacred offering. It is not Buddha's flight from suffering but rather his ability to enter suffering—and to experience it profoundly—which acts as the stimulus for him to seek enlightenment. Suffering, rather than being absent from Gotama's journey, is instead the stimulus for that struggle for enlightenment.

Brazier reinterprets the heart of Buddhist belief, the Four Noble Truths, in a far more positive, what he calls a more realistic, manner. Of the first, concerning suffering (dukkha), he notes, as seen, it is impossible to escape suffering. Gotama attempted to do so but in doing so only suffered the more. Drawing from psychology, Brazier writes, to ignore or suppress suffering is destructive, for suffering is an integral part of life. The traditional interpretation sees suffering as arising out of our desires, yet clearly much of our suffering has nothing to do with desires. Loss, sickness, and death are

13. Brazier, *Feeling Buddha*, 25.
14. Brazier, *Feeling Buddha*, 11.
15. Brazier, *Feeling Buddha*, 24.

clearly not due to desires but are rather simply a part of living. Indeed, our maturation, our deepening of our humanity, is forged through suffering.

In the Judeo-Christian biblical story, we find something similar. The Adam and Eve cycle, commonly called the story of the fall, is not so much the fall into sin but more so the falling out of a primeval innocence. To become autonomous adults, it is essential to eat "the fruit of good and evil," for it is impossible to remain in some place of protected, naive, innocence, where suffering is unknown. Suffering is something which must necessarily be experienced if we are to ever mature and deepen as human beings. Being human beings, both Gotama and Jesus are no different, the suffering through which they pass serving as a necessary part of their journey to maturation and insight.

Indeed, given the deep compassion of both, it is likely the suffering each experienced surpassed that of others. It is precisely the depth at which they experience suffering which opens each to understand how the world is deeply pervaded with pain and make their different responses. By entering into suffering at profound levels both are able to also develop deep wells of compassion.

With Jesus we find him weeping over Jerusalem as he intensely contemplates the suffering which is soon to come to that city, while later, faced with his own agonizing death, he suffers sufficiently to sweat blood. Gotama suffers intensely, as we have just seen, over something which to others would be very minor, the suffering of organisms in the ploughing ceremony. He rejects absolutely his father's understanding that suffering is something to be hidden or avoided.

In the journey to become Buddha or Christ there is no way to avoid suffering. Rather it is suffering which frames and drives the journey. In the Gospels a short Greek word, "dei" ("it is necessary, cannot be avoided") is often applied to Jesus and the necessity of his suffering. So committed was Jesus to the path of suffering that the avoidance of such presented itself as the greatest and most subtle temptation. That same subtle temptation is present also in the account of the Buddha's enlightenment, where he is tempted by Mara to pass straight into nibbana, a place where there is no suffering. Like Jesus, Gotama rejects such devious temptation, choosing instead to remain upon the earth in embodied form, where we are told he suffered to his final day.

Brazier asserts the traditional explanation that the cause of suffering is desire is too simple in that it fails to explain much of suffering. The suffering we endure is not due just to psychological causes, arising out of attempts to hold on to things or experiences, but rather is a harsh part of our life experience which cannot be avoided. Sickness, aging, and simple misfortune cannot be attributed to desire, for they would occur even if all desire were eliminated. Buddha in the enlightened state experienced all of these. Most of what Buddha called dukkha is natural and inevitable. He himself, many years after his enlightenment, suffered the pains of food poisoning sufficient to perhaps kill him. Pain does not cease for Buddha with enlightenment but rather serves as something redemptive. Mahayana tells us Buddha's consciousness of suffering is what led him to choose to remain of the earth. It is suffering which motivates his ministry. As his compassion deepens we would expect Buddha's suffering to intensify. That certainly was the case with Jesus who, out of compassion, enters suffering, also understood to be redemptive, to its most extreme level. The path to redemption in both faiths is through the deep compassion associated with suffering.

Indeed, some suffering, especially that associated with grieving, may be healthy. If, for example, I do not suffer with a friend over the loss of their child, there is something psychologically unhealthy about me. Grieving in such an instance is not only healthy but is also deeply human. As well as being psychologically unhealthy for me, an inability to suffer in such instance would also hinder human community, in this case between myself and the person suffering. Deep empathy is essential for true human community. If we are unable to understand and enter another's suffering, we are much more likely to treat them and others pathologically. A life whereby we seek to escape from suffering is both unhealthy and unnatural. It may even show us to be narcissistic. Such avoidance of suffering represents the life that his father had planned for Gotama, a delusion he rejected. To genuinely feel is to endure one's own, but also to embrace another's, suffering.

Likewise, desire is something which cannot be eliminated. It was intensely present to Buddha, even in the moment of his enlightenment where it presents itself in all manner of visions or fantasies. It cannot be extinguished for such impulses naturally arise within us, and seeking to repress or to destroy them only causes them to become only more destructive as Buddha found during his time of strict asceticism. It is better to see Buddha as rejecting desire rather than impossibly trying to extinguish it.

Rather than attempting to flee those things which by desire bring suffering, one must comprehend their true nature and thus truly perceiving, not be defeated by them. In Buddha's enlightenment account this is exactly what happens. The desires are not eliminated but rather are transformed by correct insight. Thus, as each tempting desire approached him it was transformed into its truth. Arrows meant to kill become a rainbow or shower of petals, while the demonic army was turned to flowers. In the story the adversary, Mara, is not eliminated or avoided, for that is not possible, but is instead met. The goal of Buddha through his preparation, something he had been practicing numerous years, is to meet the adversary well, to be prepared and strong in his understanding. Buddhism is not about fleeing life but rather mastering it. Brazier quotes the Zen master Dogen (1200–52) who makes clear that enlightenment is not about the avoidance of things bringing suffering, such as life and death, but rather come to appreciate them for what they are. "The most important issue for Buddhists is how to get a completely clear appreciation of birth and death. Buddha (i.e., enlightenment) exists within birth and death. So, birth and death (as a problem) vanish. Birth and death (as reality) are nirvana. If you can see this, you will not seek nirvana by seeking to avoid birth and death. This is the way to be free from birth and death. This is the most important point in Buddhism.[16]

Jesus similarly knows he cannot avoid meeting the adversary and like Buddha meets him well-prepared. He readies himself during his time spent with John the Baptist, followed by his time of prayer and fasting in the desert. There, meeting the devil in deep internal struggle, he prepares and trains himself to meet the evil one, seeing him (with vidya) for what he truly is.

As we have seen suffering causes craving or thirst to arise (sumudaya). Brazier understands these passions as something natural rather than unnatural and in them lies no shame. Through our suffering, along with the desire it engenders, we mature and deepen. "If birth and death are Nirvana, then the passions that birth and death generate are the stuff of awakening."[17] The problems are not from our feelings and passions, but rather what we do with them. "Loss is dukkha. Grief is samudaya. It arises on the back of affliction, and we can do nothing to stop it without seriously psychologically and physically damaging ourselves."[18] Suffering, and the emotions it engenders, are a part of living, to be embraced rather than fled, such flight after all being impossible, with any attempt to do so being destructive.

A goal central to Buddhism is the finding of happiness through equanimity. It is not likely a person will achieve this happiness in the impossible pursuit of the avoidance of suffering. Rather they will achieve such through their preparedness to face suffering and yet still be able to find contentment and happiness. We know we experience loss, sickness, and ultimately death, all aspects of suffering, yet we are still able to attain the happiness found in equanimity. These things, which inevitably occur need be accepted, with happiness still being found rather than being hopelessly fought.

Further, Brazier charges, the classic understanding of suffering being due to kamma has ethical problems. It is rather unfair for a person's suffering

16. Brazier, *Feeling Buddha*, 55.

17. Brazier, *Feeling Buddha*, 63.

18. Brazier, *Feeling Buddha*, 66.

to be attributable to the actions of another preceding them. In such there is no natural justice. It also presents an out from taking self responsibility for one can attribute their wrongdoing to kamma and not take responsibility for it.

The third noble truth informs us that desire (tanha) creates nirodha, a fire which burns within us. This fire is traditionally understood in Buddhism as something negative, as fires of passion needing to be doused. Brazier points out that the etymology of the word is crucial. "Ni" means down, while "rodha" is an earthen bank. The earthen bank shields from the fire, while also directing it in a certain direction. Fire, while it may be destructive, may also be something serving to refine and purify. Rather than attempting to reject or douse the fire, we need to be aware of it, consciously directing it so to achieve refining and purifying. The power of fire is dangerous and destructive, something which I well know as an Australian, but that power directed is an energy of transformation. Thus, in Australia there is a growing awareness of how Aboriginal people used and directed fire to regenerate the land.

When it comes to refining, it is the directed fire, generating most heat, which does the most work. The directed fire is the fire used in transformation, with the deep transformation called for by Buddha being achieved by use of such fire. Elsewhere the Greeks, knowing fire's destructive power when not in the right hands, punish Prometheus for stealing it. Buddha however, having developed the capacity to direct it, makes highly constructive use of the energy which fire contains.

Buddha never called us not to have passion, as such is essential to compassion and growth. To cut off feeling is asceticism, while to abandon oneself to feeling is indulgence. As we have seen in the account of his life, rejecting both, Buddha chose the middle way. "Dharma is not about destroying the energy of our passion, nor repression. It is rather about the conscious direction of the energy. It is about harnessing, not destroying.[19] Rather than calling for its extinguishment, Brazier centers on feeling and passion. Any attempt to extinguish these, he charges, is impossible and destructive. Rather their energy, like that of fire, must be harnessed and directed and as such is immensely powerful. Such directed energy can bring profound transformation, exposing the delusion of maya by cutting through to the truth of the dharma. Far from being negative, dukkha has a positive role, providing the fuel that heats the fire without which the spiritual life would remain feeble. "This would suggest that the great souls were not necessarily those who had reduced their suffering, nor those whose passions

19. Brazier, Feeling Buddha, 93.

had abated. Great souls would be people who had suffered and, in many cases continued to suffer, and who had great passion but had that passion controlled and directed to a worthwhile end.[20] Such not only describes Buddha but also Christ.

The true spiritual hero, rather than fleeing the world, in a vain attempt to avoid suffering, is instead the one who in passion great struggles with the world from within the world. This enables us to also best understand the other figure of whom we are speaking. Jesus was one full of passion, a passion for justice, including even fiery anger, which brought him into conflict with the authorities. That passion is seen in his clearing the temple of money changers, and again later, as he endured that death he was to scream out to God in a sense of desolation, "My God, why have you forsaken me?" For one who felt such deep affinity with God this cry represented an intense suffering of abandonment. There could be no greater passion than that exhibited by Jesus, hence his death being connoted as "the passion." Jesus knows he cannot avoid suffering, given his passion for what he called the "kingdom of God," the reign of righteous justice. In the passion, Jesus' passion is powerful and strongly directed. The understanding given by Brazier of Buddha certainly enables the Buddhist to have a better appreciation of Christ, for the traditional understanding of Buddhism makes Christ at best non-understandable, or at worst one who fails, being caught in passion and suffering.

Brazier opens up, I believe, a more coherent way to understand Buddhism. It is a way more in alignment with our human experience, while offering a healthier psychological dynamic. The greater realism of his presentation is not only more authentic to our human experience of suffering but greatly facilitates dialogue between Buddhists and Christians, by allowing each to enter that dialogue around suffering, and the means to transcend that suffering, while using it to generate deep compassion.

THE TEACHINGS: JESUS

We now turn to Jesus and his teachings, along with those of the religion bearing his name: Christianity.

We cannot understand Jesus and his teaching, however, without knowing the Jewish framework which so shaped him, so it is to that faith we shall first turn.

We have seen that at the heart of Judaism lies the exodus, an event still celebrated in the greatest of all Jewish festivals, Pesach or Passover. It is

20. Brazier, *Feeling Buddha*, 102.

good to again remind ourselves of its significance. In the exodus account we are told of how the Jewish people, long resident in Egypt, had fallen from their original prestigious status, to being bond servants, mistreated by their Egyptian overlords. One day Moses, on the run after killing an Egyptian overseer mistreating a fellow Hebrew in a fit of anger, has a revelation of a burning bush, "burning but not consumed," from which he hears the voice of the divine. This revelatory encounter is detailed in the key text (Exod 3:1–4:17). Upon perceiving God in the burning bush, Moses enquires as to the divine name and is informed that the divine name is "I am who I am" or "I am becoming who I am becoming." This deliberately undefinable name is etymologically linked to the name by which they are to know God but never utter, Yahweh. Later in this revelatory encounter Moses is informed that the divine, not known by name, will be understood in the divine actions to follow. Those actions are the freeing of Moses' people in the exodus, the journey from slavery to freedom in a promised land.

As seen in our examining the name of Jesus, names were deeply important in the ancient world, a means to define a person, giving some control, exercised through definition over the person with whom one is communicating. The God of the Hebrew people could not however be captured nor contained, much less controlled, by a name. The Hebraic God was not static, a supporter of some existing divine order, known by name and contained in the temple, but rather one whose significance breaks all those limitations. For like reason there was also a prohibition on the imaging of God, that being part of the Decalogue or Ten Commandments.

The ethical and political dimension, in Judaism and Christianity, and we may add Islam, finds its origin in the Exodus events. The Jewish God, unlike the gods of Egypt, could not be understood in mythic cultic-ritual terms, carried out to ensure the stability of the supposedly divinely sanctioned existing order against chaos. A god, understood in such mythic cultic-ritual terms, is named, imaged, and defined, but the God of Israel was subject to none of these.

Such is the transcendence of God in Jewish understanding, the divine name can never be said, nor the divine image be made. For God to have a name or be imaged would be to contain the divine within human categories. To this day many Jews refuse to write even the word "God," choosing instead to write "G-d."

The divine, beyond the mythic and associated cultic ritual, instead calling a for an ethical response centered on the sociopolitical, lay at the core of a long prophetic tradition. The contrast between the two understandings of the divine is most pointedly picked up in Amos, the eighth century BCE prophet who, in the context of the increasing inequalities associated with nascent urbanization, cries out, "I hate, I despise your feasts, and I take no delight in your solemn assemblies. Even though you offer me your burnt offerings and cereal offerings, I will not accept them, and the peace offerings of your fatted beasts, I will not look upon. Take away from me the noise of your songs; to the melody of your harps, I will not listen. But let justice roll down like waters, and righteousness like an ever-flowing stream" (Amos 5:21-24). In like manner, rejecting the automatic efficacy of cultic sacrifice, the seventh century BCE prophet Micah writes, "Shall I come before God with burnt offerings, with calves a year old? Will the Lord be pleased with thousands of rams, with ten thousands of rivers of oil. Shall I give my first-born for my transgression, the fruit of my body for the sin of my soul? He has showed you, O man, what is good; and what does the Lord require of you but to do justice, and to love kindness, and to walk humbly with your God?" (Mic 6:6-8).

Jesus stands in this prophetic tradition. The service of the divine was not to be limited to the temple cult but rather was something which effected how a person interacted with the world. For Jesus, and the prophets preceding him, the cult was often a major source of injustice, as it could easily identify God with an unjust order, while the nature of its injunctions made it impossible for many, especially the poor, to observe. This different comprehension of faith placed the religion of Jesus, along with his Jewish prophetic tradition, at odds with Rome. For that both faiths suffered greatly at the empire's hands.

This understanding of the divine is radically different to that prevalent in the ancient world, indeed in the modern world, where the divine was, and still is, used to sanction and sanctify the existing order. "God, king and country," as seen on many war memorials, being understood essentially as synonymous, with our way held to represent the holy will. That certainly was the case in Egypt, where the divine, whether as Amun, Horus or Osiris, was understood to be present in the Pharaoh's well-being and reign.

At the core of Egyptian understanding was the idea that the forces of chaos were always threatening the divinely inaugurated order known as Ma'at. The role of the Pharaoh was to ensure that order, understood to be true and harmonious, prevailed. This was closely linked to the regularity of the Nile flood, something essential to the survival of Egypt. If the annual flood was too small there would be drought, too large and destructive flooding would ensue. Either way crops would fail and there would be hunger in the land. This struggle is the basis of the story lying at the heart of Egyptian mythology, the struggle between Osiris and his wife, Isis, representing sacred order, and Set and Nephthys, symbolic of chaotic forces. Order was clearly important to the Egyptians, and their religion was built around both the maintenance of that order and its justification, with the Pharaoh, representing, or even being divine, being integral to that.

The above Jewish understanding of the divine broke violently into that Egyptian understanding. The stable kingdom is thrown into chaos by a slave rebellion and flight, with God understood being present in this disruptive action. This radically different conception was something new, not only for Egypt, but also for the Hebrews. Prior to that they had shared an understanding of the divine, common in the Ancient Near East, as one ensuring order, particularly against the primal waters of chaos, forever threatening to engulf the earth. Like many of the surrounding cultures, Israel believed there had once been a mighty flood, and a repeat of such catastrophe constantly threatened to overwhelm the created order. God was responsible, they held, for sustaining that order.

In the exodus however, a radically new understanding emerges with a God bearing a different name. The divine, rather than serving to justify a "divinely sanctioned order," is instead identified with the disruption of those who cry for liberation from an order understood as oppressive. Rather than the God of order, the divine becomes identified with its disruption.

Right through the Jewish Scriptures there exists a tension between those identifying the divine in the traditional style of giving order and those believing God was calling for the breaking of such, to be replaced by something more just. The former view is most identified with the priestly establishment serving the cult and ritual of the temple, while the latter is present in the prophets.

As we have seen, the idea of divine reign, the shalom, is crucial to Jewish understanding. This was marked by right relations, not only between a person and the divine, but also with others, indeed, with the entire creation, the latter crucial in our age when so much damage is being done to the ecosphere. An evocative image of that ecological wholeness is one of the wolf dwelling with the lamb, the leopard with the goat, while the calf and the lion grow fat together" (Isa 11:6).

The Law or Torah, around which the Jewish cult is built, is filled with injunctions to live justly with each other. In a society, like many in antiquity, built around slavery, there were provisions in the Torah placing limits on the use of slaves. These were codified in the Sabbatical (Shmita) and the Jubilee (Yovel). The first, reoccurring every seventh year, mandated the release of slaves, as well as forgiveness of all debts, along with the resting of the land, left fallow. "For six years you are to sow your land and to gather in its produce, but in the seventh, you are to let it go and to let it be, that the needy of your people may eat, and what remains, the wildlife of the field shall eat. Do thus with your vineyard, with your olive grove" (Exod 23:10-11). In such command ecological concern for the land and other species, along with the concern for human justice, is clearly present. Of the Sabbatical we also read,

> Every creditor shall remit their authority over what they have lent another; they shall not press them or their relative, for the Lord's remission has been proclaimed . . . If your fellow Hebrew will be sold to you, they shall serve you for six years, and in the seventh year you shall send them away from you free. But when you send them away free, you shall not send them away empty-handed. Adorn them generously from our flocks, from your threshing floor, and from your wine-cellar, as the Lord, your God, has blessed you, so shall you give them. You shall remember that you were a slave in the land of Egypt and the Lord, your God, redeemed you; therefore, I command you regarding this matter today. (Deut 15:1–2; 12–15)

This Sabbatical rest is linked with the better-known Sabbath rest, one occurring every seven years, the other each seven days.

In the book of Leviticus, after again reading about the Sabbatical year, we are given details of the Jubilee.

> "You shall count for yourself seven cycles of sabbatical years, seven years seven times; the years of the seven cycles of sabbatical years shall be for you forty-nine years. You shall sound a broken blast of the shofar, in the seventh month, on the tenth of that month; on the Day of Atonement, you shall sound the shofar throughout your land. You shall sanctify the fiftieth year and proclaim freedom throughout the land for all its inhabitants; it shall be the Jubilee Year for you, you shall return each to their ancestral heritage, and you shall return each person to their family" (Lev 25:8–17).

The Jubilee is particularly radical in its intent. By its injunctions all land, such being almost the exclusive source of wealth at that time, no matter how acquired, was to be returned to its original holders. Though views vary as to the level of observance of the Jubilee, it represents an ideal by which the Jewish people defined themselves. One is challenged to think what such an occasion would mean in many lands such as mine, taken by colonial conquest!

There were many other injunctions in the Torah likewise directed to ensuring justice. Harvests were not to be gleamed to the very edges, being left instead for the poor, while a field could only be harvested once, that missed being left for those in need. That there were poor shows that some provisions within the Torah, meant to prevent such, were not always strictly observed. These laws had as a rationale that those now called to observe them had themselves once been the oppressed and marginalized. Thus, they were constrained in their treatment of slaves, for they themselves had been slaves in Egypt. Likewise, they must deal fairly with "the foreigners in the land" for they had themselves been at one time foreigners in bondage.

Christians often misconceive the Jewish law to be a burden oppressing those to whom it applied. That is far from true. For the Jews the Torah, with its goal directed toward the holistic justice of the shalom, was, and still is, something understood as liberating.

The idea of shalom, at the heart of the Hebrew Scriptures, is central to the Torah and also motivated the prophets, from whom we frequently find a thundering rage against injustice and a religious piety which avoids social responsibility, as in the passages already quoted. Last, the third component of the Jewish Scriptures, the wisdom writings or Ketuvim, detail that style of living most conducive to creating and maintaining the shalom.

The expectation of a promised messiah, who would act as the harbinger of the shalom, came to intensify within Judaism. Each king, it was hoped in ancient Israel, would act as messiah. The messiah was understood as the anointed one, and to that end each king at the commencement of their reign was anointed in that hope. With the ongoing failure of kings to live up to the Davidic expectation, he being viewed as the greatest of all kings, the vision was increasingly pushed to the future, the hope being that someday a king would come to bring that reign. There was nothing however, in the Jewish tradition which indicated that the messiah would be divine. Rather they would be a person lifted by God to carry out the divine task. Christians, though not Jews, believe that in Jesus the messiah has come.

In Jesus we find one fulfilling the messianic role in announcing and enacting the reign of God. As we have found, only by acknowledging just how central to Jesus was the idea of the reign of God can we make sense of Jesus' public life from its beginnings in his association with John the Baptist, through to ending, death as a subversive at the hands of Rome.

Jesus' ministry is totally directed to this "kingdom of God" (the Jewishness of the Gospel of Matthew, meaning it has a reticence to use the divine name, has Jesus preach the "kingdom of heaven"). We find often in his parables, "the kingdom of God is like . . ." whereupon follows a story directed to explaining what that reign looked like, as fulfillment of the divine concern for justice and compassion. He often contrasts the vision of the divine reign with that currently pertaining. Not only Jesus' teachings, but also both his miracles and healings, are likewise directed to the shalom.

These prefigure the coming of the shalom when all will be in harmony. Thus so the feeding of the five thousand anticipates the time when one is no longer limited to praying for "daily bread," as bread will be sufficient, even abundant, justly distributed for all to have their fill. This action symbolizes a great feast, a common image for the reign of God. Again in his miracle at Cana, where he turns the water to wine, there is an anticipation of such feast.

Likewise, Jesus' healings prefigure the reign of God. Disease in the ancient world did not just have a physical aspect but also a social and religious component, the last two being totally intertwined with the physical. Within Judaism disease was held to be the result either of one's own sin or that of a forebear, therefore punishment sent by God. If the disease was chronic a person was cast out of the "holy community." This was done to protect the community from being tainted, sin being understood as both a contaminant and contagious. We may well be familiar with how leprous communities at this time were forced to live separate, needing to give warning on approach. Jesus rejected this judgment associated with disease. When Jesus, who is often viewed primarily as a healer, healed he not only was not only curing a physical ailment but also removing the stigma of divine approbation, believed to have been directed at that person, making it possible for them to re-enter the community. His healing operated on three levels, restoring a person to physical well-being, to the community, and it was believed also to God.

Jesus' concern for justice, his fearless denunciation of wrong, his special concern for the poor and marginalized, his miracles and healings are all directed by his commitment to the shalom, the divine reign of harmony and peace. As such Jesus is classically Jewish, standing in a long line of prophets who, like him shared a concern for the justice of the reign of God.

Jesus' ministry also consistently directed toward the restoring of the outsider to the community, that restoration often operating as judgment against those who had cast them out due to concerns for holiness. Hence his harsh words to "the religious."

The divine order of the "shalom" is understood by Jesus to present a direct challenge to the existing (unjust) order. We find the challenge which Jesus presents to that order retrospectively projected by his followers, even to his birth, where a fearful Herod, hoping to kill Jesus, directs a slaughter of the innocents, an episode, as found, to be without historical basis. The important thing however, is in just how strongly was Jesus understood by his followers as diametrically opposed to the order, that opposition is projected even to his birth.

Luke even projects the threat presented by Jesus to be present from before his birth by having Mary proclaim of the one she is to bear, in what was to become the Magnificat: "He has cast down the kings from their thrones

. . . and sent the rich empty away. To their place he has raised the poor"
(Luke 1:46–55).

Luke also has Jesus inaugurate his ministry with the words, "The Spirit
of the Lord is upon me, because he has anointed me to preach good news to
the poor. He has sent me to proclaim release to the captives and recovering
of sight to the blind, to set at liberty those who are oppressed, to proclaim
the acceptable year of the Lord" (Luke 4:18–19). The acceptable year of the
Lord was the year of the Jubilee.

As we have seen, Jesus' ministry begins with John the Baptist. So close
was the connection between the two, the biblical writers would have us
believe they were relatives. Jesus, we are informed, was baptized by John,
something which would suggest John being the superior figure, a source
of embarrassment for the infant Jesus movement, but so well-known they
couldn't simply erase it. Instead, as found, varying explanations are given for
it in the Gospels. Because of the embarrassment it caused there can be little
doubt as to the veracity of this event. Many viewed John as the Messiah, the
one promised, to save the people.

The short summary given in the Gospels of John the Baptist's teachings suffices to make clear the subversive nature of his message. He is cast as
a fiery apocalyptic figure, calling for repentance and renewal, proclaiming a
harsh judgment against a society perceived as so unjust it need make a radical repentance to avoid the judgment of God. John particularly admonished
those, nearly always the wealthy and powerful, who had broken the shalom.
Such criticism, directed toward Herod Antipas, would lead to his beheading.
By such the baptist stood firmly in the line of the Jewish prophetic tradition.

We may miss, however, the covert (for us) message given in the baptist's location. He baptizes on the Jordan, a place identified with Joshua's
crossing into the Holy Land, the culmination of the journey of liberation
from slavery in Egypt. Later the Jordan was again the crossing point for
those returning to Israel from the Babylonian captivity. The thousands, we
are told, who went out to John understood the significance of what he was
doing, as in baptism symbolically he had them again pass through the waters. That symbolism of both place and action, while not clear to us, was so
to both friends and enemies. Jesus, by his consent to be baptized by John
in the Jordan River, chose to identify himself closely with this subversive
action by John. That "Jesus" is the Hellenized form of the name Joshua
(meaning "God saves"), the one who had first led the Hebrews through the
Jordan, makes very clear this identification with John and his message. Jesus
continues to be presented as being intimately linked to the baptist, sharing
many of his understandings, though not all.

The subversive nature of Jesus' ministry is such that even enemies, the Herodians and Pharisees, are said to be drawn in mutual cause to kill him. We find this unlikely alliance from the commencement of Jesus' ministry given in the earliest of the Gospels, that of Mark (Mark 3:6). Again, this is almost certainly a projection back from later in his ministry, but clearly the intent by such is to demonstrate just how radical was the ministry of Jesus, in that it draws enemies together in mutual opposition to him.

Jesus' radical challenge to the system, both political and religious, is perhaps most starkly seen in his encounter with "the rich young ruler." To this man, who believes his upright religious observance and respectable ethics are sufficient, Jesus says, "go sell all you have and give the money to the poor" (Mark 10:21). His accumulation of wealth breaks the shalom, and no amount of religious cultic duties will cover such.

In much of Jesus' ministry the whiff of sedition is never too distant. Asked whether it was right to pay taxes to Rome, Jesus, far too quick on his feet to fall for the trap being set, inquires as to whose head is on the coinage, and upon being told "Caesar's" answers, "pay to Caesar what is Caesar's and to God what is God's," the implication being, as we saw, given the theological understanding shared by both him and his inquisitors, that Caesar was owed nothing, for all was owed to God.

The overturning of the tables of the temple money changers was clearly highly subversive, especially when this action took place in the lead up to Passover, the liberation celebration. Jesus' actions would clearly be understood as an attack on another empire, this time not Egypt but rather Rome and its collaborators.

So popular was the insurrectionist movement associated with Jesus, we read a few times that the authorities are hesitant to arrest him, lest there be a rebellion. They thus wait an opportune moment to do so, when in the garden of Gethsemane he is away from the crowds. Even at his arrest swords are present, Peter using his to cut off the ear of the high priest's servant. Such sword carrying is understandable for at one stage Jesus had advised his followers, "and let him who has no sword sell his cloak and buy one" (Luke 22:36). Even if such use of the word is held to be more metaphorical it is clear that Jesus in his zeal for justice was not always as pacific as one may be inclined or like to think.

The prayer, so associated with Jesus, becomes known as the Lord's Prayer and contains the line "your kingdom come, your will be done," a clear petition for the shalom. It is followed by a line which makes clear the locale of that reign, "on earth as it is in heaven." With such a reign there would be no need to pray for "daily bread" (bread only for a day being the best one could hope for under the prevailing exploitative system), for "bread" would be plentiful for all. In that prayer we next find this reign shall be marked by mutual forgiveness, including that of debt, along with deliverance from evil. Both Matthew and Luke in their versions of the prayer emphasize the primacy of the issue of debt as that which is to be forgiven, indebtedness increasingly being the experience for many under the Roman occupation. English translations hide this by speaking of "forgive us our sins, as we forgive those who sin against us." With the issue of debt, we are to think again of the Sabbatical and Jubilee. The yearning, so evident in this prayer, shows that in Jesus' judgment the divine order was certainly not present under the alliance between Rome and the Jewish establishment.

This issue of debt framed much of Jesus' ministry. It features in numerous of his parables, the best-known being the prodigal son. In that story we find the humiliation of indebtedness, with the son, having fallen into the debt, needing to tend ritually impure pigs, even forced to eat their swill.

Jesus' preaching and actions concerning the reign of God were all the more seditious when one considers the political context in which such took place. Rome held there was only one reign, that of the empire, and one lord, Caesar. While there were other kings, such as Herod, they only held power as vassals at the behest of Rome, to where all roads led, and in which all power resided. Annually, all within the empire were compelled to make an offering to Caesar, ascribing divine title to him. That pious Jews and Christians refused to do so, viewing such as blasphemy, led to fierce persecution.

Jesus proclaimed that God, not Caesar, was supreme lord, and that one's allegiance ought be directed toward the reign of God, rather than Caesar. Later, the followers of Jesus would directly cast themselves in the face of Roman wrath with such proclamation as "Jesus (not Caesar) is lord," and by their giving higher loyalty to God's reign rather than that of Rome. Those terms, like "Lord" and "Son of God," which we commonly think as being invented by the early followers of Jesus, as attributes offered to him, were anything but. Originally they were ascriptions used by Rome for Caesar. Christian use of them, ascribing them instead to Jesus, represented a direct challenge to how they ought be used. Both Jesus and the movement named after him clearly cast themselves as a seditious challenge to Roman authority.

Rome itself was happy to accept all sorts of religions and their temples, even in the capital itself, where such proliferated, so long as they restricted themselves to cult and ritual, not questioning the premise that Rome was supreme. Both Jews and Christians refused to subscribe to this accommodation, holding God to be supreme as lord of history, to whom allegiance must be pledged. Each represented movements not fitting the Roman schema of things.

The above allows us to make much better sense of the Passion narratives, which we have explored. These lie at the heart of the Christian tradition, and given the commonalities contained within each, it would seem they were written early. Even a cursory reading of these accounts makes clear just what were the charges against Jesus. They are based around his subversive preaching and enactment of the reign of God, a thing clearly at odds with Roman power. "Are you the king of the Jews?" Pilate inquires of Jesus and, not put off by his mute response, concludes that Jesus is guilty of being so, thus orders him to death by a manner, crucifixion, reserved for such rebels. To make that clear he has the charge written and placed above Jesus' head, "Jesus, King of the Jews," in three languages no less, so that none could misunderstand why he was being executed.

Much of Christianity has, despite the life and ministry of Jesus, become otherworldly. It centers around "eternal life" as life beyond death. Yet, this idea of life beyond the grave was not even universally accepted within the Judaism at the time of Jesus. We read in the Christian Scriptures of how, in their debate with Jesus, the Sadducees did not believe in it (Mark 12:18; Acts 23:8). This disbelief is understandable as such belief finds no place in that central to Judaism, the Torah. The idea of resurrection was quite new to Judaism and certainly was not universally held.

It is enlightening to reflect on how concerns for life beyond the grave arose within Judaism. Traditionally the afterlife in Judaism was conceived as being a nebulous shadowy existence in Sheol, an undesirable abode, where one was cut off from God and the divine favor. Even such a shadowy afterlife however, was peripheral to the faith.

Ideas of resurrection as reward entered late into Judaism as a response to the severe oppression of the Seleucids in the second century BCE. In face of such, comfortable theologies simplistically asserting that the righteous would be rewarded while the evil suffered were found to be hopelessly unreflective of a reality which was starkly different. Under the Seleucids the pious and righteous were suffering intensely, enduring the most horrific of tortures, there even being accounts of victims skinned alive, among other gruesome tortures. The idea of the goodness of God and graceful reward for the righteous still needed to be preserved however, and this was achieved by pushing that reward off to another world. It is possible that the idea of resurrection for the Jews had its genesis in Zoroastrianism, the faith of the Persian empire, the empire responsible for freeing the Hebrews from their Babylonian captivity, though by the second century BCE that time was three centuries past.

It is this context of the entry into Judaism of the belief in resurrection, however, which is important. That timing serves to show that those whose concern for the shalom is such that it causes them great suffering will be rewarded. The idea of life beyond the grave, far from being otherworldly, is a direct response to a sociopolitical reality of oppression.

Even with this new emphasis concern for the afterlife was still not the prime concern of faith. Although Jewish faith increasingly centered on hope for the Messiah who would bring earthly liberation, one in the meantime was to keep to the law, the 613 statutes making up the mitzvah (the commandments of the Jewish law). Even to this day Judaism built on the halakha (the wider Jewish law codices) does not show a great concern for the afterlife.

Of course, the vision of the coming reign of God, expected by Jesus, along with many of his contemporaries, never eventuated. As time passed it became increasingly clear there was a need to recast Jesus in a manner different from that of being an eschatological prophet announcing a climatic event, bringing a new epoch. The message concerning him was thus recast in a direction in which his death and resurrection became central. The actual faith of Jesus directed toward the reign of God, quickly became quite peripheral as belief became centered on Jesus, especially what his death and resurrection meant for those following him. Jesus, the Jewish Messiah, was increasingly recast as universal savior. The victory he brings becomes not a transformed order, but instead one enabling his followers to pass through death, just as he himself had done. The Hebrew term messiah is translated into Greek as Christ and accrues a whole range of more cosmic meanings.

Much of the change in understanding the significance of Jesus was driven by trying to make sense of his death. The execution of Jesus was initially viewed as shameful by his followers. Their Hebrew tradition, as found, made clear, "anyone hung upon a tree is under God's curse" (Deut 21:23). Rome had summarily dealt with any threat posed by this Galilean subversive so that the ministry and mission of Jesus, along with his followers, had surely ended in failure and shame. In fear, confusion, and disillusionment those followers had fled.

Yet seemingly not long after Jesus' demise, on the third day, we are told in the Gospels, though this may be more a parallel with Jonah's spending three days in the belly of a fish, with the actual process being longer, the followers of Jesus commence to change their understanding. They begin making the momentous claim that he had risen from the dead. His death, which had been his greatest shame and failure, was now turned into being the portal of his triumph. Jesus' disciples turn from frightened timidity to become fearless advocates of the one they follow, claiming he had overcome his shameful death, to now be gloriously resurrected into new life.

Perfunctory dismissal of this belief as mere wishful thinking or hysteria, as I have examined, is far too simple.[21]

This process of redefining Jesus begins to take place at the earliest level in the Christian Scriptures. Again, we need remind ourselves that the earliest writings within the Christian scriptures are not the Gospels, but rather those of Paul, thought to date from the early to mid-fifties of the first century, only some 25 years after the time of Jesus. These Pauline writings are a series of letters he writes to various infant churches within the Roman Empire. In them Jesus' death and resurrection are central, with Paul developing a whole theology around the idea that Jesus' overcoming death enables us to do likewise, if we pledge our allegiance to him. We then enter a paradise, not on earth in this life but post-death in a non-terrestrial heaven, though we do experience a foretaste of that in the present by living 'in Christ' in the Christian community.

Paul's corpus exhibits no interest in the Jesus of history, not even the putative historical Jesus the Gospels will later present. Some of this may be due to Paul almost certainly never meeting Jesus, but there does seem to be a conscious choice by him not to refer to events and teachings in Jesus' life. Even when he adjures his followers to act in a certain manner Paul never appeals to Jesus' teachings or actions to support his case. Paul's Jesus is the already the risen Christ of faith who has moved from being the expected Messiah of the Jews bringing the shalom to one more approximating the universal savior figure in the classical religious forms of the wider Roman Empire, a salvation figure offering life in another realm. Thus the concern for the afterlife, only peripheral to the Jewish tradition, takes center stage very early within Christianity.

This changed interpretation of Jesus we would expect from Paul because being the "apostle to the gentiles," he sought to free the significance of Jesus from confined Jewish categories to those which made sense in the wider domain. Casting the faith in a way that would have more appeal in the wider gentile world, Paul presents it in a more spiritualized, otherworldly manner. This clearly represented a radical change from the teachings of Jesus. It may be thus summarized: Jesus, the preacher of the reign of God, becomes now the one preached.

As Christian faith became ever more centered on Jesus his ontological status began to change, until in the fourth century, Jesus formally was given elevated status as second part of the Trinity, understood as both fully human and divine. That represented the culmination of something which

21. Queripel, *On the Third Day.*

in practice had increasingly become established, elevation beginning in the Christian Scriptures at the earliest level of the tradition.

The elevation is especially present in the Gospel of John, where John has Jesus making such statements as "I am the way, the truth and the life. No one comes to the father, but through me" (John 14:6). Jesus constantly refers to himself in these "I am" terms. "I am the door." "I am the life." "I am the shepherd." "I am the resurrection." This "I am" circumlocution is particularly poignant. As we have seen, these words were those received by Moses in his inquiry as to the divine name. By having Jesus use such language John is having him claim divine status for himself.

As already stated it is almost certain that Jesus never made any of these statements which have become the basis for the massive ontological claims made concerning him. Indeed it is inconceivable that anyone could have made such claim within a Jewish context and still be heard, indeed, even to survive, the common policy for such blasphemers being death by stoning. Further, if Jesus had made such a statement, he would hardly appear to be an attractive figure. As charged, of one claiming divinity for themselves we are inclined to view them most dubiously, usually dismissing them as braggarts of uncertain mental stability. The case is however vastly different if others come to that conclusion about him, especially those writing so soon after him. The same holds for Buddha.

We can conclude then that this centering of Christianity to being faith in an elevated Jesus rather than that faith in God's reign held by Jesus is probably extremely early, with Jesus' actual teaching concerning the reign of God becoming increasingly peripheral. The original "shalom" message of Jesus survives in Gospel passages concerning his teaching and most strongly theologically in the book of James, that writing coming out of a community based in Jerusalem, linked with the brother of Jesus.

This rapid change is quite distinct from Buddhism, where the teachings of the Buddha form the core of the faith, something which remains the case even in Mahayana, despite its ontological elevation of Buddha. Mahayana does represent a substantial change in the Buddhist tradition, but that change of message in Christianity goes back far earlier in the tradition and is more radical.

While it would ultimately triumph, Paul's understanding was certainly not the only view within the early church. There existed a stark division primarily between those who understood Jesus as a fulfillment of the Jewish tradition within which he remained and indeed intensified and those who believed his message to be something which radically reoriented the faith. This tension is clearly evident in the Christian Scriptures.

Matthew presents us a Jesus who not only fulfills, but heightens the Jewish Law, of which, "until heaven and earth disappear not an iota will be done away with" (Matt 5:18), while on the other side stood those views, presented most strongly, as we have seen, by Paul, strongly reorienting Jesus away from his Jewish roots, redefining him more as a classic Greco-Roman savior figure. For Paul, that Jewish Law, held so highly by Matthew's Jesus, was but a guardian, needed only until the coming of Christ who clearly abrogates it (Gal 3:23-24). Paul's emphasis on the grace of God and faith in Jesus may be contrasted with that of James who writes disparagingly of "faith without works" as being "dead" (Jas 2:26).

This discussion all took place among the earliest followers of Jesus in an overwhelmingly Jewish context using Jewish concepts (Acts 15; Gal 2). The debate, however, was also increasingly informed by a growing number of gentiles becoming part of the Jesus movement. In time they would out-number those who were Jewish, leading to a predominantly gentile move-ment moving ever further from its Jewish roots.

It is Paul's libertine view which triumphs in the church. One is able, as a gentile, to enter the church without having to embrace Jewish ritual and cultic customs, most particularly circumcision, but also the food laws.

With this triumph, a divide started to grow between this Jesus move-ment, which was gradually becoming a new religion, and its parent faith. A growing invective, already present in the Christian Scriptures, became associated with this split.

While the split between Judaism and the growing Jesus movement re-mained within Judaism it represented a type of family squabble, unpleasant but not dangerous, but as Christianity progressively defined itself a separate faith, opposed to Judaism, that was to change. That change can be seen even in the Gospels, particularly in John, where Jesus and his followers are retro-spectively presented being in continued and bitter conflict with what John disparagingly calls "the Jews."

The narratives central to the Gospels, the passion story, are written to clearly lay the blame for Jesus' death upon the Jews, absolving the Romans, their hands being washed (literally in the story with Pilate's hands) of any blame. The approbation directed by the increasingly gentile church toward "the Jews" grew until hatred and loathing ran profoundly deep.

Increasingly separated from its Jewish roots, Christianity became progressively subject to many other forces present in the gentile world. Free from his Jewish context, Jesus, as we have found, became increasingly identified a savior figure with the power to enable a person to be reborn, following their death, into another world of immortality. There were many other such figures in the world of antiquity who like Jesus were associated with dying and rising so to enable their followers to likewise pass through the portal of death. Tammuz (Mesopotamia), Adonis (Greek), Attis (Phrygia), and Osiris (Egypt), are probably the best known. Then there were the divinities associated with the mystery faiths, the Eleusinian, Dionysian, and Orphic mysteries, along with the cults built around foreign gods such as those of Cybele, Isis, and Mithras, these being the most common, among others.

Many of these faiths were in competition with Christianity in the earliest centuries, but that which most threatened to swallow Christianity was a nebulous religious philosophy, found in many forms, known as Gnosticism. This was a Hellenic thought form influenced by Middle Eastern mythology which swept through the empire in face of an official, though often stagnant, formal cult. Gnosticism, predating Christianity, greatly influenced much of the early church. Indeed, much, if not the majority, of the early church was gnostic or at least heavily influenced by it. Gnosticism represented a form of knowledge ("gnosis" in Greek), practice, and discipline, often secret, through which a person was enabled to pass through the physical realm of death to the spiritual realm of eternal life.

Gnostic schools outlined various methods of achieving this, usually through derogation of the flesh, along with acquisition of secret knowledge, such freeing us from illusion to enlightenment. Many of these means, given their secrecy, being passed therefore only to initiates, are unknown to us.

In its Christian form Gnosticism believed Jesus to be a savior figure, not through his death and resurrection but rather through his wisdom which he was able to share with others who then, like him, could find their inner divine essence, or spark and having so found, be free from material constraints, to dwell spiritually.

Gnosticism had at its core dualism, an opposition of polarities such as light and darkness, life and death, physical and spiritual, good and evil. One of each of these polarities was held to be good in its essence, the other evil. Of prime importance for Christianity was that in Gnosticism the physical was understood as the negative polarity of the spiritual. Thus the idea of a High God creating a physical world, the physical understood to be inherently evil, was abhorrent. Rather than the High God being involved in creation, gnostics understood there to be a whole series of emanations from that High God, understood to be totally remote and undefiled from anything physical, down to a demigod, an ignorant demiurge, who had created a thing so evil in essence as the material universe. Despite this, sparks of divinity are still present within our bodies, though we in ignorance are not conscious of such nor aware of our celestial origins. The gnostic goal was to extricate oneself from bondage in the physical to dwell in the spiritual realm. Means of doing this came through the acquisition of knowledge of these origins, usually through a redeemer, a docetic (only appearing to be human) type of figure. For Christian gnostics Christ was the one sent who could impart this knowledge, usually secret, to adherents. Understood as a divine being, taken apparent human form, Christ as intermediary being or aeon, understood as eternal, had come from the pleroma or "fullness," that place representing the center of divine life. This was a region of light beyond our world, occupied by spiritual beings such as aeons and archons, with whose aid humanity could recover the lost knowledge of their divine origins. Christ as one of these would lead humanity back to the light. Christian gnostics typically claimed their systems represented an inner truth revealed by Jesus, a truth deeper than that known by his other followers. In this they are similar to those in Mahayana, believing their understanding of Buddha represents a deeper, more profound way.

This, rather than concepts of sin and repentance, lay at the heart of belief. Some Christian gnostics identified Jesus as the embodiment of the supreme being who had become incarnate to bring gnosis to the earth, while others adamantly denied that the supreme being would defile their purity by taking on enfleshed form, believing rather Christ to be merely a human who, having attained enlightenment through gnōsis, had taught his disciples to do the same. Most however, held Christ to be a spiritual being, docetic, appearing to have taken human form.

The parallels of gnostic forms, Christian or otherwise, with what we have examined concerning Buddhism, especially Mahayana, are clearly strong. These center on the world as illusionary and the need for a supernatural figure to come from beyond to teach a deeper, more profound saving message.

With the triumph of what became Christian orthodoxy in the fourth century, gnostic writings were destroyed or hidden, so we had only the writings of their opponents, often selectively quoting, to understand Gnosticism. That was the case we we have seen, until a cache of documents, which have come to be known as the gnostic gospels, were found in Nag Hammadi, Egypt, in 1945. These writings, the products of different gnostic schools, give us much better access to these forms. They also allow us to better understand early Christianity, much of which was gnostic.

While most of the writings are late, therefore casting little light on the search for the historical Jesus, they do reflect the powerful influence Gnosticism had in the developing church during the second and third centuries. The Gospel of Thomas, the best known of these documents, is however an exception, placed by some (and I emphasize "some") scholars as being even earlier than the canonical Gospels. Thomas presents a Jesus, very distinct from that of those Gospels. Rather than being, as he became in the orthodox tradition, one who gives salvation, Christ in Thomas is imaged as one, who by imparting secret knowledge and practice, shows the way to salvation. Reading the Thomas Gospel is somewhat analogous to reading a Buddhist text.

In its detestation of the material, Gnosticism stands fundamentally opposed to what became orthodox Christianity, which at its core affirms the material. That affirmation is found first in the idea of an intentional good creation. Contrary to the surrounding cultures, which understood creation as an accidental by-product of the often-capricious actions of the gods, having therefore no inherent value, the two biblical Genesis creation accounts powerfully affirm the cosmos as being both the intentional and good act of a single God, who wills it into being. The divine concern for creation is further evidenced in Judeo-Christian thought in God being understood by divine interaction in the unfolding history of that creation, seen in mighty acts, especially the exodus and in the divinely inspired utterances of the prophets. By such, God is understood as being actively concerned for creation. Christians further add what stands as perhaps the most powerful affirmation of the material, God being fully present in physical human form in the person of Jesus. There could be no stronger affirmation of the material, than that the divine is clothed in it.

In gnostic forms of Christianity there was essentially nothing left of the human Jesus and his message of the reign of God.

Though Gnosticism did not fully flower until the second century CE, much of the Christian Scriptures can be understood as influenced by it, either by reaction or incorporation. Both are clearly seen in Paul's writings, wherein moving Christianity away from its Jewish roots, there are evident gnostic influences. He notes that he received his quite distinct teachings by "revelation," perhaps a sign of gnostic influence. In his correspondence with the Corinthian church (1 and 2 Corinthians) Paul is clearly in dispute with a gnostic form of Christian belief, but his argument leaves open that he himself is influenced by Gnosticism. Evidence for such may be found in such passages as "Yet among the mature we do impart wisdom, although it is not a wisdom of this age or of the rulers of this age, who are doomed to pass away. But we speak a secret and hidden wisdom of God, which God ordained before the world unto our glory" (1 Cor 2:7). Wisdom is a core gnostic category. Earlier in that same letter he writes, "Where is the wise? Where is the scribe? Where is the disputer of this world? Has not God made foolish the wisdom of this world?" (1 Cor 1:20). Paul possibly is setting worldly wisdom off against a higher wisdom of God, claiming the latter for himself, such being very much a gnostic style of argumentation. Paul seems also to be influenced by Gnosticism when he speaks of knowing a man (probably referring to himself) caught away to "the third heaven" (2 Cor 12:2). Elsewhere, in his letter to the Colossians, Paul uses that word pleroma, so core to Gnosticism, to speak of Christ, saying, "For in him the whole fullness (pleroma) of deity dwells bodily" (Col 2:9).

The concepts and language used by Paul led the second century Christian writer Tertullian to call Paul "the apostle of the heretics," while Paul's writings were often interpreted by gnostic writers in a gnostic way. Another early Christian author, Clement of Alexandria (second to third century), writes that the most famous second century gnostic writer, Valentinus, was a student of a certain Theudas, who in turn was a student of Paul. There are also in the Nag Hammadi corpus texts ascribed to Paul, including the "Prayer of Paul" and the Coptic "Apocalypse of Paul," texts which consider Paul to be the greatest apostle. That Paul claimed to have received his Gospel directly by revelation from God through the risen Christ particularly appealed to the gnostics, who likewise claimed direct gnosis from the risen Christ.

Eminent scholar on Gnosticism James Dunn charges that in some cases Paul affirmed views which lie closer to Gnosticism than to what was to become orthodox Christianity.[22]

Paul, while influenced by Gnosticism, is however not gnostic. He makes that clear in a passage, with which many will be familiar. "If I speak in the tongues of men and of angels, but have not love, I am a noisy gong or a clanging cymbal. And if I have prophetic powers, and understand all mysteries and all knowledge, and if I have all faith, so as to remove mountains, but have not love, I am nothing. If I give away all I have, and if I deliver my body to be burned, but have not love, I gain nothing" (1 Cor 13:1–3).

Communicating to the Corinthian church, Paul, while using gnostic categories, rejects the path of secret, esoteric knowledge, so valued by the them. He informs the Corinthian church, rather, that at the core of Christian belief is the more down to earth quality of love. Thus, he concludes the above with "Faith, hope and love abide, and the greatest of these is love" (1 Cor 13:13).

Paul grounds his "wisdom" in the earthy sphere of communal living, bound by love. Unlike the gnostic goal of being drawn away from the world to a mystical union with the divine, Paul understands such communion as being impossible without earthly communion with one's others.

That Paul is undoubtedly influenced by Gnosticism,makes sense of his need to distinguish himself from it, as in the above passage on love. In his radically reorienting Jesus into the classic savior figure found in the

22. Dunn, *Theology of Paul.*

Graeco-Roman world, Paul could not help but be influenced by gnostic forms, these being so amenable to his theological project. The absolute gnostic cutting away of Christ from his human Jewish roots, however, was a step too far for Paul, who after all had been Saul, "Hebrew of the Hebrews."

John may likewise have been influenced by gnostic ideas. Like Paul, he deals constantly in dualities such as darkness and light, and most tellingly flesh and spirit, that contrast, as we have seen, lying at the core of Gnosticism. John also emphasizes gnostic ideas such as the value of charisma and the abrogation of the Jewish law. The prologue to the Gospel of John (1:1-18) describes the incarnated Logos as the light which came to earth in the person of Jesus. The term "light" in reference to Jesus is a constant refrain right through John's Gospel. Those whom Jesus "enlightens" are "not born of blood or will of the flesh . . . but of God." Such language is shot through with Gnosticism.

Raymond Brown, among the most esteemed of Johannine scholars, asserts that the Gospel of John clearly displays the core gnostic idea of Christ being heavenly revealer. Yet, as with Paul, it would likewise be unfair to suggest that John is a gnostic. Following the cosmic nature of the prologue to his Gospel, something likely later added, John's Gospel immediately moves to earth his discourse, saying of Christ as divine wisdom that he "became flesh and dwelt among us" (John 1:14) anathema to gnostics. That the prologue probably existed as an independent writing before being added to the Gospel in the second century is again evidence of the influence of Christian forms of Gnosticism in the early church.

By their concern for the earthy material and communal, even when influenced by Gnosticism, the Scripture writers present an alternative to the otherworldly gnostic system. Flesh and the material are important, they strongly affirm. These writers provide us with the best of both worlds, grounding gnostic wisdom and mysticism into the world in which we exist. Christ as the manifestation of that wisdom has become incarnated in flesh and blood, those same categories in which we all have our existence.

Despite their popularity the gnostics lost out to those who established a Christian orthodoxy which holds to this day. That orthodoxy, which excluded other forms of Christianity, was set by three norms still present in the majority of churches; the development of a Scriptural canon of accepted books, the writing of creeds, and the establishment of what were held to be legitimate lineages of bishops. These served as constraints on what was considered legitimate expressions of faith, thereby excluding gnostic believers. This tightness of definition no doubt helped in the orthodox triumph. Christian belief, narrowly defined in set parameters, is very different to the breadth of understandings within Buddhism.

Though losing out and being officially suppressed, we will recognize that much of Gnosticism survives into modern popular Christianity, particularly in the dualism built around an otherworldliness and its disdain for the flesh. This dualism is so powerful that much popular Christianity understands itself as a means by which disembodied souls, having nothing to do with flesh, can pass to an unworldly (non-material) domain called heaven after death. As noted, such is a powerful mythic religious form, standing at the heart of many religions, so it perhaps understandable that popular Christianity has been cast thus. Such however stands diametrically opposed both to Jesus' preaching of the shalom, God's reign "on earth as in heaven," as well to that at the heart of Christian belief, the divine becoming incarnate taking bodily form.

There was reason then for the church to reject much of Gnosticism. Its depreciation of the flesh and rejection of the material is something rightly rejected, but unfortunately the baby was thrown out with the bath water. In its determination to be free of the gnostics, Christian orthodoxy cut itself free from needed streams of wisdom and mysticism. Rejection of gnostic forms of Christianity makes dialogue with Buddhism more difficult, as Buddhism is more analogous to these forms of Christianity rather than with what became orthodox.

Since the rediscovery of the Gnostic Gospels, however, there has been a renewed appreciation of just how broad the early church was before the censors had their way in the third and fourth centuries, along with a growing interest in gnostic forms of Christianity.

I shall examine this below as part of my presentation of an alternative view of Christianity.

As we found in examining Buddhism, there are also difficulties with the traditional orthodox understanding of Christianity. I shall now turn to examine these, before presenting what I hold to be a more credible Christian understanding.

CHRISTIANITY: AN ALTERNATIVE VISION

As I did with Buddhism I will now briefly outline a different way of telling the Christian story. I do so because not only has the old story lost, I believe, relevance and clarity but also because I hold it to have deep ethical shortcomings. I will commence with how the story has become so irrelevant in the modern world, to become non-understandable for many.

To abstract Jesus from his historical context and made of him a cultic savior figure, whose benefits are limited to a religious, even otherworldly realm, doesn't only not align with the historical reality we have just surveyed but is also, I charge, deeply unhelpful in the current context. This is because our contemporary interest is increasingly shaped by issues to do with human living, rather than asking types of metaphysical questions which can never be resolved, that especially being the case when it comes to questions to do with what happens following death. While that issue was vital in the world of antiquity, spawning, as seen, many religious movements, and was used by the church until recent times as a Damoclean sword over believers, it has now largely lost its meaning and therefore relevancy. Polls and surveys show this question has little import. The afterlife is increasingly spoken of in a light-hearted manner such as a person resuming some sporting contest "in the sky" with a deceased former opponent, or that "Jenny" will be back with her previously deceased "Peter." They are statements usually said in sentimental style, without any real conviction that something like such will really occur. Even Christian funeral eulogies make little mention of the afterlife, being centered instead on the life that has been lived, with only the formal liturgy left to speak of life being lived beyond this mortal coil.

This loss of interest in the afterlife has made much of what lay at the core of Christian theology irrelevant. Theology has long been built around the doctrine of redemption, whereby a person being "saved" is pulled out of a world, which since a primeval "fall" (Gen 3) is understood as being in essence sinful. Salvation consisted in being extracted from this dammed creation, which would finally be destroyed in an apocalypse, and being taken to another domain, often called heaven. Heaven was the goal of existence, with this world seen primarily as preparation, a place in which one committing themselves to Christ sought to live righteously with eyes set to the afterlife as reward. To be concerned for the things of this world was to be worldly, something held at best to be a distraction and at worst wrong or even evil. At its extreme such theology can even rejoice it the world's destruction, perhaps by nuclear apocalypse or environmental devastation, as this will bring God's rule. Hence, the lack of participation, mistrust, or even opposition by most conservative Christians to anti-war and environmental movements.

Speaking theologically the doctrine of redemption/salvation has been separated from that of creation, in that one is redeemed out of creation. Such understanding holds little relevancy in a world whose interest is built around world matters such as justice, peace, and ecology. In such context more earthly-minded Christian voices are needed, sought by those seeking to find any relevancy in Christianity.

In a world where prophetic voices shaped by those things at the core of Jesus' actual concern are so needed, a Christianity built around that which motivated Jesus, rather than on Jesus himself transacting some kind of

atonement with God, may provide a new relevance for a faith under challenge, either as irrelevant or nonsensical. It could be said that it is time for
Christianity to re-examine that faith of Jesus as a corrective to faith in Jesus.

Such statement may shock us as Christianity has been understood
in narrow parameters for some 1,600 years. But prior to that, as we have
seen, Christian theology had a flexibility about it, the early followers of Jesus understanding his message in diverse ways. We know it was that group
understanding Jesus' death as transactional between us and God which
won out, and having emerged victorious they set to suppressing other in-
terpretations. Now with the constraints of an authoritative orthodoxy removed—and remember, for much of Christian history orthodoxy was a life
and death issue—we are free again to explore different understandings of
the message of Jesus theological forms which will be more cognizant with
contemporary concerns.

The Christianity which will emerge from that is likely to be far different from that which has long prevailed. Those changes have already begun.
We shall return to them.

At the core of the traditional story is the doctrine of atonement. In
that story exist many difficulties, not only in regards to its relevance, something we have just explored, but also regards its logic and most damningly
its ethics.

The customary understanding of atonement, built on translation of
one to an otherworldly heaven, holds such is only possible if a person was
in a sinless state of absolute purity, for God is unable to bear impurity in the
divine presence. Such a state of sinless purity being clearly impossible for
anyone, it must therefore be vicariously imputed to them. Though there are
several variants in understanding how this occurs, the commonalities far
outweigh the differences. In summary the theory of atonement goes something like this. God as perfect cannot create anything that is imperfect and
therefore creates a perfect creation. The perfection of creation, however, experiences a "fall" when the first humans, Adam and Eve, disobey the divine
fiat by eating the fruit of the tree of knowledge of good and evil. Having lost
primeval purity, they are driven out of the perfect garden into the world of
non-perfection, cast out of divine communion. Far from understanding the
human actions (the thirst for and acquisition of knowledge) in the garden
of Eden story as being understandable, or even necessary, such is viewed as
a deeply evil willful disobedience of God. From that time all humanity, even
creation itself, has been tainted by that sin and thus alienated from God.

This dialectical theology has understood the material and earthly, at
least since the Fall, as being at odds with the divine. To be involved in the
world was to be separated from godly concern according to some, even

when that involvement was in making the world better. There was no way through worldly activity, even when good, to find God.

The schema was fully developed by the fourth-century theologian Augustine. He asserted that even if a person were perfect in themselves God would still not be able to endure their presence, due to their being infected by the species imperfection contracted in the fall. All are imbued with the original wrongdoing, "original sin," passed to them almost like a genetic code.

To this alienation a solution is posited, for while we may not be able to reach God, it is possible for God to reach us. The means to do this is by God sending his "only son," fully both human and divine, held to be untainted by sin, to the earth. He was "born as we are" (1 John 5:6) but unmarked by that original sin which had contaminated all others. He alone could atone, imputing to us a state of purity, thereby bridging from the divine side the chasm between humanity and the divine.

This could only be achieved by this perfect one appropriating all sins to himself and then undergoing the necessary punishment, death, demanded by God for sin. Jesus, having no sin, and therefore having no need to be judged by God, chooses to die in our stead by bearing our sins. "God made him who had no sin to be sin for us, so that in him we might become the righteousness of God" (2 Cor 5:21). Untainted, neither by original sin nor by any sin of his own, Jesus, taking upon himself our sins, acts as a sin-bearer. By his undeserved death, Christ is able, dying in our stead, to cleanse us. Thus purified, we are able to stand before God and be received into his heavenly domain. To achieve this we need do nothing except, acknowledging the grace of God, invoke the name of Jesus at the place of judgment and on so doing our sin is wiped clean, allowing us to receive the gift of eternal life. This schema strongly draws upon the Jewish practice of the scapegoat, the sending out of a goat which had been symbolically loaded by a priest with the peoples' sins, into the desert, so carrying those sins away (Lev 16:21–22). Jesus is often imaged as the scapegoat.

These theories of atonement are clearly drawn up based more around the need for sacrifice, divine satisfaction, and retributive justice rather than with reference to the idea expressed by Jesus, that God's love flowed to all, particularly to the outsider.

The schema utilizes the garden of Eden story found in Genesis to develop the doctrine of the fall. This, as we have found has nothing to do, however, with that story's original purpose, the provision of an explanation to the clearly perceived reality of how a good creation, created by a perfect God, had become tainted. As seen, in contrast to the older mythic stories in the biblical stories, creation in the Genesis accounts is intentional, willed by a single God, rather than accidental or even capricious. In its essence, creation is good. The Hebrews were not naïve, however, and clearly recognized that creation was obviously marked by brokenness. This brokenness they imputed to a mythic event, the disobedience of the first human couple. They did not hold this account to be literally true, the name Adam in Hebrew simply signifying "human being," while Eve means "to live, to give life." Further, they used the story as explication of the loss of the innocence with which each of us are born. We have no choice as to loss of innocence as we grow to autonomous decision making. A necessary part of our maturation is to pick from the tree of knowledge. Rather than taking the story literally, Jews understood the truth of this story to lie in the mythical domain. In no manner did they draw the detailed doctrines nor ontological conclusions from the story, as did later Christian theology.

Christian theologians wished, however, to make something different from the story. First, they inverted what we know to be true, that one is born in innocence, claiming instead, contrary to perception, that each person is born encumbered with sin. Having done such they then used the story to explain how this evil, which automatically contaminates all, came about. They thus changed the story from being an attempt to understand the brokenness evident in creation and the human reality along with our loss of primal innocence, to make of it an account which informs us of our ontological status before God.

The first step in this involved massive hubris in the claim that they could understand the divine mind, positing it being unable to bear imperfection. Along with claiming an incredible human capacity for understanding, this also places a massive restriction upon the divine, who by definition should be beyond such limitation. As for the human condition, the necessary loss of original primal innocence that Adam and Eve enjoyed before their transgression was turned into an "original sin" which infects each person from the moment of birth.

The Christian interpretation damages the original intent of the Genesis story, which was to catch mythologically something which happens to each of us. We are each born into primal innocence yet know that as we grow, we become increasingly aware of, and responsible for, moral and ethical choices. Even our law recognizes this in its understanding of diminished responsibility for minors. Sometimes the ethical choices we need to make are not straightforward but are rather more nuanced. That seems to be the case in the Genesis story. The temptation is couched in terms of having "knowledge of good and evil," that surely being a good thing, yet in the Christian understanding it is not so viewed. Perhaps such knowledge is impossible for us to achieve, or more so such knowledge doesn't exist, good and evil mostly being more ambiguous. In the modern world we also know too well that sometimes our knowledge outstrips our capacity to temper it by our ethical understanding of "good." It is as though sometimes ethical choices are too much for us and such choice has become overwhelming.

Choices, with all their ambiguity, we are however forced to make, for it is impossible to remain in primal innocence. Ethical choices are often not straightforward, sometimes calling for great struggle. I am reminded of the episode when the British broke the Nazi Enigma code during World War II. The code had allowed the Nazis to securely send orders to their forces as the chance of breaking the code were seemingly infinitesimal. Unbeknown to the Nazis however, the British broke it using a prototype of the modern computer. Having broken the code, they could not let the Nazis know of their success for they would then simply change it. So to make it not obvious that they had cracked the code the British had to sacrifice some ships to German U-boats which they could have saved. Which ships would be saved, and which would be knowingly sacrificed? Perhaps there is no other example of how complex ethical decisions can become.

Yet this complexity is our reality. There can be no retreat to primal innocence, and this is something the Genesis story makes clear. The story's intention, as it was written speaks powerfully to us, having both individual and universal significance. Its Christian interpretation seems not only archaic but strange and nonsensical.

The traditional Christian interpretation is not rooted in any experienced reality, is logically incoherent, and most damning, lacks a true ethical component.

I shall deal first with issue of logic. There is something inherently illogical about how this God is perceived by Christians. The divine is understood as having no imperfection, and that may be fair enough, but then added is the idea that in this perfection this God is unable to tolerate any imperfection, lest the divine become in some way contaminated. One of course can ask why such a limit is placed on God, ipso-facto defined as one without limit, possessing the attributes of omnipotence, omniscience, and omnipresence? Given this, the limitation placed on God regards the ability to bear any imperfection, is clearly massive, and is contrary to definition.

Where can the omniscient God be to not see sin? Where can the omnipresent God be to be not in the presence of sin? How is God omnipotent when a limit, an incredibly narrow limit, is placed on the divine capacity to forgive? God, it is asserted, hasn't the capacity to forgive even the smallest foible without some price being paid. Even one like myself has greater power than that. Surely an omnipotent one by definition must have all power including the power of absolute forgiveness. Greater divine perfection, and real power, would be to give God the capacity to dwell amid imperfection without fear of contamination. By analogy, does not the saint doing good while situated in the middle of perversion, have a greater perfection than the one whose goodness is carried out in a place of great holiness and piety? God, however, lacks that capacity.

By their supposition those proposing such a schema also display a massive arrogance about supposedly knowing the divine mind, in charging that God cannot abide imperfection. How can any human claim to know the capacity of God's acceptance? Given I fail to know the depth of acceptance by a person I know even well, the claim that I, or anyone else, can know the depth of the acceptance by God stands as perhaps the greatest example of theological conceit. Psychoanalyzing the divine would appear to be the worst type of hubris.

Again, it seems non-understandable, even illogical, that the wrongdoing connected with some archaic, clearly mythic event, the episode in the garden of Eden, is imputed to all. Why am I, or anyone else, responsible for the wrongdoing of another? Surely another's wrongdoing should not be imputed to me, nor mine to another. Imagine such in any legal system. The imputation of sin from one to another, whether to me, or to Jesus, makes no sense.

Further, we find it impossible to believe that any human would be sinless. Wrongdoing is something which accompanies even the saintliest human being. Indeed the more saintly a person is, the more they will be conscious of just how deeply they are enmeshed in sin. Yet it is claimed of Jesus that he was both fully human and yet without sin, that being even more incredible given he claims that the mere thought of a sinful act equates to the sin itself (Matt 5:21–28). That a person could achieve such absolute perfection seems inconceivable. What do we mean then by the statement that Jesus is fully human, when the quality he carries of never sinning is so infinitely foreign to the category of being human?

Yet he must be human for if not human, the whole imputation of righteousness to other humans would no longer stand. Further, it is claimed by the doctrine of original sin that even if I personally were sinless, I would still bear my and the species' taint and therefore be disqualified from standing before God. That disqualification would be precisely due to my humanity, born of the line of Adam, immersed therefore in that original sin which accompanies all humanity. Being human in this schema is to be necessarily in sin, yet Jesus, who must be fully human so to save his fellow humans, bears not this sin. As such how can he be really human?

The theory of atonement also does damage to the concept of the divine, understood as a unitive whole. What does it mean when one part of the divine unity needs the sacrifice of another part? Divine unity is surely stretched to the point of breaking.

More damning however than its being illogical, the whole atonement schema fails for being deeply unethical. The method by which human sin is expunged is deeply offensive, nothing less being involved than the torturous death of God's son, said to be untainted by sin. We must question the nature of a God who chooses to send their son to his death so to satisfy their inability to accept imperfection. Is such a type of divine neuroticism? What type of God would demand such? Any parent similarly demanding the death of their child, and even organizing it to satisfy some need, would be understood as a perverse criminal, or worse not criminally responsible but rather judged as criminally deranged. Of course, in the case of the divine, not only did God know their son was to die, but in possessing omniscience, knew the horrendous nature of that death. What type of God, in order to preserve their sense of right or purity, would demand that their son suffer the most horrific slow torturous death which the Roman Empire could develop? Hardly a God, I would suggest, with which even one, bearing even my compromised ethics, would choose to spend eternity, nor one who would hold any right to judge another like me, whose sins pale to insignificance beside that horrendous divine sin of child abuse and torture. Little wonder that the institution claiming this God has become so linked with the scourge of child abuse.

What ethic can be imputed to a God who, having such concern for their own purity, demands the death, particularly one so torturous, of anyone, even the greatest rogue, never mind their "only son"? The genuinely good person or God would not remain in selfish perfection but instead would be prepared to give up their purity and perfection to become immersed in the world. Thus, so the German theologian Dietrich Bonhoeffer, who may have wished to remain undefiled by that around him, knew that in the face of Nazi perversion he could not comfortably remain in the perfection of pacifism, something to which he was deeply attracted, but instead knew that he must place himself into the morally ambiguous struggle against the regime, even to the point of being involved in the plot to kill Hitler. His highest ethic and inclination, his desire for self-purity, would need be compromised. For Bonhoeffer, the suffering must be stopped by "putting a spoke in the wheel," as he expressed it. Keeping purity of "clean hands" was no real option in such situation. Yet God, we are informed, seeks to keep such hands to be not contaminated by evil, unprepared to compromise the divine absolute. Rather than being located in the messiness of the world, this God, concerned only for divine purity, stands back, choosing to absent the divine self from us, holding instead to a type of egotistic perfection. Such standing separate stands diametrically opposed to the central Christian doctrine of the incarnation.

Such type of methodology, used by the divine to deal with sin, only serves to dwarf the sins which it tries to expunge. Far from keeping the divine free of sin, it takes sin, unimaginable sin, to the very core of the divine being.

The traditional atonement schema built around God understood as vengeful, demanding payment to assuage his anger, is understandably offensive to many. There is after all something profoundly unethical about a God, who, from a concern for perfection, condemns all others to be excluded from divine presence, unless such an horrendous price, blood sacrifice of his son, is paid.

Ethically the traditional story also fails in its being centered on another world. In a world full of desperate need it is a dubious ethic which concentrates itself on the other world rather than this. There is something profoundly immoral about an emphasis causing a view, as put by one Christian musician, "I'm only visiting this planet." This type of theology lays itself very open to the Marxist charge that religion represents "the opiate of the masses." It does this, Marx charges, by turning genuine yearning for something better away from this world, where it could effect change, to elsewhere. As such it serves as ideology for those profiting out of the current system, who often invoke "God" or "Christian values" to support their privilege.

While such pining for an other world heaven may be understandable by those so oppressed in this world that they see no hope this side of the grave, it still does not serve as an adequate expression of Christianity as a whole. Such pure otherworldliness doesn't normally find it genesis in the poor anyway but rather is more directed at them. Theology germane to the poor, while it may appear to be otherworldly, nearly always is earthly, even if its aspirations are coded in otherworldly language, the best known being found in the religious music of the oppressed. Black spirituals like "Keep Your Eyes on the Prize" or "No Turning Back" had not just a spiritual component but also were about the very real journey to earthly freedom on the Underground Railroad. By saying this I am again not emptying them, or faith as a whole, of content and hope beyond the sociopolitical, but rather that such aspirations must not be understood, nor used, in a purely otherworldly manner. When faith is directed to the other world alone, particularly by those whose interest that serves, such fails in the domain of ethics.

There are a number of other issues which make it hard to get ourselves around such a story. Our understanding of law and how it operates makes the whole idea of expiatory punishment very difficult to understand. We believe in a rigorous examination of evidence at trial to determine specific guilt, with the one found guilty of "doing the crime, doing the time." The idea of some type of non-specific metaphysical guilt seems strange, and if I was to appeal to such in a court of law to justify my specific crime, I would not likely find a receptive ear. Again, if another were to step forward after I was found guilty with an offer to bear my punishment, this too would likewise find a non-receptive ear.

Advances in psychology also tell us that any ideas that our human condition is inherently good or evil in nature are far too reductionist. We are made up rather of a whole range of complex psychic drives, both conscious and unconscious. Ontological statements concerning human ethics are far too simplistic. Sociological understandings likewise show us that attribution of guilt to some deep disposition is rather strange. We know from court and prison statistics that crime, or more accurately punished crime, has a strong class and racial basis. The penalty for crime committed by one may fall on another in that "the sins of the father may fall on the child," but that is tied to such psychological and sociological things as how the father (and mother) raised the child, something often linked to their own upbringing, rather than having some metaphysical basis. Further, there is nothing expiatory in such passage of guilt from parent to child. The specificity and causes of crime linked to upbringing, class, race, and social status again make absolute metaphysical ascriptions of evil or wrongdoing again strange to our ears.

Again, the whole atonement theory is built on the idea that at some stage humanity fell from perfection into evil. Science makes such to be a strange assertion. Humanity, we know, rather than falling from an idyllic perfect innocence, has instead risen from a brutish existence, descended from our animal forebears. We more accurately speak of the rise of humanity than the fall of such. This is not to romanticize modern humanity, for we are all too aware of the fantastic technical capacity for evil in the contemporary world, but rather to acknowledge the enormous advances in fields as disparate as medicine, arts and culture, engineering, the social realm (racial, gender, and gender preference discrimination), and communications.

There is an alternative vision of Christianity, one which may communicate more coherently to our times, and one, I view, as being also more reflective of Jesus' message and ministry. To find and examine it we will need to lay aside many accretions which enter Christianity extremely early, present even in the Scriptures. Of course we will not be breaking new ground as the work is already underway in many quarters.

Current theological discourse is increasingly marked by a movement toward a holism which, holding creation and redemption together, understands the redemptive process, rather than being one calling us out of creation, as something taking place within creation. A person is saved or redeemed not out of the world but rather as part of the world in a renewal of the entire creation. The whole of creation, including ourselves, it is asserted, is being redeemed and renewed, a process centered in Christ. Much greater use is made of biblical texts understanding Christ as the one in whom creation is held together, and through whom it is being brought to wholeness.

"Creation itself will be set free from its bondage to decay and obtain the glorious liberty of the children of God" (Rom 8:22-23).

"For in him all things were created, in heaven and on earth, visible and invisible, whether thrones or dominions or principalities or authorities—all things were created through him and for him. He is before all things, and in him all things hold together" (Col 1:16-17).

"And there is but one Lord, Jesus Christ, through whom all things came and through whom we exist" (1 Cor 8:6).

"God purposed in Christ a plan for the fullness of time, to bring all things in heaven and on earth together in Christ" (Eph 1:10).

Finally we find in the final two chapters of the Christian Scriptures that in Christ creation will be led to a perfect wholeness beyond that which it now possesses. There shall be "a new heaven and earth" where "all things are made new." Creation will be replete with, "a river of the water of life" beside which will stand "the tree of life," yielding each month a different kind of fruit. The leaves of that tree being "for the healing of nations" (Rev 21–22). This vision posits a renewal of the whole of creation, re-establishing the primeval wholeness before brokenness entered (Gen 1–3).

Rather than being saved out of creation, so to live in another domain, we are part of the whole creation being brought to wholeness. Clearly this makes far more sense in an age of environmental crisis, in which ecological concerns have become so prevalent. While both stories, the traditional and that of which we are speaking, find roots within the Christian Scriptures, it is the latter, the holistic story, which is more relevant and sensible to our world today.

This holistic renewal of the whole of creation is a long way removed from the traditional narrow theology of redemption, wherein human beings are saved as individuals out of creation, in an after-death experience. In this alternative story the Christ event is held to have a cosmic significance, extending far beyond a meaning confining it to deliverance of individuals from divine judgment. It becomes instead the key event around which cosmic renewal centers.

This understanding, holding in a unitive manner the doctrines of creation and redemption, is truer to the broader biblical testimony, while speaking far more cogently to a time when we face an unprecedented ecological

crisis, created by human actions. For Christianity to have relevance today in the Anthropocene age it must necessarily speak to the question of ecology. Attention desperately needs now to be directed to the concrete issues facing our earth rather than to speculation concerning individual post-death existence. This being fixed on this narrow concern for my afterlife, with a marginalization of creation, has, as we saw, been charged as representing the philosophical and ideological basis for the Western exploitation of creation in a manner, which now given advanced technology, represents an existential threat.

For many Christians operating within this traditional schema, the ecological crisis is hardly a matter of concern, for one is redeemed out of the world. It may even be celebrated as signifying that world history is coming to an end and that Christ shall soon return to bring the fullness of redemption, not in this world but elsewhere.

In recent years this whole question of ecology has come to the forefront in discourse in just about every field. Discourse around faith is and can be no exception. It is impossible to do theology in the present context without reference to ecology. Traditional dialectical fall/redemption theology has nothing to say in this field. In such the world is understood to be desacralized, therefore open to exploitation, driven forward, by a teleological understanding, to an end point.

Clearly a theology where the world and God are understood as not opposed but rather analogous, with creation being the subject of holistic redemption, speaks far more cogently to this ecological concern.

Further, the holistic corporate nature of such understanding seems to approximate better the example of Jesus, who calls us away from egocentric concerns. My concern for my individual salvation seems to epitomize such.

A new emphasis on the neglected wisdom tradition is opening new, more relevant understandings of Christianity. This more cosmic understanding, built on wisdom through which all things are created and held together, again understands the divine as being analogous rather than antithetical to the world. Communion with God is held to be through a via-positiva, the divine understood as the fulfillment of what it means to be human, rather than through a via-negativa, wherein God is understood as negation of the human. This understanding, rather than negating true wisdom, calls us to uphold it. Jesus is understood as personification of wisdom, a wisdom personified in Christ as having cosmic significance. Such wisdom clearly represents another pressing need for our world faced with so many dilemmas.

This draws upon the Jewish wisdom tradition, the third great pillar of the Tanakh, the Writings (Ketuvim), wherein the divine is understood

as being present in true human wisdom. Much of the wisdom corpus consists of proverbial advice, expressive of the divine will, understood as being humanly wise. But there is also a deeper stream running through this
literature. In that stream wisdom is understood as being a creative feminine
force, present as co-creator at the point of creation (Prov 8). This divine wisdom undergirding the cosmos calls us to care for that creation, understood
to be alignment and accord with the divine will. Creation and the divine
are not understood as opposed polarities but rather as essentially belonging
together, creation being the expression of the divine will.

In the Christian Scriptures, Christ is understood as this wisdom figure in whom creation has come into being and through whom it is held
together. As just seen, Paul exclaims of Christ, "in him all things were created . . . all things were created through him and for him" (Col 1:16). John
claims of Jesus, "all things were made through him, and without him was
not anything made that was made" (John 1:3), while the writer of Hebrews
says, "whom God appointed the heir of all things, through whom also God
created the world" (Heb 1:2). Clearly by such Christ is understood as analogous to creation, indeed the principle by which it is sustained. It is as though
Christ is understood as feminine, birthing creation.

The eagerness of the developing Christian tradition to differentiate itself from Gnosticism meant that the wisdom tradition became increasingly
marginalized. It survived, however, into the evolving church, despite efforts
to curtail it. Both Justin Martyr (100–165) and Origen (c. 184–c. 253) identified Christ with the cosmic wisdom which pervades the universe, while
Theophilus of Antioch (d. 180) and Irenaeus of Lyons (d. 202/3) understood
divine cosmic wisdom as being resident in the Holy Spirit.

While the Western Church increasingly emphasized the alienation
of creation from the creator by centering on the fall, the wisdom tradition
found its place in the Eastern (Orthodox) churches. This we would expect,
given the stronger Greek influence on the Byzantine East. Greek philosophy
gave a prominent position to wisdom or sophia, who, like the Hebrews, they
personified. This strong strain of the wisdom tradition prevalent in the Orthodox Churches has led to sophia being identified with the theotokos (lit.
God bearer) Mary, the "mother of God." This is especially so in the Russian
Church where exists a whole school of sophiology in which God's essence
is identified with the divine wisdom, manifesting itself in human wisdom.

This concern for wisdom has resulted in numerous cathedrals and
other prominent churches in the eastern tradition being dedicated to divine
wisdom. Thus, the greatest church built by the emperor Justinian in the East
at Constantinople, consecrated in 538, was called Hagia Sophia (Holy Wisdom), while many other great churches built right up to the last century in

the East have borne that name. Cathedrals bearing the name Sancta Sophia in Kiev and Polotsk date to the eleventh century, continuing with St. Sophia Cathedral in Vologda (sixteenth century), Saint Sophia Church, Moscow (seventeenth century), and the twentieth-century St. Sophia Cathedral in Harbin (present day China).

Contemporary theology is also rediscovering a mystic spirituality, appropriate to this changing theological emphasis. This again offers a direction more conducive to modern concerns. Christian Gnosticism, as we have seen, understood Christ more as a wisdom figure, one showing the way to salvation rather than being the mechanism of that salvation. In the Gospel of Thomas, we are invited to drink from Jesus' mouth and by so doing to partake of his wisdom and by that action become as Christ. The wisdom which saves is latent within. "If you give birth to what you have within you, what you have within you will save you" (Gos. Thom.: 70) The spiritual practices which inform this type of Christianity are often much more conducive to contemporary interests. This stream of Christianity has always survived, often perilously, underground, as a minor key in the tradition. The theology in this key is analogous in its relating God, humans, and the world rather than dialectical, as it has long been in the West. This analogous theology doesn't place God and the world essentially at odds. Rather God is understood, though beyond the world, to be in continuity with it. Such things as human wisdom, culture, and good works are understood as having divine presence within them. Likewise, God is seen present in the ecosphere. We contain within us that divine spark, able by wise discipline to be fanned to flame.

There are a number of specific modern issues which make a theology of analogy far more understandable and appropriate to our modern context.

Flowering in the 1970s, though having buds earlier, the feminist movement has become increasingly important. We forget how quickly things have changed. During my childhood women needed their husband's permission to take out a loan, were largely restricted to the house while the men were employed, were regularly subjected to domestic abuse, which effectively was classed as a private matter, and could be legally raped in marriage. This has changed dramatically in the past 50–60 years. That change, though lagging behind what is found elsewhere, has also manifested itself in theology.

Voices of increasing numbers of women are being heard in the theological field, usually as a sharp critique of the way theology has traditionally been done. This critique is mainly concentrated on the patriarchal nature of ecclesiastical practice, which reduced women to a secondary role, but there are also deeper streams. Those deeper streams challenge the fall/redemption story which has presented women, particularly in their sexuality, specifically in the person of Eve, as being responsible for the sin in the garden. As seen, in that story Eve is presented as the temptress, leading Adam into sin, causing women to be cast in such role, the temptation usually being sexual. This type of understanding is strongly associated with rejection of that which is deeply human, particularly the body, reduced to being the instrument of temptation. As such, the female body is viewed as the instrument for men's temptation, while the male body is understood as the location of that temptation. This rejection largely served as the source of the rejection of the material as a whole.

Feminist theology has brought a renewed emphasis to sophia as wisdom, understood as a necessary corrective to the predominant masculine categories present in the traditional fall/redemption theological presentations. The divine is found in wisdom via the analogous manner of which we have been speaking. The divine as mother is conceived as nurturing/accepting, rather than as harsh judgmental father, while the body, with its power to create, is celebrated.

Also new to theological discourse are the voices of indigenous peoples. Here much work needs to be done, given previously the relationship between the coming of Christianity and indigenous people has for the most part been exploitative. Indigenous cultures and their beliefs, especially around land and the sacrality of nature, were rejected and suppressed as pagan by those bringing Christianity from within the traditional theological framework.

Holding land and nature sacred, indigenous theologies reject both the idea that these are soiled by a fall, along with the understanding that human beings are essentially alienated from the divine. These voices affirm that the spirit of the divine long existed in the land and people before Christianity. Wisdom (sophia) was present in the land and people, with the stories of creation and ongoing relationship of the material world being revelatory of God. Obviously a more holistic wisdom/creation-based theology is more amenable to indigenous spiritualities.

Such theology helps us also in the field of interfaith dialogue. In a world becoming ever more a "global village," dialogue between faiths is growing increasingly important. A wisdom-centered understanding permits Christians to better engage with other faith traditions given the exclusivist Christocentric understanding lying at the heart of the mainstream fall/redemption Christian tradition clearly presents a major hindrance to genuine interfaith dialogue. Christ, identified less as having a special ontological status and more as possessing divine wisdom, is far more conducive to interfaith dialogue. For Christians Christ as wisdom becomes analogous to Buddha as wisdom for Buddhists. Buddhists and Christians can easily enter dialogue, each bringing with them the differing wisdoms of Buddha and Christ. Though those wisdoms vary we will at least be conversing in a common currency.

I have briefly outlined two streams of Christian thought, each reaching back to the early Christian tradition. One was superseded, suppressed, only surviving as a minor underground current. In its zeal to defeat gnostic forms, the church overwhelmingly chose a fall/redemption theology, while silencing theological streams speaking in both a more holistic and analogous manner. In this dialectical theology, things "of the world" were understood to be antithetical to the will of God. Salvation was cut off from creation, with redemption reduced to being a process whereby one was saved out of a fallen world.

The marginalization of the "wisdom-holistic" tradition need change, for the Christ who calls and shows us the path to divine wisdom is one, I assert, far more attractive,and understandable than one transacting atonement between us and God by means which increasingly seem nonsensical but, as I have shown, are also ethically unsustainable. An analogous relationship between both humans and creation with the divine, allows for a more holistic understanding of redemption, one in which it is identified as being a redeemed order, a new creation as the shalom, reflective of the divine will. In an age of urgent ecological crisis such speaks far more cogently.

The original message of Jesus, the reign of God, fits far more easily with a wisdom-centered analogous theology. Though still very much a minor key, this more holistic understanding is being increasingly heard. Jesus' concern was never for saving people out of a world, understood as broken, but rather a renewal of creation, a thing clearly lying at the heart of his preaching and enacting the shalom.

True, Jesus speaks of the sin of "worldliness," but when doing so he never refers to the world as in essence evil; rather he is criticizing a self-focused thinking and action which breaks the good world by causing injustice. Egocentric worldliness is contrary to the world precisely in that it harms the goodness of creation. Jesus' rejection of worldliness was precisely because of his being for the world. That concern for the world is made clearest in the prayer with which he is so associated, the Lord's Prayer: "Your kingdom come, your will be done (where?), on earth as it is in heaven." There could be no clearer indication for the locale of Jesus' concern. Redemption for Jesus is not out and away from an earth, viewed essentially fallen or evil, but is rather upon a transformed earth, as part of the whole created order, renewed to correspond with the divine will. The world is never in essence evil (contrary to the gnostics), nor is it fallen from some pristine state as later theology would hold. It is rather in essence good but has within it a brokenness, standing in the way of the shalom, which needs be healed.

To conclude, the Christianity most widely and vocally proclaimed is hardly representative of that which scholarship is uncovering as being the message proclaimed by Jesus, nor does it do justice to the wide range of theologies present, both in the earliest and ongoing Christian tradition. Last, it offers little help on the task before us here, that of dialogue between Buddhists and Christians.

In a world of stark inequality, of political power and manipulation and ecologically unsustainable economics, the message of Jesus concerning the reign of God needs to resoundingly be heard and more importantly, enacted. Jesus, understood as wisdom, the one who challenges us to such, calling us to walk the path of salvation rather than providing us with such, is one who better enables us to travel that walk toward the peace and justice of the divine reign. That divine reign need be seen not as a nebulous other world hope but as something deeply rooted in the call for all creation to be made whole.

It is, I believe, this understanding of Christianity which we should bring to the table in this dialogue. It stands, I assert, more faithfully to the teaching and path of Jesus, speaks more cogently to the modern context, and specifically for the task we have set, enables us to more fruitfully enter this dialogue between Buddha and Christ, and the two faith traditions bearing their names.

7

THE FAITH PRACTICE

NINIAN SMART IS PROBABLY the best-known exponent of the phenomenology of religion, how we experience and practice faith, rather than in its objective reality, or what it claims of itself. Religious practice and belief, Smart held, had seven major dimensions. We shall examine each of them to see how they apply to the two faiths we are discussing.[1]

THE PRACTICAL AND RITUAL DIMENSION

All faiths have a practical or ritual dimension. These include the nature of worship, preaching, prayers, and other practices (initiation and funerary rites being important), along with patterns of behavior. These things are present in all traditions, even those defining themselves as being not sacramental. They are, however, more overt in sacramental faiths.

Ritual initially did not play a large role in Buddhism given that Theravada is a faith built around teaching, the 'dhamma" and the personal as distinct from the corporate journey to nibbana. However, it was long ago recognized that for the laity there was a need for ritual through which they could make their devotion and reverence to the Buddha. Within Mahayana such devotion plays a major part in the faith, known as puja in Hinduism. Buddhist puja, however, is very different to that found in Hinduism, containing no Vedic-derived sacrifice. Instead it is centered on the image of the Buddha, though devotion can still be carried out where no such image is available. Each person individually centers on the Buddha, meaning there does not exist the corporate nature of worship as found in a Christian

1. Smart, *World's Religions.*

congregation. The full puja comprises seven distinct sections. These are based on the Bodhicaryavatara, the writings of the eighth century CE teacher Santideva. The seven steps are worship (puja), obeisance (vandana), seeking refuge (sarana-gamana), confession (papa-desana), rejoicing in merit (punyanumodana), transfer of merit (painamana), and self-surrender (atmabhavadi-pariyagah).

Puja commences by the lighting of lamps, symbolizing wisdom or enlightenment, with offerings being placed before the Buddha image. These may include flowers, rice, fruit, or other produce, incense, jewels and water. These offerings are varied according to the Buddha or Bodhisattva being worshiped. The flowers not only serve to beautify the worship but also to show the impermanence of all things. In some Mahayana traditions the food is eaten after the ritual. During the vandana the three aspects of the triratna, the Buddha, dharma, and sangha, are honored, either by kneeling or full prostration, both before the Buddha image and the teachers, representative of the dhamma. Again, in the third step, sarana-gamana (seeking refuge), there is reference to the triratna, after which follows a ritual called sikkhapadani, wherein a worshipper makes a series of precepts around living ethically. Papa-desana (confession) is less an unburdening of sins, as in Christianity, and more a coming to terms with one's shortcomings, finding their basis in ignorance and foolishness (avidya). The next step, punyanumodana, involves the sharing of merit (parinamana), rejoicing in good deeds, both of oneself and others. A positive attitude is gained from the knowledge that one's surplus merit may be transferred to others, thereby helping to ease the sufferings of the less fortunate. The final part of the puja, atmabhavadi-pariyagah, celebrates the deep inner sacrifice of the self for the broader fulfillment of humanity. The aim of this ritual is the achievement of bodhicitta, an attitude of total altruism toward all others. This illuminates the path to that emptiness of ego, which leads to nirvana.

Another important ritual within Buddhism is yoga. Without yogic discipline it is impossible to gain the panna/prajna necessary for enlightenment. What is primarily known as yoga in the West is hatha yoga, a type of yoga based on physical exercise positions—"asanas." Yoga, however, is much more than this. Literally meaning "yoke" or "union," it is a group of physical, mental, and spiritual practices or disciplines which aim to control (yoke) and still the mind so to develop the detachment, therefore freedom from dukkha.

While there are individual observances in Christianity around devotional prayer and sacred reading, usually of the Scriptures, the ritual central to Christianity, worship, is much more corporately directed. The term "liturgy" literally means "the work of the people," though in practice it is

largely performed and led by an ordained cleric, priest, or minister, ordination being mainly concerned with that leadership role. Though in some
traditions there are private masses, which an individual priest celebrates
for themselves, the clerical role is nearly always linked with leading a ritual
for the laity, whose presence is essential. Sacraments such as baptism, the
initiation into the Christian community, and the Eucharist/Holy Communion, are best understood as being corporate. The core of this corporate
worship is weekly Sunday worship. In the Catholic traditions this includes
that which lies at the heart of the Mass, the celebration of the Eucharist
(the reception of what is understood to be literally the body and blood of
Christ in the form of bread and wine). In the more Protestant traditions
this celebration is less frequent, while the elements are believed to have less
real, and more symbolic, presence of the body and blood of Christ. In those
Protestant traditions the preaching of the word is central, the architecture
of those churches reflecting this in the pulpit being often placed above the
communion table. In Protestantism the preached word based upon the
Bible controls the sacramental side of the faith, while in the Catholic traditions the sacraments are prime. Nearly all Christian experience is built
around weekly worship.

There is a largely a set form of weekly worship, which frames even
non-liturgical forms of Christianity. Liturgical traditions will hold to this
form much more strictly, often following by rote, set orders of worship.

Worship commences by some ascription of praise to God, followed
by confession and absolution. Readings from Scripture follow, often using a
set lectionary of readings over a three-year period, following which comes
a sermon as reflection upon the readings. The worship then turns to the
prayers of intercession (prayers which petition God for the church and the
world), again emphasizing the communal (and political) focus of Christianity. Even the offering has a communal focus in that monies raised are for
the church and world. When the Eucharist is to be celebrated the offering
is connected to the offertory, in which the elements of bread and wine are
presented. The Eucharistic prayers recapitulate the communal focus of the
revelation of God, a universal community over time and space, of which
those present are part. Finally, in the prayer the elements are believed to be
transformed in some manner, symbolically (in the Protestant traditions) or
literally (in the catholic streams) into the body and blood of Christ. Worship
concludes with the congregation being dismissed with a blessing. Worship
is interspersed with hymns or songs during which the congregation, again
in a communal manner, give praise to God.

THE EXPERIENTIAL AND EMOTIONAL DIMENSION

All faiths provide experiences which elicit an emotional experience. Smart writes, "the emotions and experiences of men and women are the food on which the other dimensions of religion feed: ritual without feelings is cold, doctrines without awe or compassion are dry, and myths which do not move hearers are feeble."[2]

Profound experiences are present in the founders of the faiths we are examining and also in their followers. As we have seen the intuitive experience of Gotama in the ploughing ceremony was integral to his enlightenment, as was another arising out of compassion, the gift by the milkmaid of milk dedicated as offering. The depth of Jesus' faith experience is seen in his baptism experience where he perceives the sky opening and the voice of God confirming his call. Later his deep emotions are clearly evident in his sweating tears of blood in the garden of Gethsamane while contemplating his approaching death, and again in his cry of dereliction while hung upon the cross, believing himself to be estranged from God.

Rudolf Otto made this attribute of profound awesome/awful experience central, charging that the basis of religion lies in the numinous or the "mysterium tremendum et fascinans" (the mysterious force which draws and attracts/fascinates human beings but also raises within them an awe-inspired fear).[3]

This awe is very present in the Judeo-Christian tradition, vividly seen in such figures as Isaiah, Jeremiah, Job, and Paul. With Paul it is something so overwhelming it causes blindness. That is to be expected as God as transcendent other lies at the heart of Christianity. While Buddhism lacks the idea of a transcendent god, awe is still present, usually associated with Buddha. We find it present when the armies of Mara beat retreat before Gotama, just prior to his enlightenment, and in the elephant suddenly grown tame after being set upon Buddha by Devadatta.

Another aspect of experience, at the opposite pole to awe, with its emphasis on holiness/separation, is that cultivated in a feeling of unity with the mystical. Aldous Huxley believed this mystical unifying experience to lie at the heart of all faiths. While the unitive mystical experience of Buddha's enlightenment is clearly core to Buddhism, achieved through meditation, the means of which, as seen, is intricately elaborated, we do not find such in the Judeo-Christian tradition. We do hear of Jesus spending forty days in the desert preparing himself for his ministry and later his spending all night

2. Smart, *World's Religions*, 13.
3. Otto, *Heilige.*

in prayer, though given no details of the content of those no doubt profound experiences. Of that experience central to Christianity, Jesus' agonizing over his upcoming betrayal and death, we are given no inner experiential content, though we are told he spent the night in prayer preparing. These experiences are clearly intense, with Jesus on each occasion struggling with doubt, even alienation from God, before finally experiencing a deep unity with the divine. Thus on the last occasion he cries out asking that he be spared drinking this cup (his death) before finding a unitive role in the divine purpose saying, "your will be done" (Matt 26:42; Luke 22:42).

The corporate nature of Christianity, with its sociopolitical orientation, makes the prime experience in that faith to be not unitive but rather relational love. The love that is manifested in Christianity is one which causes an intense unity between the lover and the beloved. Thus Paul, whose conversion was a highly intense experience, can exclaim, "it is no longer I who live but Christ who lives in me" (Gal 2:20). This dissolution of the two into the one is the intense experience of differing forms of love. From such develop the mystical apophatic forms of Christian prayer, those which moving beyond words and concepts celebrate divine-human unity.

We can suspect that the profound experiential is present behind the intricately detailed processes of meditation and enlightenment within Buddhism. Given the mind nature of the faith these however have become analyzed and categorized.

The experiential dimension, probably more than any of the other dimensions, makes clear the difference of orientation between Buddhism and Christianity. In Buddhism the gaze is directed within, so we are given great detail of the inner unitive mystical path, while for Christianity it is directed outward, with the result that the mystical experience is relational, built around love. The faiths in short may be defined by one being of the mind, the other of the heart.

THE MYTHIC OR NARRATIVE DIMENSION

Religious experience is channeled and expressed through sacred narrative or myth, the story side of religion. These narratives may be historical, speak of some primordial time, or of the end of time. There are stories of founders and heroes found in each faith, along with accounts told of an evil counterpart.

Both Buddhist and Christian Scriptures make consistent use of narrative. Of the founders, Buddha and Christ, we are given extensive narrative, that being central to the belief of adherents in both faiths, strongly shaping their understanding of each. In speaking of their faith both Buddhists and Christians make constant reference to accounts given of events in their founders' lives.

These narratives found in the Scriptures pertaining to each faith are believed to have been divinely given or inspired and given that status are ipso-facto held to be true. Many other stories are present in the tradition, but not being in the Scriptures, they hold lesser authority. These are usually the accounts of disciples or followers who are inspired to follow the founders.

Most of this narrative is shaped by myth. We have examined the nature of myth, and I will return to it in our final chapter, but again, we need to remind ourselves that myth has nothing to do with falsehood. Even when it has no historical basis it is not false. Rather, it serves as a means of offering meaning. As such its truth will often be even more profound than literal or objective truth.

Especially important are myths and legends built around the events which are central to each of those faiths. Thus, a whole series of mythic events, expanding and growing more fantastic over time, get attached to Buddha's enlightenment, while likewise, fantastic events become increasingly connected to the crucifixion-resurrection cycle of Christ. In both, we found even the cosmos affected, paying homage to the great event. The mythic images used concerning these core events in each faith are remarkably similar. They each include a tree, an evil tempter, and a heroic journey or struggle.

Some suggest there are common mythic forms and archetypes which inform all human storytelling, so we should expect commonality. Certainly both Buddhism and Christianity draw upon common motifs, though as we shall see they use them diametrically different in relating the core event to each faith.

Myth is present, however, not just in these core events but rather right through the narratives which give us the lives of both Buddha and Christ. Myth informs the narratives of the births of both, each understood to be too important to be subject to normal births, while the many accounts we have in the Scriptures concerning their lives and ministries are nearly all informed by myth. The accounts of Jesus both walking upon and stilling the waters are, as we have seen, profoundly influenced by myth, as likewise is the account of Gotama's belated discovery of the obvious nature of human suffering, naively unknown to him previously, in his adulthood.

It is myth appealing to profound meaning which draws us to a faith. We may know historical events mentioned in each faith, say the ancient cities of India, and that Pilate was procurator of Judea, but it is not these facts which move and draw but rather the deep meanings of a faith as delivered in myth.

Later legend gets added to these mythic accounts of the founders and their followers. In Buddhism, accounts of the Buddhas of previous eons are created, while in Christianity we get legendary accounts of Jesus traveling to, even being buried in India, while his mother, Mary, finds eternal rest in France.

THE DOCTRINAL AND PHILOSOPHICAL DIMENSION

The doctrinal dimension underpins the narrative dimension of a faith. Being the intellectual component of faith it tends to be the domain of the experts or professionals but is present in even seemingly simple statements about faith.

As found, doctrine is particularly important in Christianity, as subscription to a belief, believed to be orthodox, is the mark of being Christian. Doctrine need be intricately developed to make sense of such concepts that God, though fully present in each of the creator, the incarnation of Jesus, and in the Holy Spirit, is one. This leads to the development of the Trinity, by which God is understood as three persons in one substance. Further questions were raised as to how Jesus could be both fully human and divine when these two categories were held to be mutually exclusive. All this needed the framing of an extensive body of doctrine.

This discussion within Christianity was framed by its presence within the Greco-Roman world, particularly in how that world was shaped by Greek philosophy. Due to the influence of philosophy in the West, Christianity necessarily has had to engage with philosophy from the time of the apologists in the second century CE until today. That philosophy is engaged in the wrestle with the paradoxes of the faith, and as a means of making sense of the faith culturally and intellectually. In the Roman Catholic tradition philosophy represents the first, underpinning step to the study of theology. What perhaps should be left as ineffable conundrums Christianity seeks to solve. To do that it makes reference to something outside itself, philosophy. Philosophy in the East in different in that it does not stand outside the faith but more so is employed within the faith.

We have examined how Buddhism, though defining itself much less by doctrinal orthodoxy, still develops a highly sophisticated philosophy. The philosophical tradition within Buddhism is, however, less engaged in sense-making philosophically as in developing rational systems of explanation for things germane to itself, known experientially. It is not so much concerned with faith making sense in the public arena, of which it essentially has little interest, it after all being maya. It is less about using logic (apologetics), as we find in Christianity, and more about making sense of intricate systems, given by experiential insight. Whole systems are constructed, especially concerning ontology, beyond outside verification or even argumentation. Buddhism plays within a very highly developed Wittgenstein "language game." In the domain it chooses, its assertions and argumentation make strong sense, having a strong internal logic. Buddhist logic is verifiable not so much through relationship to outside truth (indeed it radically and deliberately contradicts it, seeing it as avidya) but rather through deep internal experience, while Christianity seeks verification of its revelation by reference to truths outside itself.

THE ETHICAL AND LEGAL DIMENSION

The ethical and legal dimensions are concerned with how a faith manifests itself in an adherent's daily living: what they need to do and from what they are prohibited. It is that part of the faith which leads some to say all faiths are the same because they call us to live a "good life."

Ethics or "sila" are central in Buddhism, all Buddhists having to adhere to the Five Precepts or pancasila. These are that one must not kill, steal, commit sexual immorality, lie, nor take intoxicants. On becoming a Buddhist, a person commits to these, that commitment taking place in a ceremony. Without holding to sila, the first part of the Eightfold Path, it is impossible to move forward along the path to samatha (meditation) and panna (wisdom). Beyond the sila, one in the sangha, as earlier noted, is expected to then move on to the Eight Precepts (atthangasila) and Ten Precepts (dasasila), these supplementing the pancasila in detailing such things as the times when meals may be taken, until finally embarking upon the Ten Good Paths of Action (dasakusalakammapatha).

Despite coming out of Judaism, with its emphasis on the Torah and halakhah, set codes for ethical living, Christian ethics are different as they contain no mandatory ethical code which must be held. They are instead derivative. The ethic of love is central to Christianity, and while Jesus said, "love one another," Christian love does not arise so much out of a command but is more so from the example of Christ who so lived and died as the personification of love, as well as being of fruit of a life transformed in Christ. A Christian is necessarily part of the church which is called to manifest that love which is a reflection of Christ's self-giving love in its life. The result, however, is not too different. If a person truly loves they are not likely to kill, steal, or speak in a slanderous manner. While Christianity has, therefore, no set code of ethics, it is strongly implied. Christian ethics end up looking very similar to those of the pancasila.

In neither Buddhism or Christianity is ethic meant to be a burden. Buddhists understand the keeping of the Five Precepts as being the optimum way to live in that it is in accord with both our essential nature and that of the cosmos, facilitating our enjoyment of life, being in alignment with the dhamma, the underlying universal law which governs both, the physical and moral order of the universe. In the physical realm the dhamma governs all things from the rising of the sun to the phases of the moon and the changing of the seasons. Within the field of ethics and morality it manifests itself in kamma, which governs the way in which moral deeds affect our current and future lives. Enlightened beings such as Buddha have discovered this and so live deeply contented lives, while those still in a non-enlightened state, swimming against the current, experience suffering.

Something similar holds in Christianity. Christ is understood as the personification of the logos (the undergirding principle of the cosmos). Christians are called to live incorporated into Christ and as such are incorporated into the logos. The main component to the Christian ethic is love, and in so living in love we experience our greatest fulfillment. Far from being a burden, Christian ethics are understood to be a means for living most richly and fully.

THE SOCIAL AND INSTITUTIONAL DIMENSION

While the previous five dimensions can be considered in abstract external terms, the social dimension has to do with the incarnation of religion, how a religious movement is embodied in a group of people, particularly its formal organization, as sangha for Buddhists and church for Christians. This involves the study of the sociology of a religion. What is the relationship of the religion to the society as a whole? It may be that the faith stands synonymous with the group as found in small tribal groups; it may stand adversarial to the society, as did the earliest Christians to the Roman Empire; perhaps it is one denomination or faith among others; or it may be the official religion. Also within different faiths there are different forms of government. Some are strictly hierarchical such as in the Catholic churches, while others are much more loosely organized.

In its social and institutional dimension Christianity is far more corporately organized than Buddhism. With the exception of the corporate life in the sangha much of Buddhist life is private. It centers around meditation which by its nature, even when performed corporately, is an individual pursuit. Corporate worship stands at the heart of Christianity, though of course there are private pursuits such as prayer and devotional reading, normally of the Bible.

Along with the formal governance of the particular religions there are charismatic figures, be they saints, mystics, gurus, or prophets. There are some who go even beyond this final category as revolutionaries. In their time and within their religious traditions both Buddha and Christ are examples of the latter. As we saw, while they lived and died in a tradition, their thought and teaching was so revolutionary it led to new faiths being born, bearing their names. The epithets ascribed to them, Buddha and Christ, indicate just how revolutionary their teaching was.

Along with the faith founders, there are also other revolutionaries in each tradition, radically reorienting those faiths. In Christianity we find examples from the very earliest time: Paul with his thorough orientation of the infant faith; Augustine with his accommodation of Christianity to the social situation; Benedict with his codifying Christian monasticism; Saint Francis of Assisi and the advent of the friars; Ignatius of Loyola with his founding of the Jesuits and his explorations in spirituality; Martin Luther, whose theological understanding led to the Protestant Reformation; and John Wesley, from whom sprang a new denomination. Modern figures who have had great influence, taking the faith in new directions, include Dietrich Bonhoeffer; Thomas Merton; Gustavo Gutierrez, the initial systematizer of liberation theology; and Br. Roger Schutz, the founder of the Taize Community.

Within Buddhism there are such figures as Aśvaghosa, the first-century CE poet, philosopher, and dramatist; Nagarjuna, who founded the Madhyamika school of Mahayana Buddhism; the great Pali fifth-century CE scholar Buddhaghosa; and Xuanzang, responsible not only for both bringing Buddhism to China but also with establishing it in a Chinese form during the seventh century CE. Another notable Buddhist figure from that century was Dharmakirti, who taught at the great university at Nelanda and was the primary theorist of Buddhist Sankya.

From the twentieth century we have figures such as Ambedkar, the Indian advocate for the Dalits (those outside the Indian caste system); Seong-cheol, regarded by some in Korea as a living Buddha; and the aforementioned Thich Nhat Hanh. Of course, the greatest reformers in Buddhism are often anonymous, particularly those figures responsible for the radical reform of Buddhism into new schools, Mahayana and Vajrayana. Then there are those responsible for the sects within those schools such as Ch'an and Pure Land. The greatest influence on the dissemination of Buddhism has no doubt been the third-century BCE king Ashoka, though it seems strange to call a king a revolutionary. Equally the same could be said of Constantine with Christianity. There have also been those who have brought Buddhism to the West, assisting it in taking new forms, and those such as the fourteenth Dalai Lama, who have done much to popularize the faith.

Revolutionary movements, however, have a tendency to move back to the center over time, taking on older institutional structures and means of expression as they are brought back into the mainstream social structure.

THE MATERIAL DIMENSION

The social or institutional dimension of a religion also is incarnated in material form. These forms can include buildings, works of art, figurines, artifacts, and many other creations. Some faiths abstain from external symbols as believing them to idolatrous, with both Buddhism and Christianity having been marked by periods of iconoclasm.

Smart notes, "The material expressions of religion are often elaborate, moving, and highly important for believers in their approach to the divine."[4] Sometimes they appear to be almost synonymous with the faith. The figures of the cross-legged sitting Buddha or Jesus upon the cross being instances of such.

Those images however were not present from the beginning in either faith, both Buddhism and Christianity being iconoclastic in their earliest forms. Buddha, it was thought, could not be imaged as he was the Tathagata, the "thus gone" into nibbana. To image him would be to associate permanency with him, impossible with Buddha or indeed any other thing, as the doctrines of anatta and annica made clear. Thus, the earliest images associated with Buddha were ones which showed that while he had once been, he was no longer present. This was indicated by use of the Bodhi tree with an empty seat at its base, an empty throne, or most commonly the thousand-spoke wheel of the dhamma, the dhammachakra, impressed into the footprints of Buddha, footprints being a most appropriate image as they indicate movement of one once here, now gone. Not until the second century CE in the Kusana Empire of Central Asia do we begin to find images of the Buddha himself. Subsequently schools of iconography arose in northern India in Mathura and Gandhara. These images, influenced by the Greek style, often depict Buddha with specific physical signs. These include the "thirty-two signs of a great man" such as elongated earlobes, a circle of hair between his eyebrows, and a lump on the forehead known as the urna.

4. Smart, *World's Religions*, 20.

Buddha is normally presented with shaven head or with tightly curled hair, with the curls turning to the right in accord with the right-hand principle. This tightly cropped hairstyle even has a name, cudakarana. As the Buddha was elevated worship of him, "bhakti" developed and with that came an increased representation of the Buddha.

One very common image called the abhayamudra has Buddha with a raised right hand, the right hand being favored in Indian religions, as in the West (in the Western sacred language, Latin, the term for left, sinistra, has an obvious connection to "sinister"). This posture represents an assurance of security and blessing, something very similar to its meaning in Christianity as a sign of benediction.

Buddhist imagery also includes the many dhyanibuddhas, manusibuddhas, dhyanibodhisattvas, and their respective shaktis. Understanding who is being represented is helped by each, as found, being represented by distinctive colors, direction, vehicle (vahana), mudra, and by the objects they hold. The dhyanibuddha and dhyanisattva are imaged as terrifying figures, often depicted with multiple heads, legs or arms. The hands of deities often hold objects of significance, related to their being. Manjushri holds a sword, a symbol of cutting through illusion, while Avalokitesvara, identified with compassion, has many hands to help.

Art constitutes an essential element of Christianity. Until the seventeenth century the history of Western art was largely identical with the history of religious art. Initially however Christians, like Buddhists, were hesitant to image Jesus. Clement of Alexandria (c. 150–c. 215 CE) opposed all forms of art, claiming they encouraged people to worship that which is created rather than the creator. Reticence to image the divine is understandable given that Christianity grew out of Judaism, where such imaging of the utterly transcendent God was, as we have seen, strictly forbidden. Islam would later strictly align itself with this prohibition, even extending it to images of human beings. That Christians were forced to pay homage to an image of the emperor reinforced this objection.

In Christianity, the idea of the incarnation gave justification for imagery to be used, for had not the divine chosen to be represented in bodily form. This gave license for even God the Father to be imaged, the archetypal image being that of Michelangelo in the Sistine Chapel. In the Eastern church the long struggle between the iconoclasts and iconographers culminated in the eighth and ninth century, with the latter winning. Eastern Orthodox churches then became full of icons, the argument being made that rather than being fixed on the icon, one looks through the image to the reality which lies behind.

The Protestant Reformation brought a reaction against iconography with many images being whitewashed, stained windows smashed, and statues demolished. Protestant structures are marked by their stark simplicity. Yet even here images and representations are making a return.

Of that image most central to Christianity, the earliest depictions of the crucifixion show the cross as being empty, for Christ, having been resurrected it was held, was no longer upon it. Only later from the fourth century do we begin to see graphic depictions of Jesus' death.

Likewise, in Buddhism the iconographers won out with Buddhist temples having multiple images, usually statues of Buddha along with Bodhisatvas. Zen represents a type of "Protestant" movement within Buddhism with its return to stark simplicity.

The material dimension also encompasses natural features of the world that traditions single out as being sacred and meaningful. Buddhists make pilgrimage to four places identified with the four core events in the Buddha's life: his birth, enlightenment, first sermon, and his passing into parinibbana. These four pilgrimage sites, Lumbini, Bodhgaya, Sarnath, and Kusinagara, said to have been nominated by the Buddha himself in his final words to Ananda, serve as places of devotion, ritual, and monastic retreats, each of them marked by large reliquaries. In some traditions visiting these places enables one to accumulate merit and/or purify negative kamma.

The stupa is a form of architecture synonymous with Buddhism. The architectural style of the stupa, it is asserted, goes back to Buddha, who supposedly folded his robe, placed it on the ground, before putting first his upside-down begging bowl on top, followed by his umbrella. These serve as reliquaries, it being claimed that part of the remains of Buddha are in each.

Of course, as Buddhism spread, many other great sites for pilgrimage were constructed. Probably the greatest of these are found at Borobudur in Indonesia and Angkor in Cambodia. These, as earlier noted, as well as being influenced by Buddhist belief, are informed by the older Indian mythology, both symbolically designed as Mount Meru, the abode of the gods, with the large moats surrounding the latter, being symbolic of the barrier between the gods and humanity.

For Christians there is one sacred place above all others, the place of Jesus' death and resurrection, Jerusalem. Hundreds of thousands of Christians frequent the holy city annually on pilgrimage, visiting the places of the Last Supper; the Mount of Olives; the Temple; the Via Dolorosa, through which Jesus is claimed to have carried his cross on the way to his execution; Golgotha, the place of crucifixion (though there are two suggested sites); Jesus' tomb and place of resurrection. This last location is particularly important for Christians. Usually these Christian pilgrims also visit other sites in Israel and Palestine associated with Jesus, with Bethlehem, said to be the site of Jesus' birth, being especially important. Other pilgrimage sites include the Jordan River, location of his baptism, where many are baptized, along with various places in Galilee associated with his ministry.

There are other sacred Christian pilgrimage sites. The most important of these is Rome, particularly the Vatican, the place which became the fountainhead of the Western Church. For Orthodox Christians, Istanbul, formerly Constantinople, source of the Eastern churches and location of the sixth-century Hagia Sophia, built by the Eastern Roman Emperor Justinian, is especially important. Other holy places to which pilgrimages are made include Canterbury, Glastonbury, Santiago de Compostela, Notre Dame de Paris, Chartres, and Mount Athos. Many of these places of pilgrimage were claimed to hold a relic, often a part of the cross upon which Jesus died, or part of the crown of thorns he wore at his crucifixion, or even some of his blood. Due to his ascension none of his bodily parts remain, except, due to Jewish circumcision practice, the "holy foreskin," of which there are several. Given the ascension, for other body parts one had to be content with those of an apostle or saint.

Great pilgrimages were made to these places, with the promise that such pilgrimage would earn one indulgences, either lightning or eliminating sin carried by the person making the pilgrimage. Christian pilgrimage is still an occurrence, the most popular, that to Santiago de Compostela, made by many who may have little formal connection with Christianity.

Pilgrimage to holy places is strongly associated with many faiths. Aside from those in Buddhism and Christianity, we can think of the Haj in Islam, Jerusalem in Judaism, and within Hinduism, Varanasi, and Haridwar, among numerous others, along with the Kumbh Mela, the world's largest pilgrimage.

There are other material forms found in Buddhism.

One of the central symbols in Buddhist worship is the vajra. As a symbol this goes back to the vedas. Depicted as a lightning bolt or the trident associated with Shiva, it is understood to have the qualities of a diamond and as such to be indestructible while able to cut through falsehoods. The vajra has been associated with magical rituals, often used in the Vajrayana school. Given that the vajra, as we found, is understood to be the creative male principle in the universe it also has some of the phallic associations linked to the lingam in Hinduism. The vajra is held in the favored right hand, with the left hand holding a ghanta or bell. The hands are often crossed over the chest in a propitious pose symbolizing release from passions and therefore suffering.

Another important symbol is the triratna, having significance in that it represents the Buddhist triple refuge: the Buddha, dhamma, and sangha. It is often imaged as a triangle or as a trident, similar to the vajra.

Again drawing from Hinduism, the lotus is understood to be a flower of divine origin in that it germinates not from the soil but rather from itself. The lotus represents the emanation of the Buddhas in the form of enlightened speech, born from divine origination. In Vajrayana the lotus also represents the female principle and genitals, replacing the Hindu yoni.

Within Vajrayana another symbol is that of the yab-yum (father-mother). In this a god and his shakti are depicted as having sexual intercourse. The male principle here is upaya or truth, while the female represents prajna or wisdom. A member of the sangha of this school may obtain esoteric knowledge by means of sexual intercourse though, as we have seen, this is not widespread neither in numbers or frequency for those practicing such.

Sacred dress, and rituals associated with such, represent another material dimension. In the Sutta Pitaka there is frequent reference to the type of dress to be worn by Buddhist monks and nuns. Robes are prescribed to be kasaya (ochre yellow), though little is said to their style. Given that Buddha is said to have spent many years in rags, the robes worn should therefore be sewn from rags, even those sourced from burial grounds. Later however it became the norm, again drawn from the idea of "the middle way," to wear robes made of new material. Though sometimes now expensive materials are used, in deference to the original idea of rags being used, there are always several pieces of cloth sewn together.

Christianity, like Buddhism, has also other material symbols.

The prime symbol associated with Christianity is of course the cross, either as a crucifix or a simple cross, the first being more strongly associated with the Catholic traditions, the latter with Protestantism.

Another material form is the bread and wine of the Mass or holy communion, the latter being the term mostly used by Protestants. For those in the Catholic traditions, as seen, these elements are believed to materially transform to actually become the body and blood of Christ when consecrated in the Mass.

There are symbols usually associated with the clergy, again more seen in the Catholic traditions with their greater appreciation of symbolism. In celebration of the Mass a priest will make symbols using two fingers to indicate the dual nature of Christ or three fingers as sign of the Trinity. In common with many faiths the circle, often formed by a priest touching the tips of the forefinger and thumb together as a sign of wholeness, is commonly seen. At the conclusion of the Mass the priest will make the sign of the cross while invoking the Trinity. In the symbolically more sparse Protestant traditions a common symbol is that of two palms together in prayer.

Other symbols used are the ichthys (Greek for fish), this being possibly the oldest Christian symbol, used as code during the times when Christianity was still an illicit religion under the empire. The letters in Greek, as well as spelling "fish," form the acronym "Jesus Christ, God's son, savior." Thus the identification of Christianity with fish, noting also that several of Jesus' first followers were Galilean fishers. The chi-rho symbol (appearing as an Xp) is frequently found, as it represents the fist two Greek letters in the term Christ. The dove, often found with fire, is associated with the Holy Spirit. From the Noah story it is also associated with peace. The Greek letters alpha and omega, the first and last letters of the alphabet, are often associated with Christ as completeness. The triquetra, borrowed from the older Celtic pre-Christian tradition, is another symbol found, three interlocking parts symbolizing the Trinity.

Again in the Catholic traditions the clergy will wear clothing indicating their clerical status. This usually is black clothing with a white collar, worn as street wear, while particular clothing or vestments are worn when celebrating the liturgy. These may include the alb or cassock, the white dress-like garment worn innermost, a stole, the long thin scarf, and chasuble, the poncho-like piece worn as the outermost vestment. The last two are worn in different colors, indicating the liturgical season in which the liturgy is being celebrated.

We may conclude that in this last category of faith, as identified by Smart, both Buddhism and Christianity have extensive material forms. This is the part of faith most evident to an observer, so it is not unexpected that faith expression here will be most extensive.

8

TREES, SERPENTS, AND
TEMPTATION

IN THIS CONCLUDING CHAPTER I shall paint with some broad brushstrokes,
examining some of the things we have found. In so doing I will center on the
mythology informing the two faiths, much of it held in common but often
used in diametrically opposite styles.

A tree may appear to be a strange place to commence, but it is from
such a place that we will begin to understand both Buddha and Christ and
the important things, both different and common, they are saying to us.

The tree has a long tradition, both in the West and East, as the "axis
mundi" or world center. In the West originally the tree represented something positive, both life and wisdom. Right back through time from the
Sumerians and on through successor Mesopotamian cultures, the Assyrians
and the Babylonians, the tree was central, the Assyrians especially holding
it to be core to their mythology.

The best known and most relevant myth to our discussion is one which
can be traced through all those cultures, the Epic of Gilgamesh. In this story
Gilgamesh, presented as the classical mythological hero, must pass through
many trials in his pursuit of eternal life. Finally, enduring all his tribulations,
he reaches his goal, claiming that life, represented as a tree. While resting
from his labors, for even heroes tire, he loses it, stolen by another creature,
the snake. To the serpent we will return in a moment. The purpose of the
story is to inform us that eternal life is not the lot of human beings, not even
heroes, who must instead be bound by mortality.

This story informs the account of the first humans in the Hebrew
Scriptures, who share a garden with not one but rather two trees, the tree

of of life and the tree of wisdom, the fruit of which Adam and Eve partake. These trees lie at the center of a garden from which four rivers run to the ends of the earth. This place, given the older mythology on which the story draws, is almost certainly Babylon, specifically the hanging gardens of that place.

In the biblical garden human beings live in a style of blissful innocence, unaware of right or wrong, lacking knowledge needed to make such distinctions, something which changes with the snake's entrance. This creature, like the tree, has a long mythological importance right across the world, myths arising independently in unconnected cultures found in the Ancient Near East, Southeast Asia, Central America, and Australia, among others. Historically the snake has been associated with the wisdom that gives eternal life, it apparently having such, given that it can shed its old skin and seemingly be born anew. It was the snake after all, who, as we have just seen, stole the tree of eternal life from Gilgamesh. Thus, it is the snake, rather than Gilgamesh, who possesses this prize.[1] It is not as if the ancients were silly enough to take this literally. No doubt they had witnessed dead snakes. It is the symbol or metaphor that counts. Only we in the modern age are foolish enough in religious discourse to take symbol and metaphor literally. This inability to understand myth and metaphor is, I believe, the major hindrance to our religious and spiritual understandings.

Not only did the snake possess eternal life, it also possessed wisdom, particularly by its bringing the male and female traits together, with its physical form phallically being viewed as both male and female. As female it swallowed, and its flickering tongue represented female waters, while its male form was present in it being extended and in the burning of its poison like fire. By bringing these dualities into oneness the snake was seen as possessing wisdom.

The snake then has the key to both wisdom and eternal life. As such it enters the garden of primal innocence to teach these human beings how they too can acquire such wisdom and win eternal life. They need but eat the fruit of that tree, forbidden them by their creator. The patriarchal nature of the society from which the story comes ensures that it is Eve who first succumbs to the serpent's temptation, a bias having already been established by Eve being born out of Adam, such birthing clearly being in direct contradiction to biological reality. Eve, we are informed, in turn tempts Adam. The

---

1. Earlier in the West the snake had a long history being viewed positively as a symbol of wisdom/life, to be acquired. This positive view survives in the Hebrew Scriptures with the account of Moses making the bronze snake in the desert which has miraculous curative powers. That symbol of the snake entwined around a pole is still with us as representative of medical practitioners.

effect of succumbing to this temptation is immediately disastrous. Understanding their nakedness before God, and in the older Jewish tradition this is moral nakedness rather than physical nakedness connected to sexuality, they seek to hide.

As seen, to be autonomous human beings, capable of making moral decisions, means we must eat from this tree. We have no other choice for it is impossible for us to remain in the primal innocence of infancy. Having eaten, Adam and Eve can no longer live in the garden of primal innocence, instead being driven into the tough adult world where one must earn their keep by the "sweat of their brow." Is this not our universal experience? We may reminisce about our childhood, but we cannot remain there nor return to that dependent state. This awakening to adult autonomy, though necessary, can be painful.

Present also in this story however, is the idea that Adam and Eve have grasped this knowledge in an inappropriate manner, contrary to the divine will. Perhaps rather than maturing into it, they have grabbed it in a manner of egotistical possession. Wisdom, along with life, both properly belonging to God, ought then be offered by God, not grasped by humans on their own terms, in a style of hubris. Having gained wisdom on their own terms, God, fearful that they likewise will also obtain on these terms eternal life, drives them from the garden.

Due to this the serpent is viewed negatively in the West, punished by losing its legs and having, uniquely among all creatures, to slide on its stomach. This is a classic use of mythology, to make sense of an observed oddity. Likewise, the tree, originally viewed positively as a sacred locale, as in the wider Middle East in the Hebrew Scriptures, becomes something the prophets considered to be idolatrous, Israel being warned against worship of what is usually translated as the "grove of trees."[2]

The Judeo-Christian Scriptures often have means of using but inverting the myths of which they make use.

Let us now move forward to Christ. At the commencement of his ministry, he is subjected to several temptations while spending forty days in the desert. The temptations he suffers are like those first presented to Adam and Eve, the grasping of powers, properly belonging only to God, on one's own

---

2. As the snake had been originally viewed positively in the West so also the tree within the Hebraic tradition itself. God had appeared to Abraham at Moreh when he had first entered the land (Gen 12:6), while Jacob buried the foreign gods of his followers under this same tree (Gen 35:4), while Joshua established a or mazzebah (sacred Jewish pillar) in such a place (Josh 24:26). Given such a sacred history over times such places became places associated with the divine. This practice was denounced as idolatrous by the prophets (Isa 57:5; Ezek 6:13).

terms. He after all is called the "new Adam," called such in contrast to the old Adam.

The detail of the temptations Jesus rejects also parallel those to which Israel had succumbed in the exodus journey, the forty days spent by Jesus in the desert meant to parallel the forty years spent by Israel in their exodus wanderings. To turn stones to bread, to leap from the parapet of the temple with angels miraculously saving him, and to control by power the kingdoms of the world (Matt 4:11) would surely show Jesus as possessing those divine attributes which belongs properly to God alone. Unlike his predecessors, however, Jesus successfully resists these types of temptations, ones which would assail him right through his life. By the use of power and might he could prove his divine wisdom and origin, but such would be on terms lacking divine sanction. Indeed, behind all these temptations to such use of power the figure of a very subtle Satan is seen. Thus, when tempted to such means of power by Peter, Jesus exclaims, "Get behind me Satan" (Mark 8:33). This style of temptation continues even until the point of death, where, while hanging upon the cross, he is taunted to perform a miracle to extricate himself from it. Jesus, unlike both Adam and Israel, rejects taking that belonging to God, on his own terms.

In the crucifixion scene, as in the paradisiacal garden, we again find the tree and the human being, the latter again, as just seen, being subject to the temptation to grasp at divinity in miraculously extricating himself from it. While the snake is absent in the actual Gospel accounts, this creature is often found in depictions of the crucifixion, usually around the base of the cross, often crushed and defeated. The tree/cross, however, rather than being the tree of wisdom, where one seeks to grasp eternal life on their own terms and efforts, is instead the tree where life is given graciously, in a manner at absolute odds with human wisdom, for what wisdom could ever contemplate God, fully present in Jesus, being executed? What is being stated in the Christian story is that Christ, understood as the possessor of eternal life and wisdom, overcoming evil, provides for us, out of grace alone, things which we could otherwise never properly have of our own effort. Rather than being self-taken, wisdom and life must come as a gift of God in the giving of the divine self, present in Christ, on the cross.

Christ, as the second Adam, succeeds in keeping to the divine will where the former failed. In defense of Adam, it could be argued that Christ was of a different order ontologically as part of the Trinity from the beginning of creation (although paradoxically still needing to be fully human). Still Christian faith affirms that despite this ontological difference, it was not any easier for Christ to overcome temptation for being "he was tempted in every way as we" (Heb 4:15).

Christ, through his life of perfect wisdom lived to God, brings humanity to the divine by fully realizing that human potential we all carry, to live
purely before God. To those who wish to avail themselves of the grace he
offers, they too, forgiven of their wrongdoing, something they could never
receive in their own right due to their sin, thus appear pure and therefore
acceptable before God. It is that hung on this tree, not fruit but Christ, which
brings life. That life is given not through the self-obtaining of wisdom, but
through the gracious gift of another, given in love.

Christ never grasps this right to divinity, unlike human beings who,
symbolized by Adam and Eve, demand divinity, with its wisdom and eternal
life, on their own terms. Indeed the temptation for Christ is to claim the
God role by this use of power, something he rejects, though actually he,
contrary to others, has the capacity to claim such power. By grasping such
he would, however, negate the need to suffer. Suffering, born out of love, is
held to be necessary for the salvation of all. Christianity is a faith built on
love. Love involves suffering, so suffering cannot be avoided; indeed it is
redemptive.

Judaism and Christianity, and later Islam, are religions of grace, given
out of love. Salvation, unable to be obtained from within, comes from outside, from God, as grace. Of course, in Judaism and Islam grace comes directly from God with no intermediary figure needed, while in Christianity
it is given through Christ, who, so to pass that grace, must be understood
as fully God but in enfleshed human form. One's own efforts in these three
Western religions are never enough, always leaving a person short, needing
to depend on the gracefulness of God. The transcendence of God in these
faiths is linked with this. The divine is understood in terms so transcendent,
that no one through human effort could reach.

Let us now turn to the East and Buddha. Here likewise, at the key moment in the story, Gotama's meditative watch preceding his enlightenment,
we find those same symbols of tree, snake, and human being, along with
temptation, presented by an evil one, to be resisted. As in the West, so in the
East, the symbols of tree and serpent have a long and significant history. The
tree acts in a similar manner as in the West, as axis mundi, but the serpent
remains viewed, as in the older universal tradition, as positive. Siddhattha
sits under the tree in a determined effort to find knowledge, understood
as wisdom, which will free him from the ill-fare of suffering (dukkha). In
the East, Gotama's meditative turning within to seek wisdom is an entirely
appropriate thing, for in this journey within, pursued with rigorous intent,
is found knowledge, the true understanding of reality. This is salvation in
the Buddhist sense, bringing release to nibbana. This is contrary to the view
of the West where, as we have seen, salvation is a gift come from outside,

with turning inwards in the search for the wisdom of the divine being even understood as hubris, even dangerous, as an attempt at self-achieved salvation without reference to God. Hence, some Christians fear such practices as meditation, while celebrating anti-intellectualism as being contrary to wisdom.

In the Buddha story the demonic figure called Mara is understood as maya or illusion, believing those things having no reality, as having real substance. Mara, then, ipso facto has no real substance, representing instead the internal turmoil in Gotama's mind in his meditative watch.

The serpent, viewed positively in the East as the symbol of the wisdom, that which Gotama is seeking, comes to assist him in this journey by offering him protection from the rising waters, wrapping himself under Gotama seven times so he can be raised above the waters on his journey to Buddhahood, along with unfurling his cobra's hood to protect him from the rains. Of course, both the number seven and the primeval waters as forces of chaos have strong mythological content in both the East and West.

It is interesting to compare the temptation of the Gotama with that of Jesus. While Gotama's temptation is to perceive things of unreality as reality, the temptations faced by Jesus are more strongly externally and ethically based. They are to do with the temptation to power, especially that of charismatic political power, used to secure what seems a legitimate end but which uses methods so strongly at odds with that end to make that end invalid. Western religion has at its center this sociopolitical concern. Sin, literally, "missing the target," is to live corporately unjustly, while this same missing the target for a Buddhist is the missing of the target by misconception. Correct insight or mindfulness (vidya), rather than political action, lies at the heart of Buddhism. Thus, Gotama's encounter with Mara during his enlightenment watch finds him turning the misconceptions cast by Mara into true perceiving. This does not mean that wisdom is missing in Christianity nor compassionate political action missing in Buddhism. Rather, that the emphases at the core of each differ.

This contrast is built into their cosmologies in the distinction between the linear dimension associated with history/politics and the circular connected with wisdom and the ecological. Christianity operates teleologically in that it has a beginning from which it progresses toward an end, understood as perfect. God is found active in history, through both divine acts and the acts of those divinely inspired, committed to making the world a better place. As such Christianity is political. The Moses encounter with the burning bush and exodus is core to this understanding.

Christian faith supposes Jesus as bringing about a new exodus, one which triumphs even over the greatest captivity, the boundary of death itself. Liberation thus grows to include also the metaphysical sphere but in so doing never leaves the political sphere behind. That Jesus, in preaching and enacting his exodus liberation message, is essentially political is clearly seen in the Roman empire executing him as a rebel by means of crucifixion, a punishment reserved for such political figures. Jesus, in such actions as his desert sojourn, his giving a new law on the mount, and baptism in the Jordan, strongly identifies himself with the Moses/Joshua exodus tradition, in that his actions parallel that earlier tradition, as such being midrash.

In Buddhism, Buddha, understood as existing within a cyclical understanding, seeks not to conclude the cycle, that being impossible by definition, but rather to penetrate to the inner reality existing behind it. Rather than action, this calls for perception, incisive insight.

Thus the different temptations as they are presented to Gotama and Jesus speak cogently of the two vastly different cosmologies informing the two faiths. Jesus' temptation is achieve the good via wrong means, while that of Buddha is to claim that central to Buddhism, wisdom, and having done so pass beyond the illusionary into nibbana without sharing his discovery. That would be to use wisdom wrongly. Both Buddha and Christ resist these, the most subtle, and therefore dangerous, temptations.

In Western thought perfection is usually the result of a hero being involved in the struggle to overcome evil so to bring good. The Gilgamesh story is archetypal. Like Gilgamesh these heroes are usually warriors. This represents a classically male outlook and attitude to the world connected to the solar reality, having a linear aspect in that daily it has a beginning and end, while also possessing a brilliance which exposes both good and dark deeds. Within Christianity Christ is viewed as the hero figure. He, of course, is not the classic warrior figure, fighting instead his battle on a different plain. Nonetheless fight he does, against the greatest adversary, Satan, understood properly metaphorically as the internal temptation to power on any terms, that temptation made stronger by it promising the good end.

Understood in its proper manner, so comprehensive is Christ's victory, even over death, the end or eschaton is believed to have already begun in him, though it will not be complete till the end itself. That reconciliation of all things, bringing the reign of God, involves the overturning of the present "worldly" order, understood as unjust, therefore opposed to the divine will. Thus, Jesus always makes clear his identity with the victims of the current order, the poor and the marginalized.

Finally, we are told that Christ will return again at the end of time to inaugurate the perfect reign over a new heaven and earth. The fullness of peace and justice shall then prevail in the shalom. This coming reign of God is usually associated with cataclysmic apocalyptic events which will bring the overthrow of the corrupt old order so to usher in the new.

This political message centered on liberation is clearly essential in our world today. We need heroes such as Jesus who, even at the cost of their lives, strive mightily against injustice and wrong. When this is a change toward and using the right values this may be identified as true progress.

Progress, outside such an understanding however, may be problematical, justifying all manner of things with little relation to the good. Having become an absolute it has been often used for ends which are oppressive. As such it has brought us not only evil political systems, promising an ideal often associated with messianism, but also disastrous ecological ends.

We need thus always temper our concern for progress with the wisdom inherent in Buddhism and its practices, such as yoga and meditation, which enable us to see to the heart of that being promised. Is the one making the promise genuine? Is the project they are offering genuinely liberating? What type of "messiah" is on offer?

Likewise, we need to weigh progress, even when it appears good, against the environmental damage it may cause. Buddhism reminds us of the essential folly of progress for progress's sake. It calls us instead to a deep wisdom which enables us to evaluate the need for progress. It calls into question the reality of those things in which we want to progress, most radically asking the question as to whether progress is essential to our human ends. Most poignantly in our current context, do we really need to "progress" economically at the cost of the earth?

How do we face our world rife with injustice therefore needing change? There are times when we need blessed rage. With Jesus we need to throw ourselves against the great dehumanizing forces of history. Like him we need enter the world of those being crucified daily, casting ourselves in solidarity with them. Jesus' life and death stand as potent protest against wrong.

Buddha shows us a different way, a way of equanimity beyond the vicissitudes of the world. Again, we have the hero's journey, the single minded pursuit of victory, no matter with what one is assailed.

Without the clearheadedness and clarity of mind associated with such practices as contemplative meditation giving true insight (vidya), we are liable to act politically in a reactive ill-informed way, fueled by an unproductive anger, liable to take on the oppressor's methods in our opposition to them. This is the very temptation directed toward Jesus, the easy but wrong action for the supposedly good end. Jesus, before his ministry, had prepared himself for such temptation by his time in the desert, while during his ministry we find him spending time in prayer, especially immediately before his trial and execution. Both Jesus and Buddha spend time centering themselves, sharpening their thinking, and examining their deep motivations before and during their ministries.

The essential difference between the two figures is evident in the classic symbols of the two faiths, the young man Jesus crying in anguish against injustice, upon the cross, and Gotama growing old and wise in meditation. The ways of Buddha and Jesus need be held in creative tension. The stance of Jesus stands as a corrective to any spiritual passivity which too easily tempts us to retreat to the monastery, or to pious spiritual practice, living in a pure passivity beyond the world, while "the world goes to hell." The way of Buddha, on the other hand, calls us to reflect deeply upon our actions. Reactive actions may be just as dangerous as those things against which they react. We need to heed both the Christian call to the world in action and the Buddhist equanimity in the face of the world. Our passion to change the world needs be shaped by our clarity in perception on the world as is and the change we wish to make.

Is not the forced coming of the supposed reign of God, with the sure conviction that any means are permissible to bring it, and that our vision of it is true, the very temptation which threatens the West so strongly today? Think of the religious fundamentalisms found in the teleologically oriented Western faiths of Judaism, Christianity, and Islam, or how politics is subject to this same temptation to power, even for the supposedly good end. Politics in the West has regularly been subject to the temptation of messianism with usually tragic results. That has become intimately linked to the idea of inevitable progress being good. The economy must grow, and consumption must increase with change becoming understood as something good in itself. The example of Jesus shows us that we need also temper the idea of progress with how it affects those on the underside. Often it is the poor who get left in its wake. Progress need be progress for all, not just the elite.

The Jesus story shows that the "good" end by any means is a dangerous temptation. That was the core temptation faced by him right until his dying moment. The good end and true progress can only really be good when brought about by fair means with purity of intent. Christians need to temper their desire for progress, even when motivated by a good end, with the need to develop a profound wisdom which will guide them in their efforts.

The idea of progress is further called into question by the great ecological crises we face. Progress at the cost of unsustainable use of the earth's resources is short-sighted, indeed a sin against God's good creation. Uncritical thinking concerning the value of progress has led to the massive ecological crisis which threatens our world today. The idea of progress need be measured against that of sustainability, for progress cannot bring us to any ideal end at the expense of the ecosphere. Ecological thinking rudely informs us that not all progress is necessarily good.

The Christ event challenges the idea that such linear thinking necessarily means inevitable progress, any methodology being permissible to ensure that progress. It radically critiques such thinking by informing us that the reign of God does not come in some manner where a project of self-interest, using any means of power, is given divine sanction by the powerful with the invocation of God's name. That reign comes rather through the one suffering and broken on the underside of history. In Christ there is found a radical judgment cast on our manner of politics, a challenge to cast our lot with those on the underside of history rather than with those who write it. Progress, as defined and guided by the powerful, is not necessarily good.

While in the West the divine is ultimately found at the eschaton, in the East the divine is found in the constant eternal sitting behind the passing ethereal present. Meaning is found by penetrating behind that apparently real, but actually maya, to the essentially real. It can only be seen with clarity of perception. This cyclical view is much more connected to the female and to the lunar, these symbols having in common that both experience a monthly cycle. This same view informs most of the world's indigenous philosophies or mythologies. One penetrates to the divine, eschewing means of action, by turning inwards in understanding, sought usually in ritual and/or meditation. The wisdom so gained allows one to then see through unreality to the essentially real.

To the West, the East points to the ever-recurring unchanging cycle of reality, which it charges makes the efforts of Western heroes pointless. The mythologist Joseph Campbell speaks of that ever-ongoing cycle of the East "licking up the dust of heroes." To the external world, the East essentially takes an attitude of indifference. Certainly, within Buddhism one is called to compassion (karuna), but that compassion is only one of the parts of that great eightfold path which leads to self-enlightenment. The concern for karuna is derivative from the central concern of correct perception, something informing us that all around us, including any sense of "self," is but maya. Thus, in Theravada especially, the eightfold individual path is followed, as a monk, having left society, to the exclusion of all else. This lack of corporate concern with the world finds a corrective in the broader view of the later Mahayana tradition, especially in the concept of the Bodhisattva, the enlightened one who having achieved release to nirvana chooses instead to remain upon earth so to impart the saving message. Such a figure, having accumulated extra merit, is able to pass that to others for their salvation. This as grace is like that possessed by Christ whose merit is passed to all others for salvation. Yet even in Mahayana, for all its talk of compassion, the crucial central task is still to avoid avidya, wrong perception, compassion being derivative of that ultimate goal.

The different cosmologies are seen in each faith's placements, mythologically, of the climactic moment. For the Christian that comes at the end point, the eschaton; with the perfect harmony, seen externally, which that end brings, a perfection has begun in the Christ event. A foretaste of that time is seen in the cosmic signs present at the moment of Christ's resurrection. Within Buddhism the great climatic cosmological moment evidenced similarly by a profound cosmic harmony occurs with the Buddha's enlightenment, again, something in which all creation shares. In Buddhism the cosmological climax, rather than being at the end, with the physical order brought into harmony exhibited in justice and peace, comes at the moment when enlightenment, correct perception, is found by Buddha with the world as maya penetrated. The heart of one is external, the other internal.

Rather than, as in Christianity, a perfection falling to a brokenness before climaxing in perfection, the classic teleological view, we find in Buddhism each eon commencing in a diminished state before rising to a point where it is ready to receive the teaching of a Buddha and falling away again. Each cycle is linked to increasing perception of reality before it again falls away. This cycle is linked not to increasing perfection but rather to lucidity of perception. It is the lucidity of perception which drives the Buddhist cycle, that perception being the cause of either the increasing or decreasing of that which is external; longevity of life, justice of government, in each eon. In Christianity it is just actions which lead to an increasing good. The core for one is perfection of an external relational world, for the other perception of a real world behind the illusionary.

The holding of this contrast between the teleological and cyclical in tension is crucial. To understand the profoundly deep real behind the ethereal passing is important, but if it becomes a passivity in the face of the world's violence and deep injustices, a means of saying they aren't important because I am seeking the ultimate reality behind them, we fall into that type of egotism so opposed by Buddha. What Buddhism can teach us is that in the perspective we may obtain by Buddhist practice we can become more directed in our efforts to bring our world to justice and peace. What Christianity can teach us is that depth of love which creates in us the passion to change the world.

Given their differing understandings of the divine, and also where change is to be effected, Buddhism and Christianity offer different methods of communicating with that core to each. Buddhism, as we have found, is identified with meditation, by which one in stillness turns inwards to find the real essence behind the ever-changing illusion. At the heart of Christian devotion, on the other hand, is turning outward in prayer. While some forms of Christian prayer are oriented inward at personal transformation, typically prayer is directed outward, particularly in that form known as petitionary or intercessory prayer, a prayer of relation whereby one petitions God to change the external world. That prayer prayed by Jesus known as the Lord's Prayer is a classic example of petitionary prayer.

In passing it may be said that in Western philosophical terms the tension between the East and the West is that found between Plato, where reality is the otherworldly forms, this world being but a shadow reflection, and Aristotle, where things possessing potential progress toward their realization, wherein lies their true reality. In Plato's well known cave example, the one seeing shadows reflected onto the back wall, thinking the shadows to be the actual reality, suffers from misconceiving reality (Buddhist avidya), while Aristotle's understanding informs both Hegel's and Marx's very different dialectics, each speaking of progress, the former of Spirit, the latter of material, toward a perfected end.

With its concern for the world, particularly in a desire to progress it, it is little wonder that science, and its associated technology, for both better and worse, though usually the former, arose in the West. Likewise, the great political movements, capitalism and Marxism, with their belief in the need for progress, may be understood as secular versions of the Western eschatological vision of increasing perfection.

In exploring contrasts between Buddhism and Christianity we have found that their cosmologies, in their understanding of time (circular/linear), their placement of the ideal (found behind the perceived creation vis-a-vis being present at the culmination of creation), their means of attaining that ideal (meditative turning inward versus prayer directed outward), and the thing central to the human condition which causes us to miss that ideal (illusion or wrong ethics), are radically different.

Given their contrasts does this mean one must be held to the exclusion of the other in that one is right and the other wrong? I do not believe so. Equally these differences should not simplistically be explained away in a facile attempt at homogenization. Rather, I believe the differences are best held in creative tension, rather than in exclusion of one for the other. Held as such they can lead us to deeper truth of both the human condition and also its needs.

Though their outcomes in terms of behavior and ethics may often be similar, we need acknowledge the essential tension between each of the faiths' prime emphasis and how those emphases at the heart of each religion communicate in different ways to our deep human need. Both faiths, with their distinct emphases, speak of our deep human needs at different stages of the human journey. As such each can act as a corrective of the other for us at different points. The partial nature of each solution as it affects our human living is seen in that both Buddhism and Christianity develop the other side, from what was their original emphasis, so to bring themselves to completion. The faith of disciplined effort, Theravada, develops in Mahayana a side of grace, while the faith of grace, Christianity, develops a dimension of demand.

These tensions are best understood as being creative and ought not be minimized. Rather, they are best left as correctives to the other. We will briefly examine some of these creative tensions.

The first, to which I have just alluded, involves the tension between grace, where salvation is given from outside as grace, and where effort is demanded, with enlightenment as salvation being found from within. Buddhism and Christianity commence at opposites ends. The former is associated with Christianity, the latter with Buddhism. Each, however, find a counterbalance.

In Buddhism the original emphasis on effort, as seen in Theravada, finds a necessary corrective in Mahayana schools of grace. Avalokitesvara especially becomes the great symbol of compassion, extending grace to those who call upon him. In the Pure Land School, where grace is most predominant, the mere calling upon the name of Nama Amida Butsu allows a person to gracefully receive salvation, while elsewhere we are informed the reading in good faith of one verse of the Lotus Sutra can bring salvation. The Lotus Sutra, literally the Lotus of the Good Law, is understood as grace replacing the old, in much the same manner as Christians understand a new dispensation of grace replacing that of old, as found in the Torah or Jewish law. These developments within Buddhism bring it remarkably close to the heart of Christianity, which begins as a grace-filled religion in which mere calling upon the name of Christ brings saving grace.

Christianity, originally so built on grace, over time finds a corrective in the need for effort, for works. That movement begins even in the Christian Scriptures where in letter of James it is expressed, "faith without works is dead." For James works/effort are understood in terms of ethics, especially the caring for and sharing with the poor. While Christianity continues to emphasize grace, the call for effort or work emerges regularly in the Christian tradition. It is found from the desert fathers to the development of monasticism, the medieval example of Francis of Assisi to modern day liberation theology. As we have seen, Christianity along with the other Western faiths is marked by the external attribute of ethics. Christianity, originally with grace at its heart, returns to Western roots of ethical demand, in that grace, correctly understood, calls for a response.

Ethics in both Buddhism and Christianity are derivative. In Buddhism they come as a result of correct perception or understanding. In Christianity they arise from a person's conversion experience. That conversion is rooted in the acknowledgement of divine love for the world. Understanding that love, one in turn lives to love and therefore to ethics.

Within the early development of Christianity there was yet a further dimension built around self-effort. That was the need to stand firm in faith against those who would persecute believers. Those martyred were believed to have been lifted to a higher way, with some, knowing this, even seeking martyrdom. Later, when Christianity was legalized and became the official state religion martyrdom was no longer an option. Those seeking a higher way through self-effort retreated to the desert where they endured a self-inflicted martyrdom through their own strenuous ascetic as spiritual discipline. That led eventually to the development of the monastic movement where, through monastic practices, believers sought a higher form of spiritual wisdom. These forms of Christianity centered on meditative prayer and contemplation are not too dissimilar to the disciplines of the Buddhist sangha.

Another dimension of effort, something more associated with Buddhism, also enters the Christian understanding, the need for attaining wisdom, the reception of such being key to salvation. This emphasis, as we have already explored, is clearly present in the non-canonical Gospel of Thomas. Here one following the action of Christ turns inwards in self-effort attaining wisdom, and in such, finds salvation. Christ, rather than giving salvation, the schema classically associated with Christianity, instead shows the way for the individual to find their own salvation through the same type of effort as found within Buddhism. As we have seen such mainly finds expression in the eastern Orthodox churches. This concern for wisdom builds on the wisdom tradition, the Ketuvim, found in the Jewish Tanakh.

Grace and works/demand ought be left in a creative tension, two ends of one axis. There are times in which each of us need receive a message of grace. For some their whole life story, punctuated by brokenness, may have led them to a place where they need nearly always to receive a message of grace, a message affirming that salvation is a given, not demanding strenuous effort and discipline. In the brokenness we all share from time to time, each of us may need to receive this message of grace: "You are accepted," "you are loved." This needs to be a strong message, as those most needing to hear it are often least able to accept it.

Yet we know also that grace can be a justification for all sorts of things. We have seen how the German theologian Dietrich Bonhoeffer who, in those years the German church was giving justification to the Nazi regime, spoke of "cheap grace," before challenging Christians to "costly discipleship." It could be said that Christians need balance their faith in Christ with their sharing in the faith of Christ. Thus, the graceful action of God in Christ giving salvation needs to be counterbalanced with the faith held by the human Jesus, directed to the work of the justice and peace, implicit in that at the heart of his ministry, his preaching and enacting, the reign of God. For Christians when cheap grace too abounds there is a need perhaps to take cognizance of that laying at the core of both Buddha's and Christ's message, a call to commitment which radically changes one's whole orientation. This message of demand we all need to hear at points in our lives.

As some need to almost hear the message of grace exclusively, in like manner others need to hear a message overwhelmingly of demand, for true spiritual effort and life transformation. This especially is the case for those whose manner of oppressive living is all too easily justified by their often-facile appeals to religious grace alone. To the rich young ruler who appealed to his piety as sufficient Jesus calls him, "go and sell everything you have and give to the poor" (Mark 10:17–22). Such spiritual effort as prescribed by Buddha with its radical questioning of the world, even the call to leave it, will preclude such comfortable accommodation with the world in the name of grace. I would hazard a guess that some Buddhists who easily lapse into a grace justification of their lives likewise once again need to hear their founder's radical demand.

While misconception lies at the core of Buddhism, it finds also a place in Christianity, though not core as in Buddhism. Jesus warns against "storing up treasures upon earth, where moth and rust destroy, and where thieves break in and steal" (Matt 6:19–20). Immediately after he speaks of the need for one's sight to be good so that their insight may be right (Matt 6:22–23). He then critiques the needless worry about things over which one has no control. To those overly worried about their material well-being, he says, "Who not you by worrying can add a single hour to their life?" (Matt 6:27). He even speaks of teaching in parables so that only those with insight will understand, "though seeing they do not see, though hearing they do not hear or understand" (Matt 13:13). Indeed, the key event in Christianity, the resurrection, is seen by those with insight.

The messages of both Buddha and Jesus are so radical that their followers understand them as being unable to be contained within their own traditions and so create new faiths bearing their names. The radical nature of each of these faiths is again seen in that in both cases the emergent faiths developed a strong missionary impulse, something again distinguishing them from their mother faiths, both closely identified with, and defined by, a people.

More radically however, both Christ and Buddha offer a sharp critique of all religious traditions, including those named after them, with their propensity to stagnate into certainties and unchanging categories. For those who seek such comfort neither Buddha nor Christ give much in the way of succor. Indeed, a more radical interpretation would place both figures outside of what we call religion, a term derived from the Latin "to link," in that in their teachings both Buddha and Christ offer a radical critique of the type of religion understood as undergirding and linking a society, thereby providing justification (and frequently sanctification) for the status quo. Their teachings lead instead to alternate "countercultural" communities, the Buddhist sangha breaking down the caste system among other things, while the early Christian communities, house churches, were first identified as being people of "the way" because they walked a radically different path. Little wonder such radical views exist that interpret both figures as secular protests to their religious traditions. Within Zen Buddhism, as seen, we even have the shocking sentiment, "if you see the Buddha on the road, kill him." Of Jesus the Biblical scholar John Dominic Crossan charges that we "have turned the iconoclast into an icon." The iconoclastic tendencies of both Jesus and Buddha represent something from which we can draw a lesson when too comfortable in our religious systems. To such forms of religion, often comforting to those benefitting, and oppressive to those marginalized, both Buddha and Christ offer a sharp critique.

In conclusion, the ways of Buddha and Christ, each in a different manner, speak to us of our deep human needs, often casting radical, sometimes harsh judgment on how we understand our reality. They each do so in distinct ways, as evidenced in their contrasting use of primal mythological images. They cannot be simplt homogenized nor need be chosen one over the other by exclusion. Rather, they need be held in creative tension, each drawing lessons from what may appear to be its opposite. In understanding such opposites, and in the recognition of where they hold commonalities, we will be well served by our understanding of that which both Buddha and Christ bring to us.

Beyond that recognition, however, we need to be inspired to action both by their teachings and the example of their lives. We ought to have a burning zeal for what Jesus called the kingdom of God but in our pursuance of that be focused on and directed by vidya (correct seeing and wisdom) as cultivated by Buddha. Holding both in a creative tension we shall be well-equipped, with both insight and passion, to bring that needed change to both ourselves and to the world around us.

As both Buddha and Christ and their followers break open old faith categories, reforming and reinvigorating them, adherents of the faiths founded in their names have the capacity to likewise break again the bounds set for them. It is likely that each of us, Buddhist and Christian, will need to do so in an age radically different from the founders of each faith. This should not intimidate us because as seen both faiths have often been subject to change, even radical over their long histories.

Both figures, Buddha and Christ, met with an engaging, questioning mind, present to us in a manner still important, needed challenge, in a rapidly changing world.

About the Author

John Queripel B.A. (Macquarie University), B.D. (University of Sydney), M. Th. (University of Sydney), Dip. Ed (University of N.S.W.), is a minister of the Uniting Church in Australia. He has ministered widely in both rural and urban settings and as a chaplain in a university and prison environment. He has a strong interfaith interest, having chaired the "Relations with Other Faiths" committee of the N.S.W./A.C.T. Synod as well as being President of the Council of Christians and Jews (N.S.W.).

BIBLIOGRAPHY

Allen, Charlotte. *The Human Christ: The Search for the Historical Jesus*. Oxford: Lion, 1998.

Armstrong, Karen. *A History of God*. London: Mandarin, 1993.

———. *Buddha*. London: Phoenix, 2000.

Borg, Marcus. *Jesus and Buddha: The Parallel Sayings*. Berkeley: First Ulysses, 1997.

Bornkamm, Gunther. *Jesus of Nazareth*. London: Hodder & Stoughton, 1960.

Brazier, David. *The Feeling Buddha: An Introduction to Buddhism*. London: Constable & Robinson, 1997.

Cobb, John B., and Ward M. McAfee. *The Dialogue Comes of Age: Christian Encounters with Other Traditions*. Minneapolis: Fortress, 2010.

Conze, Edward, ed. *Buddhist Scriptures*. Middlesex: Penguin, 1959.

Crossan, John Dominic. *The Historical Jesus: A Revolutionary Biography*. San Francisco: Harper, 1991.

———. *Jesus: The Life of a Mediterranean Jewish Peasant*. San Francisco: Harper, 1994.

Cupitt, Don. *The Sea of Faith: Christianity in Change*. London: BBC, 1984.

Destro, Adriana, and Mauro Pesce. *Encounters with Jesus: The Man in His Place and Time*. Minneapolis: Fortress, 2012.

Dhammaanda, K. *Buddhism and Politics*. Penang: Buddhist Digest Publication Board, 1990.

Dunn, James. *The Theology of Paul the Apostle*. Grand Rapids: Eerdmans, 1998.

Fletcher, Tenshin, and David Scott. *Way of Zen*. New York: St. Martin's, 2001.

Fox, Matthew. *The Coming of the Cosmic Christ*. Blackburn: Collins Dove, 1989.

Hick, John. *God and the Universe of Faiths: Essays in the Philosophy of Religion*. London: Macmillan, 1973.

Hoover, Roy W., ed. *Profiles of Jesus*. Santa Rosa: Polebridge, 2002.

Humphreys, Christmas. *Buddhism*. Middlesex: Penguin, 1951.

———. *Exploring Buddhism*. Wheaton: Quest, 1974.

James, William. *The Varieties of Religious Experience*. London: Collins Fontana, 1960.

John Paul II, Pope. *Crossing the Threshold of Hope*. New York: Random House, 1994.

Keown, Damien. *A Very Short Introduction to Buddhism*. Oxford: Oxford University Press, 2013.

Khema, Ayya. *Being Nobody, Going Nowhere: Meditations on the Buddhist Path Wisdom*. London: 1987.

Landaw, Jonathon, et al. *Buddhism for Dummies*. 2nd ed. Hoboken: John Wiley & Sons, 2019.

Luz, Ulrich, and Axel Michaels. *Encountering Jesus and Buddha: Their Lives and Teachings*. Minneapolis: Fortress, 2006.

Mack, Burton L. *Who Wrote the New Testament?: The Making of the Christian Myth*. San Francisco: Harper, 1995.

Myokyo-ni. *The Zen Way*. London: Sheldon Press, 1977.

———. *Gentling the Bull*. London: The Zen Centre, 1988.

Narada. *The Buddha and His Teachings*. Kuala Lumpur: Buddhist Mission Society, 1988.

Otto, Rudolf. *Das Heilige*. Über *das Irrationale in der Idee des Göttlichen und sein Verhältnis zum Rationalen* [The Idea of the Holy: An Inquiry into the Non-Rational Factor in the Idea of the Divine and Its Relation to the Rational]. Translated by John Wilfred Harvey. Oxford: Oxford University Press, 1968.

Pieris, Aloysius. *Love Meets Wisdom: A Christian Experience of Buddhism*. New York: Orbis, 1988.

Queripel, John. *On the Third Day: Re-Looking at the Resurrection*. Reservoir: Morning Star, 2017.

———. *Christmas Myth, Magic and Legend*. Reservoir: Morning Star, 2018.

Sanders, E. P. *The Historical Figure of Jesus*. London: Allen Lane, 1993.

Shearer, Alistair. *Buddha: The Intelligent Heart*. London: Thames and Hudson, 1992.

Smart, Ninian. *The Religious Experience of Mankind*. New York: Charles Scribner's Sons, 1969.

———. *The World's Religions: Old Traditions and Modern Transformations*. Cambridge: Cambridge University Press, 1989.

Spong, John Shelby. *Why Christianity Must Change or Die*. San Francisco: Harper, 1998.

Staniforth, Maxwell, trans. *Early Christian Writings: The Apostolic Fathers*. Harmondsworth: Penguin, 1968.

Thich Thien Tam. *Buddhism of Wisdom and Faith*. New York: Sutra Translation Committee of the United States & Canada, 1994.

Thich Nhat Hanh. *Living Buddha, Living Christ*. New York: Rider, 1995.

Tillich, Paul. *The Religious Situation*. New York: Living Age, 1956.

Vermes, Gaza. *The Changing Face of Jesus*. London: Penguin, 2001.

Walpola, Sri Rahula. *What the Buddha Taught*. London: Gordon Fraser, 1959.

Weber, Max. *Die protestantische Ethik und der Geist des Kapitalismus* [The Protestant Ethic and the Spirit of Capitalism]. Translated by Talcott Parsons. London: Unwin Hyman, 1930.

White, Lynn. "The Historical Roots of Our Ecologic Crisis." *Science* 155 (1967) 1203–7.

Wilson, A. N. *Jesus*. London: Flamingo, 1993.

Yeshe, Thubten. *The Essence of Tibetan Buddhism*. Weston: Lama Yeshe Wisdom Archive, 2001.